A GUIDE

TO

THE MALTESE ISLANDS,

BY THE

Revd. G. N. Godwin,

CHAPLAIN TO THE FORCES.

DEDICATED

(BY PERMISSION)

WITH MUCH RESPECT

TO

HIS EXCELLENCY

GEN. SIR ARTHUR BORTON, K. C. B.

GOVERNOR

AND COMMANDER IN CHIEF

IN

MALTA AND ITS DEPENDENCIES.

PREFACE.

Go, little book! most modest, unpretending,
To guide the tourist, or the sufferer wending
His way in quest of health to Malta's shore,
Some wanderer too, perchance,' minding of days of yore.
Say to enquirers that they here will find,
Strength for the body, pleasure for the mind.
Speak thou to him whom History's Muse delights,
Of bygone days, of "Malta and Its Knights;"
Heroic deeds, Cross battling with the Crescent,
Of *"Seakings"* valiant, *"Malta Past and Present;"*
If for thy readers rocks and caves have charms,
Or if they solace find in Nature's arms;
Bid them, like misers keen, unlock the hoard,
Which Adams, Ciantar, Spratt, have richly stored.
Thy Author's ta'en some facts, for which he
Returns his thanks to Townsend, Badger, Ritchie,
To Ferris, Douglas, Gatt, Inglott and Camilleri,
Vassallo, Bennet, Gale, to Rosenbusch not chary:
To Captain Raymond, Doctor Cousin too,
The Dockyard Chaplain and Archdeacon Cleugh.
Vaunt not thyself, thine is a lowly station!
Remember what thou art,—a compilation!
Sending thee forth, the Author's labour ends,
Not without grateful thanks to all unmentioned friends.

PART FIRST.

CHAPTER I.
THE MALTESE ISLANDS.

Situation.—Dimensions.—Bays and Inlets.—Population.—
Wages.—Food.—Greatest elevation of the islands.—Appearance
from the sea.—The ancient Athalantis.—Evidenees of diminution
of area.

THE Maltese islands, viz., Malta, Gozo, Comino, and
Cominotto, are situated at a greater distance from
the mainland than any others in the Mediterranean.
They occupy an area S. E. by E. and N. W. by W.
true 8½ leagues. Cape S. Demetri the N. W. extremity
of Gozo is in lat. 36°. 3', long. 14° 10' and 50 miles
S. E. ¼ E. from the S. E. point of Pantellaria; Benghisa
Point, to the S. E. of Malta being in lat. 35° 49½ lon.
14 33¾'. The axis of the group, 29½ miles in length,
runs from S. E. to N. W. in the same direction as the
Apennines. The eastern extremity of Malta is 55 miles
S. S. W. ½ W. from Cape Passaro, and 54 miles S. ¼ E.
from Cape Scalambri in Sicily. Cape San Demitri in
Gozo is distant from Cape Scalambri S. S. W. rather
southerly, 46 miles. The intervening strait is called
the Malta Channel. Cape Spartivento the nearest point
of the Italian mainland is 190 miles away; nor will Cape
Bon on the African shore be reached nntil nearly 200
miles of sea have been traversed. Malta and the adjacent
islands which are officially styled its "dependencies"
now geographically form part of Europe, whilst as to

8

climate and productions they have much in common with Africa. Malta itself is 17¼ miles long, 9¼ broad, and about 60 miles in circumference. A boat sailing round it would traverse some 44 miles. Its area is estimated at 95 statute square miles, and its longest day is 14 hours 52 minutes. Its principal ports are the Great and Quarantine Harbours of Valetta which are separated by Mount Sceberras on which the city is built. Of these we shall speak hereafter. There are also on the northern shores the Bays of Melleha, St. Paul, Saline, Maddalena, St. George, St. Julian, Marsa Scala, St. Thomas and Marsa Scirocco, several of which could be, and have often been, extensively used by shipping. The straits of Freghi or Flieghi separate Malta from Gozo. They are about four miles in width, sufficiently deep to be navigated by large vessels, and wash the shores of the two small islands of Comino and Cominotto, which lie between the larger ones of the Maltese group. Comino and Cominotto are two miles long by one broad. Gozo is 9 miles in length and five in breadth. On the northern shore of Gozo are the Bays of Ramla and Marsa el Forn, and on the southern those of Sclendi and Dueyra. But for the most part landing is impracticable on the southern shore of either Malta or Gozo as precipitous cliffs rise sheer from the water's edge, frequently to a height of several hundred feet. There is also off the southern shore of Malta a small island named Filfla from the Arabic word "Filfel" which means a "peppercorn," on account of its diminutive size. About one third of Malta and Gozo is bare rock, and only one half is actually under cultivation. This renders it the more surprising that so large a number of people can find existence here.

9

The population of Malta, excluding the army and Navy, according to the census taken in 1871, was 124,334, that of Gozo being 17,391, making a total of 141,775. The present population is (1880) about 152,000. Malta with an area of 95 statute square miles has a population of nearly 1500 per square mile, and Gozo with an area of 20 square miles, has a population of 900 per square mile. But excluding the one third of the island which is unsuitable of cultivation, and the area occupied by buildings, the population of Malta reaches the enormous number of 2000 persons per square mile. Something must be done and that speedily to relieve this ever increasing and but too often impoverished mass of striving, toiling humanity. A few statistics as to wages, &c., may be of interest. Of a total Maltese population of 149,270 a Government report estimates the working classes to number 112,360 and the non-manual classes 33,910.

The P. & O. Company pay the men who coal their steamers 2s. 6d. per diem but the generality of Maltese coalheavers only,earn from 1s. 6d. to 1s. 8d. daily. The boatmen who ferries you across the harbour gets on the average from 1s. to 1s. 4d. per diem, the porter earns 1s. and the carter 10d. daily.

The best paid artisans are skilled engravers, who earn from 2s. to 5s. per diem according to ability. Compositors earn from 10d. to 1s. 8d., shoemakers 1s. to 1s.3d., the makers of common cigars 5d. to 7½d., spinners 2½d. per diem. Gardeners receive from 1s. 6d. to 2s. 6d. daily, agricultural labourers 1s. 0½d. to 1s. 8d. women employed in field labour from 4d. to 10d. Only two-fifths of the meat eaten on the island is consumed by the

10

Maltese, the remainder being required by the English population. The boatman eats about 4 lbs. 8 oz., of bread or *pasta* every day, the farm labourer 5 lbs., and the artisan $3\frac{1}{2}$ lbs., at a cost of $3\frac{1}{2}d.$ per rotolo of 28 oz. A little oil, fish, or cheap Sicilian cheese forms a relish to this frugal fare, which, when times are good is moistened with from half a pint to a pint of common Sicilian wine. Brandy, costing 4s. 6d. per gallon, is largely consumed. Many a dweller in the *Fior del Mondo* or *the Flower of the World* as the Maltese love to call their rocky home knows full well, from hard experience the meaning of that oft repeated phrase "the battle of life."

The highest point of Malta is a rising ground near Casal Dingli, elevated 750 feet above sea level. The hill of Dibiegi 743 feet above the level of the sea is the greatest elevation of which Gozo can boast. The Maltese islands are visible at a distance of 24 miles and when seen from the sea have the appearance of low-lying shores intersected by channels and ravines. The want of trees and the numerous stone walls which divide the fields give a dreary and barren appearance to the landscape. But there are minds on which colour makes a deeper impression than form, and there is something in the contrast between that burnt yellow soil, the intense white of the limestone where exposed, the dark verdure of the caroubier and other scanty trees which leaves its mark upon the memory when the vividness of far fairer scenes has faded away, and sunsets steal over these waters the glowing gold of which an artist may well despair of imitating. Many of the heights in Gozo are cone shaped.

11

These islands are supposed with good reason to have formed part of a much larger tract of land now submerged, and which was either a large island or islands, or else formed part of Europe or Africa, if not of both. Signor Borzesi has done his best to prove that Malta, Gozo, and Comino represent the summits of lofty mountains belonging to the island of Athalantis, and brings forward many classical quotations in support. of his theory. Signor Grongnet had formerly in his possession a stone which it is said was dug up at Città Vecchia in May 1826, on which was an inscription describing Athalantis, and also another to the effect that the consul Tiberius Sempronius in the year of Rome 536 had ordered the preservation of this stone. A fine field for discussion is here open to Archæologists. It is evident that Malta has diminished in size during the historic period. On the southern shore are to be seen near *Fom-e-Rieh* cart tracks which extend to the very edge of a cliff some 80 feet in height. Similar ruts are also to be seen at the St. George's Creek of the Bay of Marsascirocco and at Marfa from whence passengers take boat for Gozo.

CHAPTER II.

Historical Outline.

Malta in the days of the Giants.—The Phœnicians, Greeks, Carthaginians and Romans.—Arab Rule.—Arrival of Count Roger.—French and German Sovereigns.—The Knights of St. John and the Great Siege.—Decay of the Order.—Malta surrenders te Buonaparte.—Capitulation of General Vaubois. —English Governors in Malta.

ONE of our sweetest singers has saidt hat we may

> "......departing leave behind us,
> Footprints on the sands of time, "

and as it is with ourselves so has it been with those who have preceded us. Many and varied are the nationalities which have found a home in Malta and which have all left behind them footprints, more or less distinct.

The first inhabitants of whom we have any record are the Giants who dared to war with Jupiter, and to take high heaven by storm. The curious in such matters will find a long dissertation on the subject of the Giants and their doings in Ciantars Malta Illustrata (Book II). That most useful but somewhat credulous historian says "But lastly what further testimony can we desire of the habitation of the Cyclops than that given us by the gigantic bones found in Malta and their hollow burial places cut in the living rock and very often of enormous size, as for example a bone which the owner of a house used as a cross-bar for the door? We ourselves have seen a molar tooth of the thick-

13

ness of the finger and an inch in length which was extracted from a gigantic head found outside Birchircara !"

Alas for romance and the fabled kingdom of the giants ! Dr. Adams clearly shews that these remains belonged to some fossil elephant or hippopotamus, and not to any monster in human shape ! According to Homer these first gigantic inhabitants of Malta were named Phœacians, and called their island home Hyperia. Eurymedon was their sovereign, but his grandson Nausithous having taken part in the great Titanic conspiracy against Jupiter shared the fate of his brother giants. His subjects were either put to the sword or dispersed, some of them escaping to people the island of Scheria (Corfu). The fascinating nymph Calypso is said to have had two residences in these islands, viz., one in Malta and the other in Gozo, at one or both of which she entertained Ulysses on his return from the siege of Troy whilst his wife Penelope was waiting for him at home and usefully employing herself with plain needlework and shirtmaking. But to pass from fiction to reality. At a very early date probably about 1400 B. C. those daring sailors the Phœnicians who have been well styled " the English of antiquity " colonised the island, changing its name from Hyperia to Ogygia. Some authors give the year 1519 B. C., as the date of their arrival. They speedily rendered Malta flourishing and prosperous.

Traces of their occupation are still to be seen in the ruined temples of *Hagiar Khem* and *Mnaidra* near Krendi, the Giants' Tower in Gozo, and of Melcarte, the Tyrian Hercules " dispeller of evils "

14

near the Bay of MarsaScirocco. Some of the Phœnician inscriptions which enrich the British Museum have been brought to light at Bighi and elsewhere. The graves of this mysterious race cover a hillside at Bingemma, which is by no means the only resting place of their dead in the Maltese islands. Votive tablets and coins have also been upturned. In a tomb near Benghisa a square slab was found with this inscription "The inner chamber of the sanctuary of the sepulchre of *Hannibal,* illustrious in the consummation of calamity. He was beloved; the people lament, when arrayed in order of battle, *Hannibal* the son of Bar Malech." Of course many of these vestiges of antiquity belong to the second period of Phœnician occupation, when Carthage ruled supreme in these seas.

Diodorus Siculus says : " There are over against that part of Sicily which lies to the south, three islands at a distance in the sea, each of which has a town and safe ports for ships overtaken by tempest. The first called *Melite,* is about 800 stadia from Syracuse, and has several excellent ports. The inhabitants are very rich, in as much as they exercise many trades, and in particular they manufacture cloths remarkable for their softness and fineness. Their houses are large and splendidly ornamented with projections and stucco. The island is a colony of the Phœnicians, who, trading to the Western Ocean, used it as a place of refuge, because it has excellent ports and lies in the midst of the sea. Next to this island is another named *Gaulus* (Gozo), with convenient harbours, which is also a colony of Phœnicians." An ancient tradition asserts that the Phœnicians only took posses-

15

sion of the islands after a fierce struggle. They were no doubt attracted hither by the convenient position of Malta and Gozo as commercial store-houses and depôts for goods. Diodorus Siculus speaks of Gozo as possessing good harbours, a statement which shews clearly that the ships of these hardy navigators were of no great size.

For nearly seven centuries Punic governors ruled our islands in peace and the worship of Juno in the stately temple which stood on the spot now occupied by the moat of Fort St. Angelo attract-ed crowds of devotees, both native and foreign. But troublous times were at hand. Archias of Corinth founded Syracuse in 732 B.C., and it is probable that Malta changed hands soon afterwards. Some authors however variously give 755. B.C., and 736 B.C., as the date of the arrival of the Grecian conquerors, who occupied the centre of the island, leav-ing the coast in possession of the natives. The form of government during this period was repub-lican, with a Senate, high Priest and two Archons. Demetrius, son of Diodotus of Syracuse received the thanks of the Republic of Malta for some signal services which he had rendered to the island. Gozo now bore the name of Gaulos, Comino that of Hephæstia whilst the appellation of Ogygia was exchanged for the well known name of *Melita* or *Melissa.* Some say that Malta was so called "from the abundance of honey they have there, gathered by the bees from the anice seeds and flowers thereof, which grow on this island abundantly." O-thers again assert that this name was given in honour of the Nymph Melita, the daughter of Ne-reus and Doris. The learned Bochart derives the

16

name of Malta or Maltha from a word meaning "white stucco," with which according to Diodorus Siculus the houses of the natives were ornamented. It is also thought that this name is of Phœnician origin and derived from the same root as the Hebrew word *Malet* which signifies a refuge or asylum.

The Greek *Gaulos* and the Roman *Gaulum* applied to the island of Gozo, mean a cup and probably refer to its shape. The name *Hephœstia* means "the island of Vulcan," and one author speaks of Comino under the name of *Lampas* or "the Lamp."

The Greeks who did not live on the most amicable terms with the original inhabitants, greatly extended the trade in Maltese cotton cloths, and carried on a considerable commerce with Sicily. Phalaris, tyrant of Agrigentum, was their firm friend and a district near the Boschetto still bears the name of *Gorghenti* from his once famous city. The Greeks erected a temple to Proserpine on the heights of Mtarfa, and another to Apollo with a theatre attached, close to the site of the present Sanatorium at Città Vecchia, which city is honourably mentioned under the title of Melita. A Greek Pagos or village seems to have stood near the Bingemma hills, whilst another was situated near Zurrico. Greek coins, medals and inscriptions have also been met with in various places.

About the year 480 B. C. the Carthaginians obtained possession of Malta. They trafficked in marbles and gold from Greece, cotton from Malta, bitumen from Lipari, wax, honey, and slaves from Corsica, and iron from Elba. In the year 264 B. C. the First Punic War broke out and seven years afterwards the Consul Attilius Regulus on his way to

17

invade Africa took possession of Malta. After the defeat of Regulus by the Carthaginians under Xantippus the Lacedemonian in the following year, the Romans were obliged to retire and Malta again became subject to Carthage. In 242 B. C. the Consul Lutatius Catulus gained a great naval victory off Trapani, and Malta amongst other islands was ceded to Rome. The Carthaginians, whose *Punic faith* is proverbially synonymous with treachery, soon returned and resumed possession. In 220 B. C. the historian Livy tells us (Bk. xxi. c. 51): "The consul Titus Sempronius Gracchus having dismissed Hiero king of Syracuse, and having left the prætor to defend the coast of Sicily, himself crossed from Lilybœum (now Marsala) to the island of Malta which was held by the Carthaginians. On his arrival Hamilcar the son of Gisco, the commandant (a brother of the famous Hannibal) surrenders to him both the town and island with nearly 2000 soldiers. Thence after a few days he returned to Lilybœum, and the prisoners taken both by the consul and the prætor with the exception of those illustrious for their rank were publicly sold as slaves." Many of the hapless garrison are said to have been Greeks. Thus after nearly three centuries of Punic rule, Malta finally bowed beneath the yoke of all subduing Rome.

Although it is impossible to fix the date of their arrival with any degree of certainty, it is nevertheless beyond doubt that the Egyptians had formerly settlements here. This is evident from the rock chambers discovered in the year 1847 at the distance of three fourths of a mile from Città Vecchia, in the district of Kasam il Genieni, from the

2

18

Sarcophagi of terra cotta found at Ghar Barca and from other objects preserved in the Malta Museum. These Egyptian settlers were, it is thought, contemporaneous with the Phœnicians. In 1694 a golden plate covered with Egyptian hieroglyphics was found near Città Vecchia and given to Cardinal Cantani Archbishop of Naples.

The Romans treated the inhabitants of the Maltese islands, many of whom were of Grecian origin, with great kindness, permitting them to continue their ancient customs and to be governed by their own laws. Malta retained its name of Melita, and together with Gozo was raised to the rank of a Roman Municipium, so that the inhabitants enjoyed either wholly or in part the privileges of Roman citizenship. Many coins and inscriptions have been found especially in Gozo, which prove that the Romans did much to restore and beautify the temples of the gods and to enlarge the theatre at Città Vecchia. The Government was administered by a Proprætor whose actions were controlled by the Prætor of Sicily. Commerce and manufactures were encouraged and Maltese cotton cloths were looked upon as articles of luxury at Rome. The temple of Juno in Malta was an object of great veneration both to natives and foreigners. Even the very pirates who used to winter in our harbours refrained from laying sacrilegious hands, upon its treasures. But the temptation proved too strong for Verres the avaricious prætor of Sicily, as we know from the orations of Cicero. (in Verrem. iv. 46.) One of the Generals of Massinissa King of Numidia took from this temple some massive pieces of exquisitively carved ivory and presented them to his sovereign, who accepted them not knowing

19

whence they had come from. On learning the truth, the king at once restored them with all due solemnity. This story Cicero did not fail to turn to good account when detailing the iniquities of the rapacious Verres.

Some remains of a vast mole of Roman workmanship have been discovered near the head of the Grand Harbour. In the year 58 B. C. the shipwreck of St. Paul, recorded by St. Luke, is believed to have taken place in the bay which bears his name. Tradition assigns February 10th as the date of this important event. It is said that during the three months' stay of the Apostle in these islands he converted the inhabitants and his fellow voyagers to the faith • of Christ, the dwellers at Naxaro being the first to receive Christian baptism. On his departure for Rome he is reported to have consecrated St. Publius who afterwards suffered martyrdom at Athens, as first Bishop of the Church in Malta.

In 337 A. D. the Roman Empire was divided amongst the three sons of Constantine the Great, viz., Constantine, Constantius and Constans. Malta, with Italy, Illyria, and Africa was assigned to the latter. The Empire, reunited under Theodosius, was at his death again divided between his sons, Honorius reigning in the West, and Arcadius in the East. The dominions of Arcadius comprised the whole of Greece, Egypt, the provinces of Western Asia, and the islands of the Mediterranean. Malta therefore for several centuries formed part of the Eastern Roman, or, as it was afterwards called, the Byzantine Empire.

Some historians assert that first the Vandals and afterwards the Goths made themselves masters of

20

Malta, but that the latter were expelled by Belisarius in the year 534 A. D. This is however somewhat doubtful. For 475 years, viz., from 399 A. D. to 870 A. D. the Maltese islands, concerning which during this period little or nothing is known seem to have remained as dependencies of the Eastern Empire.

The Arabs were the next to take possession of Malta. Tradition recounts various predatory incursions at an earlier date, but it seems certain that in the year 870 A. D. they made a descent upon Gozo from whence they crossed over to the larger island. All the Greeks to the number, it is said, of 3000, were put to the sword, and 3614 women and children sold for 5000 pieces of gold. The government of the island was assumed by an Arabian Emir. Some historian say that the Arabs treated the Maltese inhabitants with great kindness, allowing them the free exercise of their religion, but from other evidence it seems far more probable that Christianity was proscribed here as elsewhere, and that the Christians were obliged to assemble for worship in crypts, catacombs, and similar places. The catacombs at Città Vecchia are believed by many to have been excavated during this period.

The Arabs altered the name of Città Vecchia from Melita to Medina or the "Great City," strengthened its fortifications, and diminished its area, so as to render it more capable of defence. In order to protect the Great Harbour they erected a castle on the site of the present Fort St. Angelo. Arabic coins and a stone on which is a touching epitaph have been discovered together with other relics of Arab dominion. But the most lasting

21

memorial which remains to us is the Maltese language of which the late Mr. Schlienz says " that all its words, with the exception of a very few are purely Arabic and conform in every respect to the rules, nay even to the anomalies of the Arabic grammar. " This remark applies more fully to Gozo and the casals or villages than to Valletta. The Arab rulers and their Maltese subjects frequently sallied forth from their harbours bent on piracy and plunder. The Byzantine Emperors in vain endeavoured to check their ravages, and on one occasion their admirals Nicetas and Manianes were put to flight, although in command of a considerable force.

But in the year 1090, Count Roger, the son of Tancred de Hauteville, after almost entirely expelling the Arabs from Sicily arrived in Malta, where he was °gladly welcomed by the Christian natives as a deliverer. After a short siege the city of Medina fell into his hands. The terms of surrender were that the Emir should have full liberty to quit the island, together with his property and all those who wished to share his fortunes; that a certain number of horses, mules and warlike stores should be given up; that all Christian slaves should be set at liberty; and that the Arabs who chose to remain in the island should pay an annual tribute. Many Arabs continued to reside in Malta until the year 1243, A. D. when by order of the Emperor Frederick, they were conveyed to Nocera in Apulia.

Count Roger erected a fortress at Città Vecchia which was afterwards dismantled by royal authority in 1455, strengthened "the Castle on the Rock" now Fort St. Angelo, and rebuilt the ruined Cathedral in the ancient capital. Malta having been for 220 years

22

without a regular succession of bishops, Count Roger presented to Pope Urban II. a pious priest named Walter (Gualtieri) for consecration. He also established in Malta a Popular Council for the government of the people, composed of nobles, clergy, and elected members. The Arabs were treated with lenity, and allowed to issue gold coins with the motto " There is but one God and Mahomet is the Prophet of God " and on the reverse " King Roger. " The Arms and Standard of Malta consisting of the two colours white and red were granted by Count Roger, and were taken from his own escutcheon. Having settled the affairs of Malta, the Count returned to Sicily taking with him many liberated Christian slaves, and died at Mileto in Calabria at the age of 70 in the year 1101. A. D.

The Arabs who had not quitted the island were not content to remain as a subject race. Accordingly in the year 1122, they conspired to massacre the Christians whilst the latter were occupied with the religious services of Holy Week. The plot was discovered, and the Christians attacked their would-be assassins at the fountain known as Ghain Clieb (on the roadside between Città Vecchia and Bingemma), with shouts of "Kill the Dogs," from whence the fountain derives its present name of " the Dogs' well. " Overpowered, the Arabs fled to a natural stronghold called *Kalaa tal Bahria* or " the fortress on the shore " where they held out for some time, until King Roger I arrived from Sicily with a fleet, and compelled them to surrender. Some of the chief conspirators were put to death and others banished to Barbary.

23

In spite of strenuous efforts made by the Byzantine Emperor Emmanuel Commenus in 1114, A. D. Malta remained subject to King Roger. During the reign of his son King Tancred, Malta and Gozo became a County and Marquisate. William the Fat, Grand Admiral of Sicily was one of its lords. By the marriage of Constance, the posthumous daughter of King Roger I, to Henry II. Emperor of Germany, the son of the famous Frederic Barbarossa, Malta and Gozo passed under German rule for 72 years. In the year 1224 the inhabitants of Celano in Calabria were transported hither, and did much to improve the condition and increase the prosperity of the island.

During the reigns of Henry VI. and his son Frederic II. the Maltese earned great renown at sea. Under the command of a native admiral they attacked and destroyed a squadron of the Republic of Pisa which was threatening Syracuse, took the island of Candia from the Venetians, after destroying their fleet, and taking prisoner their admiral Andrea Dandalo. The battle of Benevento on Febr. 26th. 1266, placed Charles of Anjou on the throne of Naples and Sicily and put an end to the rule of the German Emperors in Malta. In 1282, the terrible massacre known as the Sicilian Vespers took place and Peter III. King of Aragon was crowned King of Sicily with the title of Peter I. It is said on insufficient grounds that the plot from which the Sicilian Vespers resulted was arranged in Malta. A fierce contest took place off the mouth of the Grand Harbour which decided the fate of Malta. The French admiral whose name is variously given as William Corner, Cor-

24

niero, Corneille, and Cornú was defeated and slain, and the Aragonese fleet entered the Marsamuscetto Harbour in triumph. The town surrendered at discretion, and was obliged to furnish provisions as well as 2,500 crowns by way of contribution.

Charles of Anjou ruled over the islands for 18 years during which period the condition of the inhabitants was pitiable in the extreme. Nor was it improved under the government of the Aragonese monarchs. During the whole of this period the Popular Council established by Count Roger retained its influence. Its members were elected from the clergy, nobles, honourable citizens, professors of arts and liberal sciences, traders, and artizans. Each head of a family possessed the franchise. The superior clergy and the proprietors were also represented, and the casals each sent from one to three deputies to the Assembly. Amongst other privileges this Popular Council used when the See was vacant to present three names to the Sovereign one of whom was to be appointed Bishop. The Genoese led by Tommaso Morchio attacked Malta in 1371.

Over and over again were these islands given as a fief or mortgaged by the Kings of Aragon or by the Castilian monarchs who succeeded them in the year 1412. The Maltese were terribly oppressed by their feudal lords and complained with justice to Prince Louis son of King Peter II. A solemn pledge was given at Messina on Oct. 7th. 1350, that the Maltese Islands should be united in perpetuity to Sicily, and that the inhabitants should enjoy the same privileges as those of any other city in the kingdom. Also that under no pretext of lordship should

25

the islands be transferred to any private person. These promises were speedily broken. King Martin soon afterwards mortgaged or sold Malta and Gozo first to Don Antonio Cordova, Viceroy of Sicily in 1420, and afterwards in 1425 to Don Gonsalvo Monroi, a wealthy Spaniard, for 30,000 golden florins, (about £15,000). Monroi and his family ruled the island for two years until the natives weary of his oppressions determined to make a vigorous effort for freedom. They therefore rose against him, seized his ships, and forcibly carried off his wife Dame Constance as a hostage. They then offered to repay the sum for which the islands had been mortgaged. The offer was accepted, the money was paid, and King Alfonso confirmed the previous grant of 1350 by a decree signed at Valencia on June 20th, 1428, which conferred upon the Maltese the same privileges as those enjoyed by the citizens of Palermo, Messina, and Catania. On this occasion the ancient capital received the name of Notabile. King Alphonso having spoken of it as "Jocale Notabile regiæ coronæ," the brightest jewel of his crown.

Until the year 1530, no other cession of the islands took place. In 1427 an army of Moors 18,000 strong invaded Malta, and were pressing the garrison hard, when, it is said, that St. Paul, accompanied by St. George and St. Agatha completely routed and dispersed the enemy.

Plague followed in the train of war, and the population of Malta which before the Moorish invasion amounted to 24,000 whilst Gozo had 8,000 inhabitants, was terribly diminished and the survivors left in great poverty and misery. About this time measures were taken to provide an efficient militia and

26

also a cavalry force, 200 strong. The Maltese were forbidden to arm ships under a penalty of 1000 florins. On April 16th, 1431, King Alphonso, in consideration of the poverty of Malta and Gozo granted them full exemption from custom house dues in Sicilian ports. In 1466 the Jews resident in Malta, petitioned that they might no longer be under the jurisdiction of the Hakem or Captain of the Rod at Città Vecchia, and that they might cease to wear the *Little Red Wheel*. This was a round piece of red cloth which men and women alike were obliged to wear constantly on their breasts, as a distinctive badge of nationality, under a penalty of 15 days imprisonment. Their requests were denied, and in the year 1492, King Alphonso banished them from Malta and the rest of his dominions. The 70 oz. of gold, which was the University's share of the property of the Hebrews was applied by that body on Sept. 14th. 1513, to the repair of the castle in the Great Harbour.

From 1467 to 1470 Malta suffered greatly from drought, no rain having fallen for three successive years. In the year 1488 eleven Turkish galleys landed men in the Marsamuscetto Harbour and made an unexpected attack upon the Borgo, plundering it, and carrying off 80 of the inhabitants as slaves. In consequence of this surprise, the Tower of St. Elmo was ordered to be constructed, consisting of a small fort with a shallow ditch of which more hereafter. In 1519 the plague again made its appearance and in 1526 some Moors landing by night near Benuarrat, plundered the village of Musta, carrying off 400 captives into slavery, amongst whom were a bride and a party of wedding guests. The relatives of the

27

prisoners were obliged to reduce themselves to poverty in order to ransom their unhappy kinsmen.

But brighter days were at hand. On January
1st. 1523, the Knights of St. John of Jerusalem left
Rhodes for ever, after having made such a gallant
defence against an immense Turkish force as to cause
the Emperor Charles V. to exclaim "There never
was anything so well lost as Rhodes." Into the previous history of this famous Order it would be foreign
to our purpose to enter, and the reader is referred
to *Malta and its Knights*, by Lieut. Col. Porter, R. E.
the *Sea Kings of the Mediterranean*, by the Rev. C.
F. Townsend, *Malta Past and Present*, by the Rev.
H. Seddall, and the *Storia di Malta* by Dr. G. A.
Vassallo, the histories of Boisgelin, Vertot, Bosio, and
other kindred works. Suffice it here to say that from
the erection of a small hospital at Jerusalem in the
year 1050 A. D. gradually developed that famous and
illustrious Order of Knighthood which long formed
one of the bulwarks of Christendom against the sword
of Islam.

Expelled from Palestine in 1291, the Knights re-
tired to Cyprus, from whence in 1310 they removed
to hardly won Rhodes. Driven forth once more, as
we have seen in the year 1523, they wandered in
search of an asylum for nearly seven years until at
length by a deed of gift signed at Castel Franco
near Bologna, and confirmed by the Pope on the
25th of the following month, Charles V, Emperor
of Germany granted "to the Most Reverend the Grand
Master and the Knights of St. John, as a noble,
free and uncumbered fief the castles, fortresses, and
towns of Tripoli, Malta, and Gozo, with their entire
jurisdiction, both civil and military, with no other

28

condition than that they should annually on the day of All Saints, (Nov. 1st.) present a falcon to the Viceroy of Sicily, in the name of the Order." L'Isle Adam the hero of Rhodes and 44th Grand Master of the Order also agreed that the Knights should never make war against the Emperor or the kingdom of Sicily; that the Emperor should select the Bishop of Malta from three candidates chosen by the Order, one of whom must be a Spanish subject; that the admiral of the fleet or his lieutenant should always be an Italian; and that the Order should not be able to transfer the sovereignty of the island to any other power without the consent of the Emperor.

The Maltese might, in accordance with the decree of 1428 before mentioned, have resisted the cession of their island home to the Knights, but as the latter solemnly swore to observe and keep inviolate all their ancient laws and privileges they after some little demur received them with open arms. An oath to the same effect was taken by each Grand Master on his entry into office. The University or governing body relinquished in favour of the Order the sum of 30,000 florins due to it from the royal treasury.

Commissioners sent by the Knights to examine their new possession reported that Malta was about 60 miles in circuit, that it was but an arid rock covered in many places with sand, and here and there with a small amount of soil, without river, rivulet, or spring. That the inhabitants were dependent for their water supply on tanks and a few brackish wells, that the supply of corn was insufficient for the people, some 12,000 in number, that wood was sold

29

by the pound, that dried cowdung and thistles were in general use as fuel. The houses of the people were miserable huts, the old capital and its fortifications crumbling to decay, whilst the two or three guns of Fort St. Angelo were insufficient for the defence of the little town which had grown up around it. Figs, melons, fruits, cotton, cummin, honey, and locust beans were its principal productions. Gozo with a population of 5,000 and defended by one ruinous fortress was described as being smaller, but in comparison with Malta fertile and pleasant. Pirates and sea rovers made constant attacks upon both islands. The natives wore quilted cotton vests thick enough to stop an arrow, or even sometimes to turn a bullet.

The magnificent harbours and the central position of the islands were irresistible temptations to the Knights of St. John, and after arranging for the establishment of a mint in Malta and for the importation of corn from Sicily duty free, L' Isle Adam and his knights took possession of their new dominions on October 26th 1530 with a squadron composed of the three galleys, S. Croce, S. Filippo, and S. Giovanni, a galiot and a brigantine.

Only in briefest outline can we sketch the residence of the Knights of St. John in Malta. The members of this illustrious Order were divided into three classes, the first being styled Knights of Justice, who were obliged to produce proofs of nobility. None but those who had already received the honour of knighthood were eligible for this class. The second class which was composed of ecclesiastics was subdivided into Conventual Chaplains who were attached to the Church of St. John, the Hospital, and the Galleys, and the Priests of Obedience who were not obliged to reside in Malta

30

but were attached to some of the churches belonging to the Order or under the authority of a Grand Prior or Commander. The third class was composed of servants at arms and *brothers de stage* or *donats*. The former of these were esquires and eligible for the honour of knighthood. The latter were menial servants who wore the demi-cross, but who nevertheless possessed many privileges. Each knight took the vows of poverty, chastity, and obedience, none of which, in later times, were scrupulously observed. There were also houses of Religious Dames of the Order of St. John of Jerusalem in France, Italy, and Spain, admission into which was reserved for ladies of most ancient and noble lineage.

The Ursuline nuns in Malta received from the Order an annual pension of £51. 18. 10. The nuns of Toulouse, received £ 73. 0. 0. and those of Martel in Querci, £ 29. 10. 6. annually.

The knights were divided into eight Languages, viz., Provence, Auvergne, France, Germany, Italy, Aragon, Castile, England, and Portugal. At the Reformation the Language of England was suppressed, the Anglo-Bavarian Language being substituted for it in the year 1784. Each of these Languages had its own Palace or Auberge, presided over by a chief called the Pilier, who received from the treasury either money or an equivalent in grain for the supply of his Auberge. All members of the Order of whatever grade might eat in their respective Auberges but Commanders seldom did so, and those holding Commanderies worth £ 200 per annum or servants at arms holding Commanderies of more than £ 100 per annum were not admitted.

31

The Pilier of each Auberge found his dignity somewhat costly, aud was usually rewarded with the next vacant Commandery. The nondining members received an allowance in money. The Grand Master presided over the Great Council which was composed of the 54 Grand Crosses of the Order. Besides this, there were other tribunals with less authority, and the Grand Master had numerous important offices in his gift.

To each Language were attached various lucrative Bailiwicks, Commanderies and Priories, the attainment of which was naturally an object of ambition. Letters were addressed to the Grand Master (whose office was elective) thus: "To his Most Eminent Highness the Grandmaster," and in official documents he was styled "Most Eminent aud Reverend Signor Grand Master."

The general income of the Order was derived from Responsions or fixed contributions from the various Commanderies and Priories belonging to the Order in various countries, which produced about £ 47,520 annnally. Two years income of Commanderies vacant by death brought in nearly £21,472. Fees paid by all admitted into the Order or receiving promotion in it amounted to £20,334 per annum. Four fifths of the income of deceased knights, was estimated at £24,755 yearly. The first year's revenues of certain Commanderies was reckoned at £477 per annum. Priory and other presents £197. The sale of forest trees on the estâtes of the Order (mostly in France) £4,798. Renounced pensions, various foundations, rent of houses, &c. £7,630. One per cent of the value of the goods stored at the Lazaretto produced annually £130. The Government Printing Press and the sale of a permission granted

32

by Papal Bull to eat eggs and butter during Lent realized £1,055 yearly. The ransom of Turkish slaves brought in on an average £7,661. Omitting other items, we may estimate the annual general income of the Order between 1778 and 1788 at £136,417.

The expenditure included—Ambassadors £3,802, Receivers in various countries £6,643. The Conventual Churches £2,991. Alms given to the Capuchins, clothing to all liberated Christian slaves passing through Malta, allowances of bread and meat for services rendered to the Order, £140 given to the infirmary at Floriana, and a yearly distribution of 600 qrs. of corn and £245 in money amounted to £1,730. The Great Hospital cost £7,947, and that for women £2017. Foundlings and children of poor parents £614. Pensions £4,032. Nuns of the Order £154. The Navy and the Port cost £47,494; the Land Forces and fortifications £17,303, and Public works £3,454. The Grand Master received annually £600 in aid of his table and £20 towards the repairs of palaces. Each member of the Order was allowed annually 4 qrs. of wheat, 9 gallons of oil, and £4. 8s. in money, amounting in all to some £15. Clothing was allowed annually varying in value from £2 4s. for a knight to 11s. for a novice. The falcons presented yearly to the Viceroy of Sicily and the Kings of France, Spain, Portugal, and Naples, involved an expence of £103. Public offices £1,002. Slaves and slave prisons £4,275. Conveyance of letters, £2,036. Maintenance of state silver plate £327. Workshops and magazines £1,826. These and other items make the average annual expenditure £128,533. The Grand Masters received £29,689 in 1797 from the Treasury of which £2,527 were expended for the direct be-

33

nefit of the inhabitants. The yearly expenses of the Grand Master for himself, his household, bodyguards and state attendants for the same year was £13,861. Altogether the Order spent for the benefit of Malta not more than £200,000. These figures are taken from the valuable pamphlet of W. H. Thornton, Esq., formerly Auditor General.

The Revenue for 1880 is estimated at £176,800, derived from Customs, £115,100; Land sales, £100; Land Revenue £14,700. Rents exclusive of Land £22,140. Licenses £3,020; Postage £140; Fines, Forfeitures, and Court fees £5,710; Fees of Office £1,290. Reimbursements to Government £2,600; Interest £8,370; Special Receipts £3,580. Estimated Expenditure, Establishments £76,657; Works £20,734; Other Services £65,603; Sanitary Office £690. When we add to this the enormous amount spent annually by English residents and visitors, by the fleet and garrison, and by the numerous ships which crowd our harbours, we shall see at a glance that financially, as indeed in many other respects Malta has no cause to regret the vanished dominion of the "White Cross-Knights."

Greatly to the regret of L'Isle Adam, the Emperor Charles V. insisted that the Order should undertake the defence of Tripoli in addition to that of Malta. On November 13th, 1530 the Grand Master made his public entry into Città Vecchia, and formally commenced his government. One of the first cares of the Order was to take possession of the Church of San Lorenzo in the Borgo as the Conventual Church of the Order, and to establish a Hospital. L'Isle Adam did much to strengthen the fortifications, and died at Città Vecchia in 1534 at the age

3

34

of 65, revered and beloved by all over whom he ruled. His remains were interred in the chapel of Fort St. Angelo, from whence they were subsequently removed to St. John's Church.

In this year Henry VIII. confiscated the possessions of the Order in England. Many of the English knights died on the scaffold or in prison, others abjured the Order, and the rest fled to Malta where they met with a most kindly reception, and were allowed to retain all the dignities attached to their Language. The post of the English knights during the Great Siege was between those of Castile and Germany. A Turkish fleet of 10 sail threatened Malta and landed troops who penetrated as far as Casal Gudia, but the invaders were obliged to retire to Comino " the nest and lair of Saracens " where they waited in vain for a chance to plunder. The knights did not fail to make reprisals in various directions. In 1540 the celebrated corsair Dragut first attacked the island, and eleven years afterwards Sinam Pasha after threatening the Borgo made a descent upon Gozo, and committed great ravages. In May 1553 the Forts of St. Michael and St. Elmo were completed, as well as some bastions at the head of the Borgo.

During the fatal expedition of Charles V. against Algiers in 1546 the Order lost eighty knights and four hundred soldiers. During a terrible storm, Charles V. exclaimed: "They must indeed be Maltese galleys to outride such a tempest." The Grand Master Claude de La Sengle in 1554 enclosed the whole of St. Michael's Mount with a line of fortifications within which soon arose the town of Senglea, called after its founder or defender.

35

Three years before Tripoli had been captured by Dragut, and its brave defender De Valier stripped of his habit and imprisoned in deference to popular clamour. On the night of Oct. 23rd, 1555 a sudden and unexpected storm sank four galleys in the Dockyard Creek, then known as the Port of the Galleys, 600 slaves and two knights being drowned. Early in 1556 Dragut effected a landing in the Bay of Marsa Scirocco, but was repulsed. In the following year a Maltese knight boarded a Turkish galley, and, finding escape impossible, boldly set fire to some gunpowder, and was blown to pieces with the ship.

The Maltese Admiral Romegas having captured many prizes at sea the Sultan swore "by his own head" to be revenged and to make himself master of Malta at all costs. Fortunately for the Order they had at their head a true hero. The name of La Vallette is synonymous with genius, courage, and piety, and when on the 18th of May, 1565 the Turkish fleet of 130 vesels besides 50 smaller craft, and a number of storeships having on board 38,300 men, 5000 of whom were janissaries, and 63 guns of large calibre hove in sight the knights, 474 in number with 87 servants at arms, and 8,155 soldiers were not taken by surprise. The starshaped Fort St. Elmo was almost the first point of attack. Glorious indeed is the story of its defence. The first attack was made on May 31st, but it was not until June 22nd that the victorious Crescent floated above its ramparts, and the Ottoman fleet entered the Marsamuscetto Harbour. "What may we not expect the parent to cost us when we have purchased the child at such a price!" exclaimed the Pacha Mustapha as he examined the fortifications on the other side of the

36

harbour, of which a knight said "this is the place which we mean to surrender to the Bashaw and we reserve it on purpose to bury him and his janissaries!" But why prolong the story? The Turks dragged boats across the isthmus which separates the two harbours, tried to destroy the stockade which closed the entrance of the French Creek, repeatedly attacked and almost carried by assault Fort St. Michael and the Bastion of Castile, and did all that brave men could do, but in vain.

On the 7th of September, a day ever since memorable in the annals of Malta, tardy succours arrived from Sicily, and landed in Melleha Bay. An engagement took place near Musta, after which the Turks quitted the island with all speed, having lost no less than 25,000 men, whilst on the side of the Order 200 knights, 2500 soldiers, and 7000 inhabitants had lost their lives. The Borgo received the proud title of "Citta Vittoriosa" or "the Victorious City," whilst Senglea has ever since been styled "Invicta" or "Unconquered." The Turks prepared fresh armaments but incendiaries in the pay of La Vallette destroyed the arsenals at Constantinople, and Malta was left in peace. On Thursday, March 28th, 1566, La Vallette laid the foundation stone of the city which has ever since borne his name. The daily sum expended for building purposes varied from £150 to £200, and Città Notabile thence forward bore its present name of Città Vecchia. On August 21st, 1568 La Vallette died, lamented and honoured, from the effects of a sunstroke. His grave is in the Church of St. John.

On March 17th, 1570, the Order removed from the Borgo to the new City. Each Language had

37

its own post to defend, and its own Auberge or palace. In 1570 Admiral St. Clement was defeated near Girgenti by a Turkish squadron, but on Oct. 7th, in the following year Maltese galleys took part in the great victory of Lepanto. In 1575 the Inquisition was established in Malta, and retained its power until the arrival of the French in 1798. The Grand Master John de La Cassiere (1572-1582) expelled all Jews from the islands, and tried to remove from Valletta all women of bad character. In 1582 the city of Valletta contained 2000 houses, there were on the ramparts 150 brass guns, besides 12 mounted at St. Angelo, 20,000 qrs. of wheat were imported annually from Sicily, and Malta produced about 100 casks of wine yearly. The Maltese strictly performed their religious duties, but, adds the Pope's Legate "Would to God the same could be said of the knights!" During this year, we are told by Dr. Vassallo, that a dispute having arisen between Bishop Gargallo and the Canons of the Cathedral at Città Vecchia, the Bishop seized the Canons in the Cathedral, dragged them, arrayed in full canonicals, behind his horses to the prisons of the Borgo, and confiscated their property. For this high handed proceeding the Bishop was justly condemned by the Pope to suspension, banishment, and fine.

The Turks having again carried off slaves from Gozo the Grand Master Cardinal Verdala erected fortifications for the protection of the western portion of the island. In 1592 some Tuscan galleys coming from the Levant introduced the plague to which 3,800 fell victims. The population of Malta and Gozo in 1590 was 30,500. The Jesuits were first introduced into Malta in 1593.

38

In 1601 a successful attack was made by the galleys upon Lepanto and Patras, and in 1614 the Turks again landed in the Bay of Marsa Scirocco. On April 21st of the same year the Grand Master Alofio de Wignacourt completed the acqueduct which has ever since been such a priceless boon to Malta, and admitted the water to the fountain in St. George's Square, amidst great public rejoicings. In 1619 some of the young knights raised a riot, and were with difficulty prevented from throwing an unpopular suffragan bishop into the Marsamuscetto Harbour. This would indeed have been throwing cold water on the episcopate!

The Grand Master Alofio de Wignacourt built a tower for the protection of Comino, and at his death in 1622 left to the Order the large sum of £20,460 besides 200 slaves and 4000 qrs. of corn. A few months afterwards the Bishop of Malta removed his official residence from Città Vecchia to Valletta, not without considerable opposition from the Grand Master Vasconcellos. In 1623 the island was slightly visited by the plague. In 1631 the last General Chapter but one was held. Of this assembly the Grand Master Pinto said: "Were I king of France I would never assemble the States General; were I the Pope I would never convoke a Council, being the head of the Order of St. John I want no General Chapters. I know that these assemblies always end in an attack upon the rights of those who have convened them." The last General Chapter was held in 1776.

According to the census taken in 1632 the total population amounted to 54,463 persons. There were 4171 cattle, and 2132 beasts of burden. The produce

39

of that year was 5289 qrs. of wheat, and of other kinds of corn 29,776 qrs. In 1636 the fortifications of Floriana were commenced, which are named after Col. P. P. Floriani an Italian engineer. After two years labour and an expenditure of £8000 the lines were left unfinished, and were not finally completed for nearly a century. In 1638 the defences of Margarita Hill were commenced, under the auspices of Father Firenzuola. Want of funds compelled the suspension of the work until the year 1716. An attempt was made in 1639 to revive the language of England, but the troubles between Charles I. and his Parliament put an end to the design. Tumults having arisen the Jesuits were for a short time expelled from Malta in 1639, and six years afterwards a riot of the Maltese women took place at Città Vecchia in consequence of a proposal to dismantle that ancient stronghold.

The year 1644 witnessed the capture at sea of the Great Turkish Galleon, an event which is still often mentioned with pride by the Maltese. In 1650 the Public Library first had a beginning, and about this time the islands of St. Christopher, St. Bartholomew, St. Martin, and St. Croix in the West Indies were purchased by the Order for £5000.— an unfortunate speculation!

In 1656 the Maltese galleys had a great share in a signal victory gained over the Turks near the Dardanelles. Plague and famine threatened the islands for some years, and to repel invaders 14 watch towers were generously built upon the shore by the Grand Master De Redin at his own expense. On August 28th 1670 in the Bastion of St. Nicholas the first stone was laid by the Grand Master Nicholas Cotoner of the stupendous fortifications which bear his name;

40

and which are nearly three miles in length. Some 50 years elapsed before these works were completed. At the close of the year 1675 the plague reappeared, and it is said that 11,300 persons perished. A terrible earthquake in January 1693 which lasted several days, caused great damage to buildings and destroyed the Cathedral at Città Vecchia. It was however rebuilt by the year 1700.

The Grand Master Raymond Perellos y Roccafull did much to increase the navy, but when engaged with a Turkish foe the flagship sank with five hundred men, the Admiral Spinola and a few others escaping with difficulty. In 1709 the Turks attacked Gozo, and in 1722 they endeavoured in vain to excite a revolt amongst the numerous Mahometan slaves in Malta. The Grand Master Manoel de Vilhena did much to strengthen the fortifications, and built at a cost of £2,500, defrayed by himself, the fort on the island in the Marsamuscetto or Quarantine Harbour which bears his name. Grand Master Pinto improved the Palace, established a printing press under Government control, built the "Pinto Stores" near the Great Harbour, erected the Castellania or Courts of Justice, finished Fort Chambray in Gozo, encouraged the planting of mulberry trees, and the manufacture of silk, built bomb proof shelters at Fort St. Elmo for women and children in the event of a siege, armed men of war, commenced the excavation of a dock and the building of the Custom House, and successfully resented the interference of the King of Sicily in the internal affairs of the island.

There were in the year 1749 about 4000 Turkish or Moorish slaves in Malta and a conspiracy was formed amongst them to murder the knights

41

on the festival of S. S. Peter and Paul (June 29th). The appointed signal for the rising was to be the exhibition of the head of the Grand Master Pinto from the balcony of the Palace. The plot was discovered, and about 60 of the ringleaders were put to death. A great storm did much damage in 1755, and the church of Melleha fell, burying many persons. The Public Library and the Church of St. John owe much to the Grand Master Pinto, who in 1768 expelled the Jesuits, forbidding them ever to return, and confiscated their convent and property. In 1775 a popular rising known as the "Rebellion of the Priests" took place against the unpopular Grand Master Ximenes de Texada. It was soon put down, and the leader Don Gaetano Mannarino was imprisoned for 23 years until the arrival of the French in 1798.

The Grand Master Emmanuel de Rohan did much for Malta. Amongst other benefits the laws of Malta were revised and embodied in the celebrated Code Rohan. In 1783 a terrible earthquake caused much misery and destruction in Sicily and Calabria, whereupon the Maltese galleys at once put to sea, carrying timely relief to the distressed inhabitants of Messina to the value of £1,703. The year 1784 saw the establishment at a cost of £1,405 of the new Anglo-Bavarian Language, and the union of the Order of Jerusalem with that of St. Antonio of Vienna. In 1793 Fort Tigne was completed, at the entrance of the Quarantine Harbour. It is named after the Grand Prior of Champagne who designed it. But the fall of the Order was at hand.

On Septr. 19th, 1792, the National Assembly of France decreed that the Order of Malta in France

42

should be entirely annulled, and its property annexed to the national domains. The decrease of annual income at once amounted to £51,816. German and Arragonese, Spanish, Sicilian, Portuguese, and Neapolitan Commanderies shared the same fate. A party which desired the surrender of Malta to France was formed in the island. The plate belonging to the men of war, galleys, Palace, and Hospital was entirely or in part coined into money. The greatest economy was practised, and the Navy greatly reduced. The deficit, however, continued to grow larger day by day.

On June 6th, 1798, a French fleet commanded by Commodore Sidoux, consisting of eighteen men of war and seventy transports appeared off Malta, followed three days afterwards by a still larger one under Admiral Brueys, composed of 18 sail of the line, 18 frigates, and more than 400 transports. There were 282 knights capable of bearing arms out of 332 who were present in Malta, besides land and sea forces numbering 6,800. Refused permission to enter the harbour, the French effected a landing on the morning of Sunday, June 10th at 4 a. m. at eleven different points in Malta and Gozo. Within the walls of Valletta all was panic and confusion, and on the 12th of June a capitulation was signed on board the man of war L' Orient by which Malta was surrendered to Bonaparte. The Grand Master Hompesch was promised his income for his lifetime; and French knights might return to France. Private property belonging to the knights was to be respected, and each knight was to receive an annual pension of 700 francs and those above 60 years of age 1000 francs. The religion, privileges,

43

and liberties of the Maltese were to be respected.

The same afternoon 15,000 French troops took possession of the forts, and the victorious fleet entered the harbour. Two men of war, one frigate, four galleys, 1200 guns, 1,500,000 lbs. of powder, 40,000 muskets, besides shot and shell in abundance were found in Malta. The weak and feeble-minded Grand Master Hompesch embarked with 12 knights on the night of June 17th on board an Austrian merchant ship bound for Trieste. He died in obscurity at Montpellier in the year 1804. Thus fell the Order of St. John.

The French at once set to work to make Malta a Gallic colony. Knights under sixty years of age were obliged to leave the island within three days, all coats of arms and escutcheons were to be defaced, and nearly all the church plate together with that belonging to the Palace and the Auberges found its way to the crucible. On June 21st Buonaparte left Malta, carrying with him the Maltese regiment, the Grand Master's guards, and many Maltese sailors.

General Vaubois who was left behind with 3,053 infantry and five companies of artillery to garrison Valletta carried on the work of spoliation, until at length on September 2nd 1798 the Maltese, exasperated beyond endurance by an attempted sale of church property at Città Vecchia, rose against and put to the sword the 65 men who formed the garrison of the town. Next morning a French detachment proceeding to Città Vecchia was compelled to retreat into the town by some peasants led by Vincenzo Borg. All Malta heroically rose in arms against the oppressors, and, unaided by any European power, formed the blockade of Valletta. At

44

the request of Lord Nelson to whom messengers were despatched by the insurgents, a Portuguese squadron blockaded the harbour, until the arrival of Lord Nelson himself. The city of Valletta was several times bombarded, both by sea and land. The Maltese mortgaged every thing to raise money, and suffered terrible hardships, but still the French held out. A plot to give up the city to the insurgents was detected, and the conspirators were put to death without mercy. Famine and disease did their work, and, during the two years siege, 20,000 Maltese are said to have perished. A congress was assembled, which sat at the Palace of St. Antonio, and of which Sir Alexander Ball who had been left by Nelson to direct operations, was the president. The English flag was first hoisted in Malta at Città Vecchia on the house of Baron Gauci, at which Major General Pigot was a guest, and at which the Anglo-Maltese Convention was signed.

In Dec. 1799 Brigadier General Graham landed with the 30th and 89th Regiments and some artillerymen, numbering in all 1,309 men. These were followed by two Neapolitan regiments, and in June 1800, Major General Pigot took command, having brought with him the 48th Regiment and the two Battalions of the 35th Regiment. Still the French held out gallantly, and made 86,000 qrs. of wheat supply the garrison for two years instead of for seven months. In September 1799 a lb. of fresh pork was sold in Valletta for 6s., a lb. of salt meat for 2s. 10d., the commonest fish for 2s. 2d. a b., a fowl cost 50s., a pigeon 10s., a lb. of sugar 18s. 4d., a lb. of coffee 21s. 8d., and a good fat rat 2s. 7d. The ships which tried to escape from the

45

harbour were captured by the English fleet, and it was not until only four days' provisions were left in the fortress that General Vaubois surrendered Valletta to the allied English, Maltese, and Neapolitan forces. On September 8th, the anniversary of the defeat of the Turks, the French troops sailed for Marseilles in English transports, and the two years' siege came to an end.

On February 19th, 1801 Major General Pigot issued a proclamation to the effect that his Britannic Majesty took the Maltese under his protection, and granted them the full enjoyment of their religion, property, and liberties. This was confirmed by Sir C. Cameron, Civil Commissioner, on June 15th, 1801. In 1802 the English government spent £3,783 for the redemption of Maltese slaves at Constantinople. According to the terms of the Treaty of Amiens, Malta was to be restored to the Knights of St. John. A Maltese Langue was to be established, those of France and England being suppressed, and the English troops were to evacuate the islands within three months. The Maltese at once despatched a deputation to London to protest against this arrangement, and to claim either entire freedom or the protection of England. The Governor Sir Alexander J. Ball did all in his power to prevent the cession of the islands, war broke out once more, and in 1814, by the 7th article of the Treaty of Paris it was declared that "the island of Malta with all its dependencies shall appertain in full authority and sovereignty to His Britannic Majesty."

The Latin inscription placed on the Main Guard by order of Sir Thomas Maitland has a pleasant

46

sound to English ears, but is nevertheless true "The love of the Maltese and the voice of Europe confirms these islands to great and invincible Britain." The Order of St. John of Jerusalem still exists at Rome, but has no longer any connection with Malta.

"Happy is the nation that has no history," and our record of events since the departure of the French is, fortunately, but brief. In the autumn of 1809, Sir Alexander J. Ball died at San Antonio, lamented by the whole population. Two years previously, on April 3rd, 1807 the magazine of Fort Ricasoli was blown up by some mutineers, of which more hereafter. In 1812 the plague committed terrible ravages, carrying off no fewer than 4,668 persons. In 1818 Sir Thomas Maitland put an end to the Università, an ancient municipal governing body, and also to the office of the Giurati, another of the time honoured institutions of Malta. On February 4th, 1820 six of the crew of the *William* of Liverpool were executed for piracy, and hung in chains on the redoubt near Fort Ricasoli which is popularly known as "the Pirate's Tower."

On May 1st, 1835 Sir Frederick Ponsonby issued a proclamation notifying "the creation and establishment of a Council of Government within this island of Malta." This Council was reformed in 1849, and is now composed of 18 members, 10 of whom are appointed by the Crown, and the other eight elected by the people. The Judges of the Superior Court of Justice are ineligible, and not more than two ecclesiastics can be Members of Council at one and the same time. Member of Council are styled "Honourable." The session commences in November and ends in June.

47

On October 25th, 1836 John Austin Esq. and George Cornewall Lewis Esq. (afterwards Sir George Cornewall Lewis Esq. Bart.) arrived in Malta as Royal Commissioners and resided in the island for some 18 months. They recommended the abolition of the censorship of the press which was accordingly effected by an Ordinance of Council promulgated on March 16th, 1839. Many changes were made in the Customs and other dues, the Charitable Institutions were re-organized, Primary Education received due attention, and schools were established in the various casals or villages. The only three situations reserved for Englishmen were those of Chief Secretary, First Assistant Secretary, and Auditor of Accounts. The administration of justice was simplified, and the police force was assimilated to that of England. In the year 1837 more than 4,000 persons died of cholera. Under the administration of Sir H. Bouverie much was done to make good roads, and to drain the Marsa at the upper end of the Great Harbour. The Dowager Queen Adelaide spent the winter of 1838 in Malta, and on March 20th 1839 laid the foundation stone of the English Collegiate Church of St. Paul, which was erected at her sole expence at a cost of £18,000.

In 1847 the Right Honourable Richard More O Ferrall was appointed as Civil Governor, and two years afterwards a reform took place in the Council of Government. Sir William Reid the next Governor did all in his power to raise the standard of education in Malta. He also widened and restored Porta Reale. The foundation stone of the new structure was laid on June 28th, 1853 by the Governor in the presence of the principal officers of the gar-

48

rison. Within the stone was placed a scroll from whence it appears that in 1858 the population of Malta and Gozo exclusive of the garrison was 123,496. Of these 40,200 had no fixed occupation, 1,040 were priests and 125 nuns. There were six educational establishments under ecclesiastical control, 18 supported by Government, and 156 private schools. There was one English church built by the Dowager Queen Adelaide, two military chapels, and one Scotch church. The annual revenue amounted to £227,000.

Sir Gaspard Le Merchant did much whilst Governor for the improvement of education and to increase the water supply. He planted trees in various places, reconstructed 23 roads, widened more than 20, and made 14 new ones. During his term of office the lunatic asylum near Città Vecchia was completed and opened. The Ospizio or Poorhouse, the Hospital for Incurables, the Orphan Asylum, and the Central Hospital were all modified for the better, and it is to Sir Gaspard Le Marchant that Valletta is indebted for its new Market and magnificient Opera House. During this period also the public offices were concentrated at the Palace, telegraphic communication was greatly extended, the prison system was re-organized, alterations were introduced into judicial procedure, and the former home of the Grand Masters was beautified at a cost of £1100. The Marsa at the head of the Great Harbour was extended and deepened, the fortifications were rendered more easily defensible, the works at Pembroke Camp were commenced and completed, and the old palace of the Giurati at Città Vecchia was converted into a Military Sanatarium.

49

In 1864 and again in 1867 Malta suffered from visitations of cholera, and in 1865 Sir Henry Storks appointed a Commission of Enquiry into the condition of Primary Education. The foundation stone of Holy Trinity Church Sliema was laid on September 20th 1866, and the Church was consecrated by the Right Rev. Dr. Trower D. D. late Bishop of Gibraltar on April 23rd 1867. On May 25th 1873 the interior of the Opera House was destroyed by fire. The consecration of the Most. Rev. Count. D. Carmelo Scicluna, D. D., Archbishop of Rhodes and Bishop of Malta took place in St. John's Church on April 11th 1875, the Archbishop of Reggio officiating. H R. H. the Prince of Wales first visited Malta on July 5th 1862, again on October 30th of the same year in company with the Crown Prince and Princess of Prussia, and also on his return from India in the Serapis in April 1876. On each occasion there were great public rejoicings. The Palace of San Antonio was the residence during a portion of the year 1877 of the Duke and Duchess of Edinburgh. The ex-Empress Eugenie visited the island in 1876, and T. R. H. the Duke and Duchess of Connaught included Malta in their wedding tour in 1879.

Though the history of the islands has of late years been uneventful, the inhabitants have been prosperous and happy. In 1878 Malta was selected as the European place of sojourn of the Indian Contingent. None of those who saw the great review on the Floriana parade ground by H. R. H. the Commander in Chief, or the Levèe at the Palace, will ever forget those imposing spectacles. On Jan. 31st. 1880, H. M. S. Thunderer once more left port

50

after remaining in harbour for more than a year, to repair damages caused by the terrible bursting of one of her 38 ton guns on Jan. 12th 1879, by which several valuable lives were sacrificed. Great storms in Sicily and heavy weather prevented the arrival of the Italian mail steamers for a whole fortnight of the month of February 1880. Important reforms of the Civil Establishments of Malta, recommended in the Official Report of Sir Penrose Julyan C. B. are under consideration. The present Governor of Malta is H. E. Sir Arthur Borton K. C. B. to whom this handbook is with much respect (by permission) dedicated.

LIST OF GRAND MASTERS WHO RULED IN MALTA FROM 1530 TO 1798.

L'Isle Adam	1530	Martin de Redin	1657
Peter du Pont	1534	Annet de Clermont Gessan.	1660
Didier de St. Jaille	1536	Raphael Cotoner	1693
John D' Omèdes	1536	Gregory Caraffa	1680
Claude de la Sengle	1553	Adrian Wignacourt	1690
John de la Vallette	1557	Raymond Perellos	1697
Peter de Monte	1568	Mark Anthony Zondadari	1720
John de la Cassiere	1572	Anthony Manoel de Vilhena	1722
Hugo de Verdalle	1582		
Martin Garzes	1595	Raymond D'Espuig	1736
Alophius Wignacourt	1601	Emmanuel Pinto	1741
Louis Mendes Vasconcellos	1622	Ximenes de Texada	1773
Anthony de Paule	1623	Emanuel de Rohan	1775
Lascaris Castellar	1635	Ferdinand de Hompesch	1797

PART SECOND.

CHAPTER I.

THE CITY OF VALLETTA.

Situation of Valletta.—Foundation of the City.—Streets of stairs.—Arrangement of Streets.—Houses, Lodgings, and Hotels.—Boat and Carriage fares.—Postal information.—Telegraph Companies.—Medical Men and Merchants.—Lines of Steamers, and Steam Ship Agents.—Consuls.—Weights and Measures.

THE city of Valletta is situated on the north eastern shore of the island, in Long. 14°. 31'. and Lat. 35° 53'. N., and stands upon a promontory or tongue of land which separates the Quarantine and Great Harbours. This promontory bears the Arabic name of Mount Sceberras, which is variously said to mean "the lofty place" or "the jutting out of the cape." It was. also formerly styled "Guardia" from the constant watch maintained here both by day and night. From its shape it has also received the English appellation of "The Hog's Back." Mount Sceberras, which projects into the sea in a north easterly direction, is 3200 yards in length by about 1200 in breadth, except at its seaward extremity where it narrows considerably. Its highest point is about 200 feet above sea level, but this elevation becomes much less towards its junction with the mainland. Under favou-

52

able circumstances the snow-clad summit of Mount Etna 128 miles distant may be seen from Valletta, and the eruptions of this volcano are distinctly visible at night.

Mount Sceberras was formerly the property of a Maltese family of the same name, to whose representatives the Grand Masters were accustomed to present annually a small coin as an acknowledgment of their rights. An ancient chapel formerly stood at the seaward extremity of Mount Sceberras dedicated to St. Erasmo, or St. Elmo, the patron saint of sailors. In 1488 a small star-shaped fort was ordered to be erected here, which received the name of St. Elmo from the already existing chapel. A fort of the same name formerly defended the entrance to the harbour of Rhodes. Fort St. Elmo was captured by the Turks in 1565 after a most heroic defence, and after the departure of the besiegers the Grand Master John de la Vallette determined to carry out his preconceived design of fortifying Mount Sceberras, and of making it the site of a flourishing city. Accordingly on the 28th of March 1566 the foundation stone of the new city was laid amidst great public rejoicings, on the spot whereon now stands the Church of Vittoria. La Vallette's name was given to his projected city, and he desired that the only epithet applied to it should be that of "Umilissima" "Most Humble." From the day of its foundation, Valletta has continually increased in population and importance, being admirably situated for commerce, and strongly defended against all attacks either by sea or land. The history of Malta has therefore for the last three centuries been intimately and inseparably linked with that of Valletta and its sister towns.

53

According to the census of 1871 the population of Valletta amounted to 24,818, the three cities of Vittoriosa, Cospicua, and Senglea on the other side of the Great Harbour having almost the same number of inhabitants.

Many of the streets are very steep, being upon the sloping sides of Mount Sceberras, and are either broad flights of stairs, or are flanked with steps for the convenience of foot passengers. It was the intention of the engineers who drew the plans for the city to level the summit of Mount Sceberras, and to form a level platform on which the city was to stand, defended by ramparts, which were to be in great measure formed from the solid rock scarped down to the water's edge. False alarms of a threatened attack from Constantinople prevented the execution of this design, and only the central portion of the work was completed. Hence the well known lines

"Adieu, ye joys of La Vallette.
Adieu, scirocco, sun, and sweat,
Adieu, ye cursed streets of stairs,
How surely he who mounts you swears!"

Under the full blaze of the July sun, to which however it is currently reported that only newly arrived Englishmen and mad dogs expose themselves, the streets of stairs are decidedly a weariness and a toil to mount!

Ten streets traverse the peninsula lengthwise, and are intersected at right angles by eleven others which, with but few exceptions connect the Great and Quarantine Harbours. The principal street is Strada Reale which runs from Porta Reale to Fort

54

St. Elmo, a distance of three quarters of a mile. Many of the best shops are situated in this street. Valletta was first lighted with gas in 1857. For commercial information we recommend all visitors to Malta to purchase the "Malta Almanacks" published annually by Mr. Critien, Bookseller, 28 Str. San Giovanni, and by Mr. Watson, Bookseller, 248 Strada Reale, which contain a mass of useful information. We can only note a few matters of general interest.

The houses in Malta are for the most part large, roomy, and convenient. The walls, especially those of the older houses, are of considerable thickness, for the sake of coolness. The roofs are flat and form terraces which serve to collect the rain-water, which is carried by pipes into underground tanks affording a supply during the rainless sultry days of summer. The terraced roofs also form a pleasant and favourite promenade during the summer evenings. The city is abundantly supplied with fresh water which is brought from the Bingemma Hills and their neighbourhood by means of an aqueduct more than nine miles in length. A great deal of attention has lately been directed to the question of drainage, and numerous sewers have been constructed under the superintendence of Colonel H. Wray, C. R. E.

Most of the houses in Malta are provided with one or more balconies, which, projecting over the streets, give a pleasant appearance of irregularity to the general outline, and afford both shelter and a view of the street to those within. Charcoal is generally used as fuel. Houses are usually hired by the month, quarter, half year, or year. The rent of a furnished house in Valletta is about £12 per month, unfurnished

55

houses being obtainable for half this amount. Furniture can be hired, and lodgings are fairly plentiful. Beef and mutton cost about $8\frac{1}{2}d$ per lb. Fruit and vegetables are abundant and cheap.

The principal hotels are the "Imperial," 91 Str. S. Lucia, also another of the same name, and belonging to the same proprietor at Sliema. Dunsford's Hotel, 254 Str. Reale; Morell's Family Hotel, 156 Str. Forni; Hotel d' Angleterre, 34 Str. Stretta; Great Britain Hotel, 42 Str. Mezzodì, St. George's Hotel, 74 Str. Teatro; Australian Hotel, 53 Str. Stretta; British Hotel, 267 St. S. Ursola; Europe Hotel, 58 Str. Zaccaria; Duke of Edinburgh, (Landing Place Sliema); Rising Sun Hotel, 7 Str. Giardino, Floriana; Old Minerva Hotel, 141 Str. Stretta; Crown Hotel, 69 Str. Stretta; and the Oriental Hotel, 29 Str. Stretta. Boats are easily obtainable at the various landing places. The usual charge for a boat to cross either of the harbours is 3d. Those who cross in company with other passengers pay $\frac{1}{2}$d. Between one hour after sun set and sunrise, and on festival days these fares are increased one half. When a blue flag is hoisted as a sign of stormy weather, double fares are chargeable. The tariff fare for a boat by time is $6d$ for the first hour, and $3d$ for each succeeding one. A carriage drawn by two horses if hired for less than half an hour $1s. 8d.$, for each succeeding quarter of an hour 8d. Any time beyond one hour to be paid for at half the above rates. For a carriage drawn by two horses, the fare for any distance not exceeding one mile is $8d.$, and for every half mile beyond that distance, 4d. Return fares one-half. For a carriage drawn by one horse two-thirds, and for a cart or "go-cart" one-half

54

of the above fares. Carriage, coachman, and pair of horses £8 per month. One horse carriage or saddle-horse £4. A carriage and pair for the day about 10 *s*. Shorter periods in proportion. Settle terms before starting. Tariff changes proposed.

The Post Office is at 197 Strada Mercanti, and is open daily from 9 a. m. till 5 p. m. On the arrival of mails during the night the office is open for a short time. Mails for England viâ Italy are made up on Mondays, Thursdays, and Saturdays, but we are promised five mails per week ere long. Postage for all countries within the General Postal Union $2\frac{1}{2}d$. Mails are also despatched on the 29th of each month viâ Naples. Mails for India are despatched every Thursday viâ Brindisi, and letters specially addressed "per P. & O. Steamer" are forwarded every Saturday. Local letters $\frac{1}{2}d$. per oz., newspapers free. Where time is an object, local letters should be sent by a messenger. The Mediterranean Extension and the Eastern Telegraph Companies have offices at 7, Strada Marsamuscetto. The first named of these Companies has Branch Offices at the Borsa (Strada Federico), and the Marsa, Great Harbour. The Branch Offices of the latter are at 95A Strada Santa Lucia, and 3 Strada Ghar Illembi, Sliema. Charge for a telegram of 20 words to London by either Company about 10*s*. Messages may be sent to Gozo by means of the Military Telegraph at very moderate rates.

There are many able and skilful medical men resident in Valletta, and Police Physicians are appointed in every district. There are also throughout Malta numerous Government Dispensaries where the poor can obtain medicines gratuitously. The pro-

57

fessional fees of Physicians and Surgeons are regulated
by a Government Ordinance. The Chamber of Commerce appointed annually by the mercantile community of Malta has its head quarters at the Borsa
or Malta Exchange in Strada Reale, as have also
the Malta Bank and the Anglo-Maltese Bank. Hours
from 9 0. a. m. till 4. 0. p. m. Messrs. James Bell.
and Co., 118 Strada San Domenico, and R. Duckworth
and Co., 14 Strada Ponente, are English Bankers.
Shipping Suppliers and Bankers; C. Caruana, 31 Str.
Nuova, Marina, Mortimer and Co., Molo, Marina, and
Michael and Sons, 7 Marina.

Weekly P. and O. steamers, nine days outward
bound from Southampton arrive about Friday.
Homeward bound steamers on Monday, but sometimes
later. Stay in Malta 6 hours. Fares to Southampton:
first class £15: second class and servants £9: soldiers,
sailors and their wives £6. Office, 41 Strada Mercanti.

The Fraissinet Cies mail steamers (Agent T.
G. Micallef Esq., 157 Strada Mercanti), arrive from
Marseilles and Naples every fortnight, and also from
Alexandria for Naples, Genoa, and Marseilles, twice
monthly, leaving the same day. Fares to Marseilles:
first class £ 8., second class £6. Fares to Alexandria:
first class, £6 : second class £4. 8s. 0d. Fares to
Naples : first class 80 francs: second class 60 francs.
To Genoa: first class 170 francs, second class 130
francs. Messrs. Smith and Co., 12 Strada Cristoforo,
are Agents for the British India Line of steamers.
Fares to London: first class £12. 12. 0: second class
£8. 0. 0: Fares to Bombay and Calcutta: first class
£40, second class £ 24. Also for the Moss Line
to Liverpool, first class £12 0. 0: second class
£10. Fares to Alexandria: first class £5, second class

58

£ 2. 10. Also for the Ocean Steamship Co., Corinthian Shipping Co., Northumberland Steam Shipping Co., Wilson's Line, and the Orient Line. Fares by these steamers as per Moss Line.

C. Lowe Esq. 94 Strada Forni, is the Agent for the Cunard Line to Liverpool, Constantinople, Syra, Smyrna, &c. Fares to Liverpool: first class £12. Fares to Constantinople £6, to Smyrna £5, to Syra £3. 10s. A. Camilleri Esq. 9 Strada Levante, is Agent for Leyland's Steamers and the Papayanni Line to Liverpool. Fares to Liverpool: first class £12. Fares to Alexandria, Constantinople and Smyrna £5. Syra £4. Malta has also steam communication with Holland, Belgium, North Africa, the Levant, Calcutta, and Shanghai.

Messrs. Addison Duncan & Co. 73D. Strada Mercanti, are Agents for steamers trading to the Black Sea and Levant. O. F. Gollcher Esq. 2 Strada Zaccaria, is the Agent for the Anchor Line, Henderson's Steamers, for London, Liverpool, and Rangoon, Royal Netherlands Steam Navigation Co., the Hall Line for Liverpool and Bombay, also steamers for London, the Levant, and Black Sea, as well as for Tunis (every Saturday).

T. G. Micallef Esq. 57 Strada Mercanti is Agent for the Clan Line. Fortnightely from London and Liverpool to Bombay. Fares to London: first class £12: second class £9. S. Micallef Eynaud Esq. 114 Strada S. Paolo, is Agent for steamers from Liverpool and North Shields to the Mediterranean and Black Sea. P. Eynaud and Co. 11 Marina, are Agents for the Florio Co's steamers which arrive on Monday, Thursday, and Saturday, returning the same evening. Fares to Naples: first class £4.

59

second class £2. 15: deck passage £1. 2. Also for the Rubattino Line to Tunis and Tripoli. Fares to Tunis: first class 61 francs: second class 41 francs. To Tripoli: first class 41 francs, second class 31 francs. For Tripoli on Wednesdays, and for Tunis on Saturdays. R. Ferro & Co. 34 Strada Federico, are Agents for steamers between Italy, Antwerp, Egypt, the Black Sea, also to London and India. R. Soler Esq. 15-16 Marina, is Agent for the Ottoman Steamer Trabulus Garb to and from Tripoli. Fares: first class 40 francs: deck passage 15 francs. Weekly departures. Messrs. Walker and Pace, 44 Strada S. Giovanni are Agents for various lines of steamers, and also for the Shipping and Mercantile Gazette.

The other principal merchants are W. Hearn Esq., 219 Strada Reale, Messrs. Turnbull Jun. and Somerville (Agents for Messrs. Henry S. King & Co.) 20 Strada Reale, and C. B. Eynaud Esq., 21 Marina, Barriera.

Ships of 3000 tons register can have hull or machinery repaired at the Clarence Hydraulic Lift Dock at the head of the Quarantine Harbour.

The following States have either Consuls or Vice-Consuls resident in Valletta—United States of America, Austria, Belgium, Brazil, Denmark, France, Germany, Greece, Italy, Morocco, the Netherlands, Persia, Portugal, Russia, Spain, Sweden and Norway, Turkey, and Tunis. The Rotolo is the usual standard of weight, and is often spoken of as if it were equivalent to two lbs. English, but it is actually 28 English or 30 Maltese oz. The Maltese salm is the same as the English qr., and the cantar contains 100 rotolos.

60

CHAPTER II.

CLIMATE.

Mild in winter.—Prevailing Winds.—Gregale and Scirocco.—Sultry in Summer.—Winter attractions for invalids.

FROM the end of October until May, the climate of the Maltese islands is exceedingly pleasant and healthy. Rain falls abundantly during the winter season, the annual average being about 24. 23. inches, but only at intervals, and many bright and sunny days are enjoyed even during this season. Hail sometimes falls, but snow never. Ice may occasionally be found, though only in thin layers, on calm winter mornings, or when a very light breeze is blowing from the N. W. It has been seen at Polverista Gate, in the Dockyard Creek, at the Marsa, and at Pietà. Throughout the winter an entire day without sunshine or an entire day of rain is equally rare, though they do sometimes occur. Rain falls chiefly during the night, and, though almost tropical in its violence, is speedily absorbed by the highly porous soil. Invalids may with due precautions take open-air exercise at some time or other on almost every day of the year, but no one suffering from debility should remain in Malta during the great heats of summer. No place can boast of a greater equality of temperature. During the eight cool months the thermometer at no period of the 24 hours falls below 51°, except on rare occasions, nor does it rise above 71. During the four summer months 86° is the highest temperature usually attained, 73° being the

61

lowest. The average annual temperature of Malta is 67° 3'. The prevailing winds are from the N. W. and S. E. The Commander Dolomieu has calculated that the former blow on 200 days in the year, and the latter during the remaining 165. The Northerly winds called by the natives *Venti alti* are bracing and invigorating, passing as they do over a wide expanse of sea, but those from the south called *Venti Bassi*, with their attendant clouds and mists are warm and enervating, having first swept over the burning sandy plains of Africa.

Many of the poorer clsases habitually sleep out of doors during the summer months without experiencing any ill effects. The coldest winds are from the N. W. Westerly winds generally bring rain. The Gregale cr N. E. wind sometimes blows with hurricane force. Ships have been sunk in the harbours, the quays torn up, and the lower tier of merlons at Fort Saint Angelo, with an estimated weight of 90 tons each, uprooted and shifted for several yards. Fortunately the gregale is not a frequent visitor, and is not in the habit of prolonging its stay on these shores. Easterly winds are mild, but the S. E. or Scirocco wind is close, damp, and misty. This wind is especially prevalent in September but also visits Malta at other times. Whilst it is blowing the pavement of the streets is quite wet, and every thing is covered with a moisture resembling heavy dew. Paint applied during the prevalence of a Scirocco never thoroughly dries, metals become tarnished, and gum loses its adhesive properties. Many feel languid, depressed, and in low spirits, but others seem insensible to its influence. It appears to affect the natives quite as much if not more than the English

62

residents. Though a "black sciroc" does not deserve quite all the hard things that have been said against it, its advent is nevertheless by no means welcomed by dwellers in the "Fior del Mondo." In Africa it is an exceedingly dry and rather strong wind, but when it arrives in Malta, having traversed a considerable expanse of sea, it has become heavily charged with vapour, whilst retaining the heat accumulated in its passage over the deserts of Africa. Iced beverages are very pleasant during a "Sciroc," and in the time of the Knights whenever supplies of snow from Sicily were small, the contents of the icehouses were reserved for the use of the hospital. An old author says that a century ago the Maltese used to emerge from a bath by degrees without making use of a towel in order to ward off inconveniences resulting from this wind. Windows and doors should be kept closed whilst it blows. The mean quantity of moisture in the air of the Mediterranean basin is only equal to one half of that in the atmosphere of England.

The summer days are sultry, but the mornings and evenings are deliciously cool. The sun remains so long above the horizon, and the countless stone walls absorb abundant heat which radiates from them so copiously after sundown that the nights are often uncomfortably hot and sultry. Both by night and day there is frequently a sensation of heat far greater than that warranted by the actual indication of the thermometer. The Mediterranean currents which run not less than three knots an hour considerably modify the temperature. It is the decided opinion of the medical authorities that regiments and departmental officers ought not to be

63

stationed in Malta for a longer period than three years at a time.

The Maltese enjoy good health and often live to a great age, the peasantry being especially robust and vigorous. The "colpo d'aria" or sudden cheeking of perspiration must be guarded against, as speedy and fatal illness results from it. During the winter months, invalids will do well to visit Malta. It is easy of access and the climate is delightful. The markets are well supplied with both luxuries and necessaries, green peas being in season from November till May. The houses are spacious and airy, and much attention has of late been paid to drainage and sanitary measures. Amusements abound, and cosmopolitan Valletta the meeting place of nations, can offer much during the season to divert the tourist or pleasure seeker. To the archæologist, geologist, botanist, or artist, as well as to him who voyages in quest of health Malta presents many objects of interest, whilst the lover of animals will be pleased to learn that hydrophobia is said to be an unknown disease in Malta, and that horses never suffer from glanders or from grease.

CHAPTER III.

The Months in Malta.

The following valuable observations are kindly contributed by Sig. G. Abela Pulis.

JANUARY.

THE Japanese medlar, almond, caroubier, Neapolitan medlar, hortensia, elder, and mulberry trees are in leaf, also the jessamine and various roses. The almond, and lemon trees are in flower, also the Asiatic ranunculus with its numerous varieties, and hyacinths. The lime (*Citrus limetta*), sweet orange (*C. Aurantium*), mandarin (*C. aur. nobile*), and Seville (*C. Bigaradia*) orange, bear fruit. The countryman sows cabbages, turnips, cumin, tomatoes, lentils, maize, vetches, and anise: plants potatoes, using foreign tubers, and onions: weeds beans, corn, garlic, &c., reaps green barley for forage, and stores winter potatoes. Meanwhile the gardener sows the almond: prunes and grafts the vine and gum-producing trees: and plants vines, mulberry trees, and strawberries. Of spontaneously growing plants there are in flower the *Anemone coronaria, Erica multiflora,* red cornucopia, and rosemary, &c. The Channa is plentiful, also mullet of exquisite flavour. On January 25th 1865 was captured a female *Alopus filamentosus,* called by Sicilians the imperial blackbird. All the species of sea mews and gulls are plentiful, with starlings, woodcock, &c. and many aquatic birds. The Actinia Fordaica with other species of shellfish swarm in all the harbours.

65

The proverb says "Dry days in January make plenty of fruit!"

FEBRUARY.

The nectarine, service, banana, apple, pomegranate, sweet pepper, sulphur rose, and plane trees are in leaf: the apricot, strawberry, pine, and laurel are in flower: limes, lemons, peas, and beans yield their stores. Meanwhile the peasant sows March grain, cumin, and potatoes: weeds corn, late beans, potatoes, and cumin. Ground intended for cotton must be ploughed; sulla or clover, and trefoil are cut for green forage. The gardener sows gourds, sweet pepper, and pumpkins: *Adonis æstivalis, Viola odorata, Oxalis cernua, Coronilla Emerus, Coronilla stipularis,* the laurel, African pea or *Krempuc,* and other species are in flower. Birds approach our shores, also several species of the Cockrell, which are caught during April, and sometimes even as late as June. On February 7th 1866 several large band fish were captured, and on February 17th 1854 a very fine sword fish. Lizards and wood snakes awake from their winter sleep. Some woodcock arrive, also the robin redbreast, and other birds. The farmers' proverb says: "February's rain is as good as a dunghill, and fills every garner."

MARCH.

This is the month of leaves, sun-strokes, colds, and rheumatic fevers. Amongst the trees and plants in leaf are the vine, oleander, peach, pine, pear, lemon, plum, caroubier and cotton plant: the lime,

5

orange, laurel, Japanese medlar, pear, apple, artemisia, plum, and barley are in flower. Lemons, peas, and beans are productive. In the country, common anise, vetches, March corn, beetroot, kidney beans, maize, melons, water-melons, cotton, and white Indian wheat are sown. Corn, cumin, and anise are weeded. Labour in the gardens is directed to the sowing of oranges, cucumbers, sweet basil, and sweet pepper, to the transplanting of vegetable marrows, and the pruning and grafting of olives. The *Nigella damascena*, various poppies, the *Crategus oxyacantha*, and many other plants are in flower. March is the best month for botanical rambles. The districts with the greatest variety of species are the Wied Babu on the south side of the island, Gneina, on the S. W. shore, Puales, near St. Paul's Bay, and the whole of Gozo. Fish begin to be plentiful, and the whiting is caught until the end of June. Many birds arrive. The Catalogue by Mr. C. A. Wright will be found very useful by the ornithologist. Silkworms are hatched, but the manufacture of silk is no longer carried on. " If March be not seasonable June will not be festive! "

APRIL.

The month for flowers. Cases of apoplexy are not uncommon. The jujube, black mulberry, walnut, olive, apple, cherry, prickly pear, and pistacchio trees are in leaf. Spinach, mushrooms, onions, olives, quinces, potatoes, artichokes, pomegranates, and the white mulberry are in blossom. Strawberries, Japanese medlars, tomatoes, and vetches yield their increase: the orange tree sheds its leaves. Rural occupations in fields and gardens are: sowing cotton, white Indian wheat, melons, water-melons, maize, the Syrian marsh-mallow, and fennel: thinning cotton, and mowing clover for hay. Clover and beans are uprooted, and potatoes dug up. The gardener sows pumpkins, cauliflowers, and Cayenne pepper, transplants pumpkins, and uproots the bulbs of garlic. Many flowers bloom, amongst which are the varieties of the caper. The botanist is still busy. Blackbirds are caught in large numbers, swordfish appear, and various crustaceans are caught. See Dr. Gulia's "Pesci di Malta." Sheep are shorn. Bees prepare to swarm. "April brings flowers of which May gets the credit."

MAY.

The month for mowing. The jujube, olive, cassia and cotton plant are in leaf: spinach, onions, saffron, vines, and wild marjoram, prickly pear, iris, and a thousand others are in blossom, whilst barley, black vetches, kidney beans, almonds, cabbages, apricots, and chick-peas, cherries, cumin, cucumbers, tomatoes, gourds, and coriander have reached maturity. Cotton is sown on clay soils, cumin is gathered, and barley being mown the threshing-floor is got ready. The gardener transplants pumpkins, sweet, and Cayenne pepper, sweet basil, and gourds. He also prunes his vines, and hoes his pot-herbs. The willow, wild plum, the star of Bethlehem, called in Maltese speech "Fowl's milk," convolvulus, and many others blossom. The learned rock-fish, which is caught with the net, is excellent. Gozitans fish for the boops: quails, roller birds, starlings, and

68

other birds arrive. Migratory locusts are frequent but unwelcome visitors. "A careful man is never poor!"

JUNE.

The month for threshing. The first signs of epidemics usually appear during this month. The Japanese medlar puts forth branches for the second time, and the anise, sweet and wild marjoram, sweet plum, jujube, and pomegranate trees are in flower. Cherries, corn, beetroot, St. John's figs, black mulberries, water melons, pears, anise, and horse radish are gathered.

The peasant toiling beneath a burning sun plants cauliflowers between his cotton and water-melons, weeds and thins his cotton, reaps, and threshes his corn. Onions and potatoes are dug up. The gardener, less exposed to the sun, sows mulberries and leeks, caprificates figs, prunes, grafts, and irrigates the orange trees. Meanwhile the women pick the buds of the caper, which are sold by measure. Thyme, thorny endive, myrtle, and Jerusalem sage are noticeable plants. During the heat of the day, the grasshopper chirps in the fields; the lesser daw incubates at Filfla; glow-worms shine, and the tortoise lays its eggs. The cockrell is abundant, as are also several varieties of the ray and skate. The tunny fish taken off Trapani supplies our markets. When silkworms were reared, the cocoons were collected during this month. "Sickle in hand in June!"

JULY.

The month for heat, sun-strokes, lock-jaw, typhoid fevers, &c.

The orange, elder-tree, laurel, endive, mint, and caroubier are in leaf. Maize and cotton flower, and the apricot, melon, pear, apple, plum, pumpkin, onion, prickly pear, sweet pepper, nectarine, fig and vine are laden with fruit. The almond tree sheds its leaves. The peasant is busied in gathering anise, pulling up beetroot, in beating the heads of saffron, threshing corn, or sowing clover. Gardeners sow different kinds of cabbage, and gather almonds. Two species of Verbascum, the Orsinia Camphorata, on the forts and seaside cliffs of Gozo, the agnus castus. For Maltese Flora see Dr. Gulia's "Repertorio Botanico" and "Repertorio di Storia Naturale." Several species of the genus Sparus are caught by fishermen, also delicious white bait, and the Marroon or Castagnola, good for cats and men. A specimen of the *Smaris insidiator* was captured on July 6th 1865. Honey is collected, and weasels are born. "He who doubles his dunghill doubles his field!"

AUGUST.

The month of fruit and fevers. The wild and sweet marjoram, artichoke, and lemon are in leaf: the tuberose blossoms, and the peach, vine, pumpkin, pippin, walnut, Cayenne pepper, maize, caroubier and cotton yield increase. Figleaves fall, cotton is cut, and winter potatoes are planted, with the produce of Malta. Farmers begin to manure their land. Onions, horse-radish, and peas are sown. On the

70

sea shore are in flower the sweet smelling ambrosia, the marine critmo, and the medicinal squill. The lampuca, one of the best fish of the Mediterranean, is caught from August until the end of the year, and sometimes till the end of March. Mullet are plentiful, and also the boops which is caught in bownets, and we see shoals of sardines. The old saying is often true. "S. Antonio (17th Jan.) great cold.—S. Lorenzo (Aug. 10th) great heat.—Both of short duration!"

SEPTEMBER.

The vintage month. Catarrhal ophthalmia, liver complaints, and bilious fevers are prevalent. The date palm, onion and laurel are in leaf, and the jujube, walnut, yellow peach, bergamot, lime, lemon, sweet basil, and white Indian wheat are fruit bearing. The black mulberry and sweet plum shed their leaves. Fields are ploughed and manured before the sowing of vetches, barley, and garlic, the planting of winter potatoes, and the transplanting of various sorts of cabbage. The peasants are busily engaged in picking cotton-pods, and gathering the ears of maize. In the gardens tomatoes, endives, turnips, horse-radish, lettuce, onions, and artichokes are sown: pot-herbs are thinned and grafted, ripe pumpkins are cut, and exposed to the sun. Of spontaneous plants there are in flower the *Nepela Calamintha, Timo capitato,* several of the Hypericum tribe, *Inula viscosa,* and the *Datura metel,* poisonous to birds. In the waters are the razor-fish, the pearl-fish, (a delicacy), and the basse which pursues its prey especially into the Quarantine Harbour. Ladybirds and beetles are plentiful in the country, as well as other insects, such as the *Acherontia atropos, Deilephila lineata, Epilachna chrysomelina,* and *Asida sicula.* "The September moon draws seven moons."

OCTOBER.

The month for sowing. Colds and rheumatism are the order of the day. During this month diphteric affections, such as croup, &c. are common. Garlic, squills, saffron, and strawberries are in leaf, and the caroubier, fennel, and the Japanese medlar bloom. Fruit is yielded by the vine, olive, pomegranate, pear, laurel, service tree, quince, and apple. The peach, quince, pear, apple, jujube, apricot, and service trees shed their leaves. The fields are manured and sown with barley, vetches, peas and beans; tomatoes, and various turnips are planted. Spinach is sown, and olives, asparagus, and artichokes planted. Leeks are uprooted, and pumpkins cut. Fennel and the late narcissus are among the few flowers of this month. Various kinds of anchovy are caught, and Sig. Borg's tonnara at Melleha lays snares for the tunny which visit our shores. Shoals of the delicious white tunny are often caught at the same time. The cross spine is caught off the Great Harbour. This is the lambing season, and various birds arrive, such as the robin redbreast, water wagtail, bullfinch, greenfinch, chaffinch, &c., and some aquatic species. "If you would reap well sow quickly!"

NOVEMBER.

This leaf-falling month is very trying to persons in *the last stage* of consumption. The Japanese medlar is in leaf: the cauliflower, artichoke, and saffron bloom. The Japanese medlar bears fruit. We remark the shedding of leaves by the vine, pomegranate, Cayenne pepper, and elder tree. In the fields saffron, barley, and wheat are sown; onions and winter potatoes are planted. Carrots are sown and cabbages planted in gardens. Vines and pomegranates are pruned and cultivated. A sacred plant which formerly wrought many wonders blossoms in lonely places. It is collected by herbalists and sold to poor women to be used in baths for ricketty children. Sage *(clandestina)* and the ranunculus are in flower. Several kinds of sharks, amongst which are the Small Spotted and the Great Shark are caught in large numbers, except the last named, which is, fortunately, rare. From November until the end of February they have savoury flesh, which is more or less esteemed. The needle-fish and the flying-fish are plentiful in the markets, and are obtainable until the end of May. "A good manager's eye is worth as much as a dunghill!"

DECEMBER.

A rainy month. The sweet orange, mandarin, and the other species and varieties of the genus Citrus continue to bear fruit: the cherry, pistacchio, caper, and cotton shed their leaves. Wheat is sown, onions and figs planted: and fennel pulled up. The gardener sows almonds and beetroot, plants

73

the peach, plum, vine, apple, and strawberry: grafts the apricot, the plum upon the wild variety, and the pear upon the quince: he also prunes his vines. The flowers of the daffodil make the fields gay. Mullet are excellent: the Maltese say that red fish should be eaten in winter, and azure fish in summer. The Streaked Sparus appears from time to time. Storks arrive, and the caves of Ghar Dalam and Ghar Hassan are full of hybernating bats. We must not forget the bees, which, as flowers are scarce, require to be fed. "December sells and gives not back!"

CHAPTER IV.

STREETS AND BUILDINGS.

Porta Reale.—Strada Reale.—Opera House.—Union Club.—Church of St. John.—Courts of Justice.—Public Library.—Governor's Palace.—St. George's Square.—The Borsa, and Fort St. Elmo.—Strada Stretta, the old Duelling-ground. Strada Forni—Auberge de France, the Bakery, and the Auberge de Bavière.—Strada Zecca, and the Mint.—St. Paul's Church, and the Auberge d' Aragon—Marsamuscetto Steps and neighbourhood.—Walk round the Ramparts, &c.

AS we approach Valletta from the country, and note its thickly clustering houses of stone, we are reminded of the ancient prophecy that "every palm of Mount Sceberras (on which the city stands) would be worth a zecchin of gold" and of the words of Lord Beaconsfield: "Malta is certainly a most delightful station. Its city, Valletta, equals in its noble architecture, if it even does not excel, any capital in Europe. And although it must be confessed that the surrounding region is little better than a rock, the vicinity nevertheless, of Barbary, of Italy, and of Sicily, presents exhaustless resources to the lovers of the highest order of natural beauty. If that fair Valletta, with its streets of palaces, its picturesque forts, and magnificent church, only crowned some green and azure island of the Ionian Sea, Corfu for instance, I really think that the ideal of landscape would be realized."

We cross by a drawbridge the ditch which extends from the Great to the Quarantine Harbour,

75

950 yards long, 55 feet deep, and 30 wide, and enter by the principal gate called Porta Reale or "the Royal Gate," but which the French used to style "the National Gate." It is adorned with two statues, one of which is that of L'Isle Adam the heroic defender of Rhodes, and the other that of La Vallette the hero of the great siege of 1565, and the founder of the city which bears his name.

Above the gateway which was rebuilt in 1853, is an inscription commemorating the commencement of the city, which was probably formerly attached to the foundation stone. Passing the guard-house on the left we enter Strada Reale the principal street of Valletta, which runs in a straight line, though not on the same level for three quarters of a mile to Fort St. Elmo at the other extremity of the city. This street was formerly called Strada S. Giorgio, and on Mayday was used as a race-course in the days of the Order. Many of the best shops are in this street. We pass on the left a handsome block of new buildings, on the site of the old Ordnance Office, which was formerly used by the Knights as their "Ferreria" or foundry. On the opposite side of the road is a fountain with the words Omnibus Idem, "alike for all."

Close by is the noble Opera House with its Corinthian portico, one of the greatest architectural ornaments of Valletta, which stands on the site of the building known as the Auberge d' Inghilterra, the former home of the English knights. The demolition of the old building was commenced on February 24th 1861, and the foundation stone of the new Opera House was laid on September 11th 1861. It was opened on October 9th 1866 with

76

Bellini's Opera of "I Puritani." Mr. C. Barry was the architect. On May 25th 1873 a fire destroyed the interior fittings and decorations, but on Oct. 11th 1877 the Theatre was re-opened with Verdi's Opera of "Aida."

It is under the superintendence of a Committee appointed by the Government. The Opera season commences on October 15th of each year, and closes on the following 14th of May. Performances are usually given on Mondays, Tuesdays, Wednesdays, Thursdays, and Saturdays, with the exception of certain festivals, days of public mourning, &c. The *impresario* is bound to produce not less than 18 operas during the season, two of which must be entirely new to the Malta stage. Performances commence at 8. 30. p. m. Boxes for the season, per month from 6 *s*. 3 *d*. to £1. Stalls per month £1. 11. For the season, per month 12 *s*. 6 *d*. For one night 2 *s*. Amphitheatre 9 *d*. For further information see Malta Almanacks.

Strada Reale No. 7 is the Palazzo Azzopardi, and on the same side as the Opera House is the Church of Sta. Barbara with the inscription "Sanctæ Barbaræ Dicatum." The first church on this site was erected in 1573. Having fallen into decay it was rebuilt in 1740 and solemnly blessed by Mons. Rull Grand Prior of the Order on December 1st of that year. The principal picture is by the Cavalier Favray. Connected with the church is the very ancient Confraternity of the Bombardiers, which has existed for three centuries. Many of its members are buried beneath the church, Sta. Barbara being the patroness of artillery and all things therewith connected.

77

A few yards farther down Strada Reale at No. 20 are Messrs. Henry S. King and Co's suite of commodious Reading and Writing Rooms, Offices, &c. for ladies and gentlemen, which are specially intended for the use of passengers to and from the East. These Rooms which are under the management of Messrs. Turnbull Jun. and Somerville are kept open day and night when mail steamers are due. Passengers can receive and answer letters, see the latest telegrams, as well as English, Indian, and Colonial papers &c. free of charge. Instructions can be given here as to the forwarding of baggage and the execution of commissions in Malta, or by Messrs. Henry S. King & Co. either in London or at any of their Branch Houses. These Rooms are a great boon to travellers, who can here obtain all information relative to Cook's Tourist Arrangements, and also O ye smokers! good cigarettes! Members of the Indian Co-operative Agency will find the Malta Branch at Mr. Archer's, 303-306 Strada Reale, nearly facing the Opera House.

Opposite Messrs H. King's Reading Rooms are the Franciscan Church and Convent. The first Franciscan Convent in Valletta was founded in the year 1600 mainly through the exertions of Father Daniele La Greca a Sicilian priest. On April 5th 1730 the work of rebuilding it was commenced, the Grand Master Manoel de Vilhena giving £300 and lending slaves, convicts, and two carts. A large picture in the choir represents this Grand Master superintending the erection of a large convent. In 1681 the church was rebuilt by the Grand Master Gregorio Caraffa, whose portrait is in the sacristy. It is simple in architecture and consists of a nave. It

78

was beautified in 1862. There are several pictures here by Mattia Preti, and that of S. S. Cosmo and Damiano is by Paladini. Amongst other confraternities connected with this church is that of physicians and surgeons whose patron saints are S. S. Cosmo and Damiano. The confraternity of artists and painters formerly used to assemble here on St. Luke's Day.

Close at hand on the same side of the street is the Auberge de Provence, now occupied by the Union Club. This was the head quarters of the knights of the Language of Auvergne who had an annual revenue of £19,791. 10. 0. and who seem to have usually numbered about 60 resident in Malta. The head of each Auberge was called a Pilier who was responsible for the common table (see p: 30). The brethren were evidently sometimes unruly, for " If a brother be guilty of any insolence or indecency in the inn where he eats : if he break the doors, benches, tables, or any thing of the like nature or fling them away carelessly, he shall be punished by the master and the council. Whoever shall strike the piliers, pages, servants, or slaves, though he draws no blood shall be punished with the quarantaine, (40 days fast, confinement to quarters, attendance at all church services, bread and water on Wednesdays and Fridays eaten on the ground, in addition to a flogging in a state of nudity by a priest), with 6 months imprisonment for the second offence. " The giving of ill language to a brother in the Master's Palace was punished with the loss of three years' seniority: if in an inn, of two years' seniority. "If they draw their sword, or give a box, or kick, they shall be expelled without a possibility

79

of pardon. The brothers shall not bring any dogs with them to devour the bread that might else be left for the poor. If any dogs come in they shall be drove out, and if their master offers to oppose and complain of it, he shall suffer the same punishment."

This Auberge formerly contained many fine pictures, amongst which was one of La Vallette taking possession of Malta by the Cavalier Favray, and another of the Grand Master Rohan. The superior of the Auberge de Provence was called the Grand Commander; who by virtue of his office was perpetual president of the common treasury, comptroller of the accounts, superintendent of stores, governor of the arsenal, and master of the ordnance. He had the nomination (subject to the approbation of the Grand Master and Council) of all officers from the different Languages; and to this he added the power of appointing persons to various places of trust in the church of St. John, and in the Infirmary. The church of Sta. Barbara belonged to the Language of Provence which also had a chapel in the Church of St. John.

The Union Club was established in 1826, and is to consist of 150 members present in Malta. Officers of the Army and Navy, Civil employés of the Malta Government, and gentlemen residing in Malta are eligible. This Club is under the management of a Committee of nine members, including an Honorary Secretary and Treasurer. Members are elected by ballot. Visitors to Malta may be introduced for one week by a Member. The ceiling and walls of the Ball-room are very handsome, and are very good specimens of antique mural decoration. Quarterly Subscription £1. Entrance £5.

80

Pursuing our way down Strada Reale we speedily reach an open square which was planted with trees under the administration of Sir Gaspard le Marchant, and which was formerly a sanctuary. A criminal, however, who once dared to insult the Grand Master as he passed was dragged forth and hanged on the spot. We note a granite fountain surmounted by a lion, and another over which a unicorn presides, and have now reached the crowning glory of Valletta.

The Church of St. John.

On either side are two large houses. The one on the right was formerly the residence of the Grand Prior of the Order, and the upper portion is now occupied by the Circolo Maltese, one of the Maltese clubs. Entrance 8s. 4d. Annual Subscription £1. Admission by ballot. The house on the left was the abode of the Vice Prior, who guarded the treasures of the church, almost all of which were unfortunately carried off by the French in 1798. The facade, which is built in the semblance of both church and fortress, as belonging to an Order at once military and religious, has nothing striking in its appearance. It is surmounted by a Maltese cross, beneath which is a figure of Our Saviour, the work of Algardi of Bologna, which was brought from the now demolished church of S. Salvatore on the Marina. Above, is the inscription "Salva nos" (save us). The clock constructed by a Maltese called Clerici, has three faces, which mark respectively the hour, the day of the week, and that of the month. The two flanking bell-towers contain ten bells, seven of which give warning of the church services whilst

81

the other three are connected with the clock. Two of the largest were given by the Grand Master Pinto, and were consecrated by Bishop Alpheran de Bussan. The building of the church was commenced during the rule of the Grand Master De La Cassière, who employed the architect Girolamo Cassar, who also drew the plans for the city of Valletta, and designed the Auberges of the various Languages. The first stone was laid in November 1573, and in 1578 the Church was sufficiently far advanced for consecration. The see of Malta being at that time vacant, Bishop Gargallo not being as yet consecrated, Mons. Ludovico di Torres Archbishop of Monreale in Sicily came to Malta, and consecrated the church on the 20th of February, 1578. The coats of arms of the Grand Master De La Cassière, and of Archbishop Torres, together with two Latin inscriptions over the entrance record the erection and consecration.

Let us raise the large mat which hangs at the door and enter. It is impossible not to be struck with the magnificence which is everywhere displayed. The church is of an oblong form, 187 feet in length. The nave is 50 feet in breadth, or including the side chapels 118 feet. The height to the centre of the roof is 63 feet 6 in., and the walls were inlaid with slabs of green marble between 1663 and 1680 by the Grand Master Nicholas Cotoner. The corridors date from 1735. As we enter we notice two marble fonts, which were presented in 1641, and another of plain marble which was brought in 1648 from the Church of Vittoria.

The church consists of a choir and apse, nave, and two side aisles, the latter being divided into side chapels, one of which was assigned to each

6

82

of the various Languages of the Order by the first General Chapter held in Malta in the year 1604.

We cannot fail to notice the pavement which is composed of some 400 richly inlaid marble slabs, commemorating many famous and illustrious members of the Order. These slabs are adorned with many quaint and appropriate emblems, and bear suitable epitaphs. Any one who wishes to study these monuments should consult the able work of the Maltese artist Caruana, which can be obtained at the Libraries and elsewhere.

Successive Grand Masters and Grand Priors vied with one another in adding to the treasures of the Church of St. John, individual knights gave costly gifts, and every member of the Order on promotion was bound to give a "gioja" or present to the church, the amount of which was recoverable by a lien upon his property. The "gioja" of the Grand Master was limited to 50 oz. of gold. The carved ornaments of the nave and side chapels were gilded with sequin gold at the expense of the Grand Master Nicholas Cotoner. The paintings on the roof are worthy of special notice. They are the work of Mattia Preti generally known as "the Calabrese" from the place of his birth. He came to Malta in 1661 at the invitation of the Grand Master de Redin, and resided here until his death in 1699. The Grand Master Nicholas Cotoner was also one of his patrons. During this whole period he was more or less engaged in adorning and beautifying the Conventual Church. He refused to receive payment, whereupon the Order bestowed upon him the rank of Commander, and each of the Languages granted him a pension. He was a very pious man, and much of his income gladdened the hearts of the poor. He has found a last resting place beneath the roof which he did so much to beautify. His portrait and a brief biography are to be seen in the sacristy. Mattia Preti specially excels in what is termed by artists the "Sotto in su," or the power of making figures painted on a flat surface appear to the spectator below as though standing out in bold relief. Preti specially prepared the stones and then painted his figures upon them in oils.

The roof is divided into seven zones; one of which at the west end above the gallery is narrow, and the other six separated by projecting bands of stone, sculptured with numerous gilded palm branches. Above the gallery is "The Religion" holding in one hand the standard of the Order, and in the other a drawn sword. On either side are the figures of the Grand Masters Raphael and Nicholas Cotoner. The small arch has on the left the figures of St. Elizabeth, mother of the Baptist, and of Raymond du Puys, the second Grand Master, whilst on the right are Zacharias and S. Geraldo, the founder of the Order. In the first large zone we see Zacharias ministering in the temple, and on the right the naming of St. John Baptist. Above is depicted the meeting of the B. V. Mary and St. Elizabeth. In the second zone the Baptist is pointing his disciples to Christ as "the Lamb of God," whilst on the right we see the multitudes coming to his baptism. On the roof is depicted an angel presenting the infant saint to the Heavenly Father. The third zone pourtrays "The Baptism of Christ" and "St. John preaching in the Wilderness." Above are the

84

Heavenly Father, angels, and a scroll "Hic est Filius meus dilectus."

The fourth zone represents the arrest of St. John by Herod. On the right the Baptist makes reply to the messengers from Jerusalem, and in the centre he gives advice to the soldiers. The fifth zone shews how Herod was reproved by St. John, on the right the Baptist's followers are being sent with a message to our Lord, and in the centre is the daughter of Herodias with the severed head in a charger. The sixth zone represents on the left the dance of the daughter of Herodias, whilst evil spirits whisper to her mother, and on the right the executioner does his work. Above is a chorus of angels. In the apse St. John carrying the banner of the Order kneels before the "Holy and blessed Trinity." At the corners of each of these arches are twenty four figures of martyrs and heroes, illustrative of the history of the Order.

The pavement was partially restored under the administration of Sir H. F. Bouverie, and the pictures under that of Sir Charles T. V. Straubenzee, G. C. B. by Sig. Cortis between December 21st 1867 and the year 1874. Turning to the right as we enter the church we see before us the Chapel of the Decollation of St. John or the Oratory. This was erected in 1603 by the Grand Master Alofio Wignacourt for the instruction of novices and other pious purposes. The Altar is formed of rich marbles, and is surmounted by a group representing the Crucifixion by Algardi of Bologna. The three lunettes are by Favray, who has also enriched by his pencil several other churches in Malta. The large picture behind the altar is by Michael Angelo de

85

Caravaggio. This painter who derived his surname from a castle in the Milanese in which he was born in the year 1560, was the son of a mason, and was at first employed to prepare colours for painters in fresco. He studied at Venice where he learned to imitate the colouring of Giorgione, and in 1608 came to Malta to paint the roof of this church, was knighted by the Grand Master Wignacourt, departed, and died in the following year. The remaining pictures in the Oratory are by Preti. Over the altar in a special monstrance made by Bernini at the expense of the Grand Master Caraffa, was formerly preserved the most highly prized relic of this church, viz., the right hand of St. John the Baptist. It was originally kept at Constantinople in a church built by the Emperor Justinian expressly for its reception, after its removal from a church in Antioch. The Sultan Bajazet presented it to the Grand Master D' Aubusson, and when the knights were expelled from Rhodes L' Isle Adam conveyed the precious relic to Malta. It was encased in gold, and adorned with many precious stones. By its side with many other votive offerings was a costly diamond ring. This Napoleon appropriated, but returned the hand itself to the Grand Master Hompesch, who carried it away with him to St. Petersburg, where it is still carefully preserved in the Winter Palace. In the Oratory are kept the splendid tapestries presented to the church by the Grand Master Perellos at a cost of £6000. These tapestries, which are well worth seeing, were executed in Brussels by the firm of J. D. Vos. They form part of the decorations of the church on St. John's Day, from the festival of Corpus Christi to that of

86

S. S. Peter and Paul, and from Christmas Day until the Epiphany.

The first side chapel in the south aisle is dedicated to St. James, and was assigned to the Language of Castile. The bronze monument of the Grand Master Manoel de Vilhena is very handsome, and recalls to mind the building of Fort Manoel on an island in the Quarantine Harbour. Grand Master Emmanuel Pinto who was a great benefactor to the church, giving to it amongst other gifts two large bells, is also buried in this chapel. His tomb is adorned with a fine portrait in mosaic which was painted by the Cav. Favray for fifty magisterial zecchins (£17. 14. 2.) at the expense of the Venerable Assembly in gratitude for the mace granted to that body by Pinto.

We next visit the Campo Santo, which consists of a large plain stone slab with a pyramid in the centre, in memory of many a valiant soldier. The Chapel of St. John was assigned to the Language of Aragon. Grand Master Despuig whose bust and arms are seen here gave the altar. In this chapel are preserved the relics of St. Fidéle given by Pope Clement the Twelfth in 1738 and solemnly translated hither in September 1789. The Grand Master Martin de Redin, the two Cotoners, and Perellos are buried here. The monuments of Perellos and of Nicholas Cotoner who was a great benefactor to the church, were executed in Bernini's studio at Rome, in which the Maltese sculptor Melchior Gafà was a pupil. The allegorical figures of Asia and Africa which are copies from the celebrated bronze originals of Giovanni di Bologna, support a well executed figure of Fame.

87

The Chapel of St. Sebastian, assigned to the Language of Auvergne is adorned with numerous figures of dolphins, the emblem of Auvergne. It contains a picture of St. Sebastian by Paladini and the tomb of the Grand Master De Gessan. On the South side of the Choir is the Chapel of the Most Blessed Sacrament or of "Our Lady of Philermos." This latter title was given because this chapel formerly contained an image of the B. V. Mary, of which many miracles are recorded. This image was carried to St. Petersburg by the last Grand Master. Monsignor Alpheran, formerly Bishop of Malta, was the donor of the silver tabernacle, and the silver rails valued at £800 were given in 1752 by the Bailiff Guérani, and a knight named De La Salle, as a votive offering of one-fifth of their personal property. These costly rails escaped the notice of the all-plundering French, thanks to a coat of paint.

Notice those ancient keys. They are those of Patras, Passava, Lepanto, and Amameta. This last was an African city, captured by the galleys in 1603. We now enter the choir which dates from 1598.

The marble Baptism of Christ was worked at Rome at the expense of the Grand Master Caraffa, after the designs of Melchior Gafà. This eminent sculptor was born in Malta in 1635, and studied at Rome under Ferrata. He commenced this group, but an accident prevented him from completing it himself. The sculpture was placed in position in 1714.

The Grand Master Perellos gave the marble altar at the extremity of the apse. The high altar of lapis lazuli and other marbles cost 4,500 Roman scudi, and was designed in Rome by Bernini in 1686. A former prior gave the six large silver candlesticks, and in 1669 the large silver lamp was the gift of the Bailiff Rospiglion. The Grand Master Garzes gave the pulpit and choir seats in 1598. Two silver statues brought from Rhodes representing Moses with the Tables of the Law, and the Angel of the Apocalypse, in the choir were melted down in August 1761, for fear of a threatened Turkish invasion. The old service books are : very curious. The Crypt below the Choir is called the Chapel of the Crucifixion. Here lie twelve Grand Masters amongst whom are L' Isle Adam and La Vallette. Here also rests Sir Oliver Starkey the faithful secretary of La Vallette, who was the last English Turcopolier, and one of the three Englishmen who took part in the famous siege of 1565, and the writer of the epitaph on the tomb of La Vallette. The frescoes are by Nasone.

The Chapel of St. Carlo or the Chapel of the Relics. Here are preserved in two handsome reliquaries above the altar a thorn which was formerly a portion of the crown worn by Christ, a fragment of the cradle of the infant Jesus, one of the stones which slew St. Stephen, the foot of Lazarus, and some of the bones of St. Thomas of Canterbury. The crucifix over the altar is said to have been made from the basin used at the washing af the disciples feet. A very ancient wooden figure of St. John the Baptist, which is preserved in this chapel, was formerly attached to the stern of the flagship of the Order. This chapel was assigned to the Anglo-Bavarian Language, established in 1784 by the Grand Master de Rohan.

89

The Chapel of St. Michael assigned to the Language of Provence, contains the tombs of the Grand-Masters Antonio de Paula (died 1636), and John de Lascaris (died 1657). The tabernacle contains a portion of the wood of the true cross. Above the altar is a copy of Guido Reni's celebrated picture of St. Michael doing battle with the Dragon.

The Chapel of St. Paul was assigned to the language of France, and contains the monuments of the Grand Master Alofio Wignacourt and his brother John, of the Grand Master Emmanuel de Rohan, and of the Comte de Beaujolais. This last monument is by Pradier, and was erected by Louis Philippe, brother to the deceased Count. The Chapel of St. Catherine, the altar of which is elaborately ornamented, was assigned to the Language of Italy. The Grand Master Caraffa is buried here, and the chapel contains relics of St. Catherine and the body of St. Euphemia. Notice the picture of S. S. Gerolamo and the Magdalen by Caravaggio, and the picture of St. Catherine by Mattia Preti.

The Chapel of the Magi was assigned to the Language of Germany. The two lunettes and the picture above the altar are by the Maltese Stefano Erardi. In the entrance to the Sacristy is the tomb of Preti, who so greatly beautified the church. The Sacristy contains 15 pictures, and an ancient painting of a Christ on wood which is said to have been brought from Rhodes. A Mass of requiem is sung annually on the 7th of September for those who fell in the famous siege of 1565. As the bells of St. John's toll mournfully at 10 a. m. the people exclaim "It is the Deliverance of the Knights."

90

The clergy of St. John's enjoy several special privileges. After plundering it of its treasures, the First Napoleon restored the church to Bishop Labini, and it has since borne the title of Co - Cathedral. The clergy forming the Chapter of the Diocese officiate. The cost to the Local Government of the restoration of this church between the years 1867 and 1875 was £5,886. 8. 5. The niece of the Grand Master Rohan was permitted by Sir Thomas Maitland to find a grave at the feet of her uncle.

Quitting the church and returning to Strada Reale we pass another open space planted with trees, and ornamented with an obelisk of red granite which serves as a drinking fountain, erected during the rule of Sir Gaspard Le Marchant.

On the opposite side of the street is the large, massive, and unadorned Auberge d' Auvergne. The revenue of the Languaga of Auvergne was about £7,198, and its emblem was a dolphin.

The head of this Auberge was called the Grand Marshal. He had the military command over the whole Order, excepting the Grand Crosses or their lieutenants, the Chaplains, and other persons of the Grand Master's household. He entrusted the standard of the Order to the knight whom he judged most worthy of such distinction. He had the right of appointing the principal equerry; and when at sea commanded not only the general of the galleys but even the grand admiral himself.

The upper floor is occupied by the Archives, with the Courts of Appeal and the Commercial, Civil, and Criminal Courts, in which H. M. Judges preside, whilst on the ground floor the Magistrates of Judicial Police administer justice. There are police

91

cells for persons awaiting trial, or sentenced to not more than three days' detention, and also a small chapel. The Language of Auvergne had a chapel in St. John's Church (see p. 87), and also another within their Auberge. The paintings on the roof of Messrs. Crockford's Drapery Establishment which forms part of the Auberge, were executed some years since at a cost of £200.

Adjoining the Auberge d'Auvergne is a large building formerly called the Conservatorio. This was the repository for the gold, plate, and money of the Order, and from hence payments were made when authorised by the Treasury. This Conservatorio was under the control of a knight called the Conservator, who was appointed every three years from the several Languages in turn according to seniority.

Adjoining the Conservatorio was the Treasury, situated in the large block of buildings forming the left hand side of St. George's Square. This building was formerly devoted to the keeping of account books and records. It was managed by a committee, of which the Grand Commander or some knight of the Language of Provence was the president. The expenses of the Treasury and Conservatorio amounted to £833 per annum. The magnificent rooms of the latter were a few years since occupied by the Casino Maltese.

On the opposite side of the street is Victoria Square formerly called "the square of the knights," which was enclosed by Sir Gaspard Le Marchant. The Café de la Reine with its pleasant seats beneath the trees and plashing fountain is much frequented. In the centre of the square is a statue of the

92

Grand Master Manoel de Vilhena, the work of the Cav. Savasse, which formerly stood in the centre of the square at Fort Manoel, (Part ii. Chap. v.), but was removed hither by Sir 'Gaspard Le Marchant. Surrounding this Square, opposite to which is Dunsford's Hotel, are covered arcades lined with shops, forming an agreeable promenade on wet days and during the great heats of summer.

The entrance to the noble Public Library is by a staircase on the eastern side of Victoria Square. This Library first had a beginning in the year 1650, when the room above the Oratory at St. John's Church was set apart for its accomodation. The books were afterwards transferred to a room over the larger sacristy. The general Chapter of 1612 had also ordered that books, instruments, and curiosities belonging to deceased knights were not to be disposed of.

The Cardinal Portacarrero died in August 1760, and on the 26th of that month was honoured with a solemn funeral in St. John's Church at the expense of the Treasury and the several Languages. In the following year the Bailiff Tencin bought for £700 granted by the Treasury, the books of the deceased Cardinal to come to the Order as universal heir, on condition that a Public Library should be provided, together with rooms for a librarian. This was agreed to, and the Bailiff Tencin sent for French workmen to bind the volumes, converting at the same time the cases in which the books were sent from Rome into the present book-shelves. He then added his own books and those of his lieutenant 4,030 in number, making a total of 9,700 volumes.

93

Dr. Fra. Gius. Zammit who died at the age of 94 on Nov. 2nd 1740, and was buried in the parish church of Casal Balzan, bequeathed to the Hospital 15,000 volumes, many of which were afterwards added to the Public Library, which possesses portraits of the Bailiff Tencin, of Dr. Bruno, of Dr. Zammit, of Cardinal Portocarrero by the Cav. Favray, and of Sir H. Oakes. Additions were also made from the Libraries of the Camerata, St. John's, and the Order of St. Antonio. The first librarian appointed in 1763 was Canon Agius di Soldanis of Gozo, with a salary of £1 per month and lodging. The knights' books accumulated, duplicates being always sold, so that the library cost only £8. 10s. per annum. In 1782, Dr. Gerolamo Bruno left £1000, the yearly interest of which was to be devoted to the purchase of new books. The Library was afterwards established in the present building, which was built during the rule of De Rohan, but not used until 1812. There were then 30,000 volumes, to which 20,000 have since been added. This Library to which additions are constantly being made, and which is well supplied with magazines and reviews, is rich in unedited manuscripts. Open on every working day from 9. 0. a. m. till 3. 0. p. m. and also for two hours in the evening during the winter months. Admission free. Books are lent with the sanction of the learned and kindly Librarian C. Vassallo L. L. D. F. S. A. to whom I return grateful thanks for much valuable information, always most readily and patiently given.

Close to the Public Library, is the large, massively-built Governor's Palace, about 300 feet square, and surrounded by four of the principal streets.

94

The front has two entrances from St. George's Square, of which it forms one side. Each gateway opens into a large courtyard planted with orange and other trees and gay with creepers. The other three sides of the Palace have each an entrance in the centre, and open and covered balconies almost surround three sides of the building. One courtyard was allotted to the sedan-chairs of the Grand Crosses, and in the other were the stables of the Grand Master.

The right-hand gateway, opened by the Grand Master Pinto who greatly beautified the Palace, leads into Prince Alfred's Court, so named in honour of the first visit to Malta in 1850 of H. R. H. the Duke of Edinburgh, who planted here a thriving Norfolk Island Pine about 40 years of age. There is a fountain in the centre of this courtyard, which is surrounded by the Head Quarters' Office, Chief Secretary's Office, the Government Printing Office, Public Record Office, and the Offices of the Controller of Charitable Institutions, and the Crown Advocate. We may remark in passing that the Grand Master Lascaris was the first to establish a printing press in the year 1643, over which, however, he exercised strict control. This square was first planted by Sir Gaspard Le Marchant in 1858. The clock resembles that of Old St. Dunstan's Church in Fleet Street fifty years ago. Quaint Moorish figures have been striking the hours and quarters with hammers ever since June 22nd 1745.

Beneath the archway leading into the second courtyard are two fieldpieces, and a tablet commemorating the visit to Malta on Oct. 30th 1862, of T. R. H. the Prince of Wales and the Crown Prince and Princess of Prussia. The courtyard has borne

95

the name of H. R. H. the Prince of Wales since his first visit to Malta on June 5th 1862, and has in it a statue of Neptune by Giovanni of Bologna, holding the escutcheon of the Grand Master Alofio Wignacourt who defrayed the cost. This statue was brought from the fish market in 1853 by Sir Gaspard Le Marchant.

The Treasury and Land Revenue Office, the latter of which was formerly used for Divine Service by the English residents in Valletta before the erection of the Collegiate Church of St. Paul by the liberality of the late Dowager Queen Adelaide, are beneath the arched portico which surrounds this courtyard.

The knights intended to build the Grand Master's Palace on the site occupied by the Auberge de Castile, but Eustace de Monte nephew to the Grand Master of the same name, having erected this building in 1572 from the plans of Gerolamo Cassar, it was purchased from him. The grand marble staircase on the right of the entrance erected in 1866, with broad steps of no great height, is a copy of the old one up which the Grand Master was carried in his chair of state, and which the young knights said was specially designed for the benefit of gouty dignitaries. A staircase on the left led to the Grand Master's summer apartments. The floors of the corridors are inlaid with escutcheons formed of variously coloured marbles. The walls of the Council Chamber, and other parts of the Palace are adorned with frescoes, most of which are by the two principal pupils of Giuseppe d' Arpino. There are also portraits of various Grand Masters, some of which are by the Cav. Favray. That of the Grand Master Alofio Wignacourt is by Caravaggio. The

96

Grand Master Zondadari enriched the picture gallery, which was full in days of old.

There are in the Dining Room portraits of Louis XVI. by David presented by himself, and of his son the hapless Dauphin. Also portraits of Louis XIV., George IV., and Queen Victoria. The inlaid marble mosaics on either side of the fireplace in this room are very fine. Along the corridors are ranged figures of knights and men at arms in full armour, bearing on their shields escutcheons in chronological order, commencing with that of the first Grand Master, and ending with that of the present Governor.

In the Council Chamber are the velvet chairs and neat desks of the Council, and the Governor's throne on which are the gold-embroidered arms of England. Upon the walls are frescoes, but the costly tapestries, some 22 in number, each about 15 feet square, crowded with colossal figures, representing scenes in India, Africa, and South America, are the chief attraction here. They were purchased in Brussels by the Grand Master D'Espuig from the firm of J. D. Vos.

In the Armoury (253 feet long by 38 broad), are the old colours of the Malta Regiment. Carefully preserved in glass cases are the original Bull of Pope Paschal II., sanctioning the foundation of the Order, the deed of gift by which Charles V. transferred Malta to the Order of St. John, and the trumpet which sounded the retreat from Rhodes. Also the sword, axe, and surtout of Dragut the famous Algerine Corsair who held high command during the famous siege of 1565, and the batons of office of the two celebrated Grand Mas-

97

ters La Vallette and Alofio Wignacourt. The suit of armour formerly worn by the last named Grand Master richly inlaid with gold is also in the Palace. None but a giant could wear armour nearly seven feet in height, and a helmet weighing 37 lbs. must have been an unconfortable head dress. This figure is commonly called by the Maltese "John Bull." There is a remarkable cannon in the Armoury which is said to have been taken from the Turks during one of their attacks upon the city of Rhodes. It is about five feet in length, and the bore is three inches in diameter. This probably unique cannon is made of tarred ¾ inch rope bound round a copper cylinder and covered with cement, the whole being painted black. Notice the various ornaments made with weapons which adorn the Armoury. Fourteen thousand muskets were formerly kept in store, and as late as the year 1761 a number of new arquebusses were placed in the Armoury, the old ones being worn out.

At the foot of a staircase near the Armoury is the state carrriage of the last Grand Master, which is said to have been used by Buonaparte. Baron Azzopardi however expressly states that Buonaparte declined to use it, preferring to march into the city at the head of his guards. Within the palace is the noble hall of S. S. Michael and George so called as being the scene of all investitures and assemblies connected with that Order. This distinguished Order, instituted by Letters Patent dated 27th August 1818, consists of the Sovereign, Grand Master, 35 Knights Grand Cross, 120 Knights Commanders, and 200 Companions, and is limited to the British Colonies. The insignia are, the Star, inscribed with

98

the motto "Auspicium Melioris Aevi" and the Collar
and Badge suspended from a watered Saxon blue
riband with a scarlet stripe. On the highest part
of the Palace is a small square tower from whence
signals are made announcing the approach of ships,
which, by means of the signal stations at Gozo and
Delimara, are sometimes reported at a distance of
56 miles to the East, and 20 miles to the West
of the anchorage. Sheets shewing these signals can
be obtained from the local booksellers.

An observatory, whereat many important meteorological facts have been recorded, is established
in this tower. It owes its origin to the Grand Master Rohan, who provided an astronomer, and scientific instruments to the value of £5000. During
the French occupation these valuable instruments
were concealed in the tower, which is called the
Torretta, and their hiding place was discovered in
1816 by Captain Smyth. Sir A. J. Ball converted
the room in which astronomical observations used
to be made into a store for signals. The Torretta
commands a fine view of the city and island.
Lamartine said that from this point "Valletta resembles the shell of a tortoise stranded upon a reef,
and appears as if cut out of a single piece of living rock!"

In the basement of this tower were carefully
guarded amongst other treasures the sword and dagger presented to the Grand Master La Vallette by
Philip II. of Spain. The golden hilt of the sword
was set with diamonds, and the sword and dagger
were annually carried in procession before the Grand
Master on Sept. 8th. The French seized them, and

99

Macgill states that before leaving Malta Napoleon had the sword balanced for his own use.

Visitors who intend to remain some time in Malta will do well to inscribe their names in a book kept at the Palace for that purpose. The side of the Palace towards Str. Teatro was formerly assigned to the Pages of the Grand Master and was called the Paggeria. These young gentlemen of noble birth, were 16 in number and were received into the Order as Knights of Justice at 12 years of age instead of 16, as were other candidates. Their position, although ivolving heavy expenses, was much coveted. Two of them attended the Grand Master on all occasions, one acted as taster when he dined in public, and during the Carnival they made a brave show in a splendidly decorated car, drawn by six richly caparisoned mules and preceded by two trumpeters and a kettle drummer on horseback.

Two centuries ago the Grand Master Nicholas Cotoner ruled in this palace with more than regal state. He never addressed a knight except *en Maître*, and was attended at church by 400 knights, who also ranged themselves in the hall when he dined in public, and did not move until he gave them permission. Brydone says that in 1770 no European sovereign, with the exception perhaps of the king of Sardinia, was as well lodged as the Grand Master. Though the Grand Master did not pay state visits to the dignitaries of the Order, he nevertheless always received them in his own palace standing and uncovered. At state banquets whenever the Grand Crosses drank a health they uncovered, as did also the Grand Master. On these occasions it was contrary to etiquette to leave the table before the Grand Master had pledged his guest

100

in wine. The summer apartments were gay with hangings woven in the looms of Damascus, and during the month of May flowers and branches of poplar from the Boschetto were constantly to be seen in the balcony overlooking St. George's Square. The exhibition of the head of the Grand Master Pinto from this balcony was to have been the signal for the general rising of the slaves in 1749, and from hence permission was given to commence the popular amusement of the Coccagna.

In front of the Palace is St. George's Square, which was formerly called in common with the present Victoria Square "the Piazza dei Cavalieri" or "the square of the Knights." No Maltese were allowed to walk here except such as received a permit, of which they were expected to make but moderate use. The French called it the Square of Liberty and it was here that the Festival of Liberty was held on July 14th 1798. The conspirators who wished to give up Valletta to their insurgent countrymen during the siege of 1798—1800 were shot in this square. It was the scene of numerous festivities under the Knights of St. John, and it is still the heart and centre of the Carnival and of various festivals. During the winter months a weekly public guard mounting, a monthly trooping the colours, and an occasional brigading of regimental bands attract crowds of spectators. At the right and left hand corners of the square are drinking fountains. Closely adjoining the one on the left is the house formerly occupied by the family of the Vice-Chancellor Abela who first described Malta, (at present the head quarters of the Maltese Casino San Giorgio). Entrance 6s. 3d. Quarterly subscription 9s.

101

In the centre of the square is the Main-Guard with an electric clock. The Latin inscription above the entrance is to the effect that. "The love of the Maltese and the voice of Europe confirm these islands to great and invicible Britain." A. D. 1814. There are some clever sketches here done in hours of leisure by successive officers on guard. The Knights' Main Guard occupied the same site. To the right is the Brigade Office, adjoining which is the Garrison Library. This building was the former depository of valuable documents and papers, and was under the charge of the Vice Chancellor of the Order. The Garrison Library which contains about 20,000 volumes is well supplied with newspapers and periodicals, and is much frequented by residents and visitors. Naval and Military Officers and Civil Servants whose yearly salary is not less than £100, are eligible as Proprietors. Entrance for Officers 10s., for Civil Servants £1. Quarterly subscription 10s. payable in advance. Visitors to Malta may be introduced for one week. Yearly Members are elected by ballot. Entrance £2. Quarterly Subscription 10s. Visitors to Malta pay in advance 5s. per month; 7s. 6d. for two of the same family, and 10s. for any number exceding two of the same family. The Reading Rooms are open daily from 9. 0. a. m. till 9. 0. p. m. The Library is open daily from 9. 0. a. m. until sunset during winter, and until 6. 0. p. m. in summer, except on Sundays and certain other days when it closes its doors. On Festivals the Library is closed at noon. Visitors to Malta will do well to subscribe to this Library.

In the Strada Vescovo on the left of the square is a block of buildings with a handsomely carved

102

stone facade, one of which is the residence of the Ven. Archdeacon Cleugh. This is the Hostel de Verdelin, and was the old home of the Cavalier de Verdelin Commandant of Artillery, whose portrait is in the Palace. The next house in the same block, which was then an hotel, was the temporary home of Lord Byron when in Malta.

Leaving St. George's Square and pursuing our way down Strada Reale, we pass Bisazza's or "the sick man's" (No. 63), whereat a great consumption of ices and confectionery is continually in progress, and the handsome Borsa or Exchange "where merchants most do congregate," and whereat the arrivals and departures of ships are carefully recorded. Sig. Gius. Bonavia was the architect, and it was opened on April 11th. Two days afterwards, 800 guests assembled at a ball, and the visit of H. R. H. the Prince of Wales in June 1862 was another memorable event in the history of the Borsa. The upper floor is occupied by the Casino della Borsa. Entrance 10s. Quarterly subscription 12s. 6d. The rooms contain some curious old pictures of Valletta. Admission by ballot. Members may introduce visitors for a month (see also p. p. 56-7). When King Louis Philippe came to Malta to visit the tomb of his brother, the Comte de Beaujolais in St. John's Church, he lived at the house now occupied by Sig. A. Despott. Up this sloping street at an early hour on Easter Day a procession headed by the R. C. Priests of the Greek Rite carries a life-size figure of Our Lord at full speed with shouts of "Viva! Christ is risen!" amidst crowds of spectators. On the left are the church and nunnery of Santa Caterina. The nunnery originated in an orphanage founded by a Jesuit priest

103

in 1606 near St. John's Church. The present building was commenced in 1714, but want of funds hindered its completion until 1766. The architect was the Cav. Carapecchia, and the sisterhood of Sta. Maddalena were received here when the French converted their nunnery into a hospital. Bishop Labini consecrated the church on July 15th 1783. The Bailiff Pereirà lived at No. 219.

An open space is now reached, studded at intervals with large round stones, which cover underground granaries wherein corn may be kept for years without detriment, and 70 of these "Fosse" contain nearly 40,000 qrs.

An ancient chapel dedicated to Sant' Elmo or Telmo the patron saint of seamen, stood on this site, and a watch was kept for all vessels entering or leaving port. In 1488 the Viceroy of Sicily gave orders for the construction of a fort in consequence of a Turkish invasion, which was rebuilt and armed in May 1553. It was of no great size, somewhat resembling a star in shape, protected by a ravelin on the side of the Quarantine Harbour, and having a cavalier or elevated work on the sea face. The Prior of Capua was the architect, and some of the workmen were, Sicilians. The narratives of Porter, Townsend, and Seddall tell how in 1565 the heroic garrison held out from May 25th until June 23rd, and preferred death to surrender. On May 28th 1687 the engineer Don Carlos de Grunemberg commenced extensive additions, and a few years afterwards the Grand Master Perellos added several bastions which have lately been materially strengthened. This heavily-armed fort, which is built of "zoncor" or hard limestone, has accomodation for more than

104

200 men. A few years since Col Montague R. E. discovered a little, forgotten chapel just within the gate, wherein the garrison assembled to receive the Sacrament on the night before the final assault. The date 1649 probably refers to a restoration. The stone carvings are elaborate, and the chapel has been partially restored by Colonel Montague. Another chapel with the date 1729 is used as a schoolroom. On the night of September 9th 1775, a band of priests and conspirators against the Grand Master Ximenes obtained possession of the fort, by the aid of a corporal who admitted them. Their leader was Don Gaetano Mannarino, and they disarmed the garrison, imprisoning the commandant De Guiron, and hoisting the ancient Maltese standard. The revolt was however speedily put down, some of the conspirators being executed, and Don Gaetano Mannarino remained in prison for twenty three years until the arrival of the French in 1798.

Over a gateway is a large eye carved in stone emblematic of vigilance. General Abercombie who fell at Alexandria and Sir A. J. Ball the first English governor of Malta are buried in two bastions which bear their names. Above the fort is a lighthouse erected in 1766 and formerly lighted only in winter, with a white light visible fifteen miles away, the lantern of which commands a fine view, and of which the Duc de Rivas says

"Across the dark blue waves,
Thy colossal form and diadem
Flames on a level with the stars."

In the last century a new lantern cost £110.

105

The approach of ships is notified by signals from this fort. The barracks of Lower St. Elmo (occupied by an Infantry Regiment) with a fountain formed of four stone shells, were built in the last century by the Chevalier Tigné as a treble row of casemates to be used either as stores or as a refuge for women and children in a case of bombardment.

Skirting Fort St. Elmo we pass along the French Curtain, to the foot of Strada Stretta "the Narrow or straight Street" as it is variously interpreted to mean. This street runs the whole length of the city, and contains numerous hotels and lodging houses.

The Garrison Library, Brigade Office, Courts of Justice, and the Commissariat Bakery have entrances in this Street which, from its narrowness, is much used during the shadeless days of summer. The Masonic Hall is at No. 27. The following are the Masonic Lodges, &c. in Malta. St. John and St. Paul Lodge, No. 349, E. C., Zetland Lodge, No. 515, E. C., Union Lodge, No. 407, E. C., Keystone Mark Lodge, No. 107, E. C., Broadley Mark Lodge No. 248, E. C., Royal Arch Chapter Melita, No. 349 E. C. Rose Croix Chapter, "Rose of Sharon," Melita Preceptory of Knights Templar, and Priory of Knights of Malta, Provincial Priory of the Mediterranean, District Grand Lodge of Malta, Sanct' Elmo Lodge of Royal Ark Mariners, Provincial Grand Mark Lodge of Tunis and Malta. Also the Wignacourt Conclave of Knights of Rome, and of the Red Cross of Constantine, as well as the William Kingston R. A. Chapter, and the Melita Council of Royal and Select Masters. The Leinster Lodge, No 387, Irish Constitution is held in Strada delle due Porte, Senglea.

106

A Mark Lodge and Royal Arch Chapter are attached to this Lodge.

Strada Stretta was the duelling ground of the knights, who were strictly forbidden to fight elsewhere, and were obliged to sheath their swords at the request of a woman, a priest, or a knight. A cross on an adjoining house marked the scene of a fatal fray. One such cross at least is still to be seen.

Strada Forni is the next street which traverses the whole length of Valletta. At its upper end is the Presbyterian Church, in connection with the Free Church of Scotland. This church which can accomodate 450 persons was commenced in 1856 and completed in 1857.

The house of the Revd. G. Wisely M: A. is at 210 Strada Forni, adjoining the church. The services are announced in the local papers. Opposite the church is the plain massive and unadorned auberge de France. In 1687 this Auberge contained some fine pictures, many of which were blackened by age. The best were by the Cav. Favray. The Language of France had an annual revenue of £30,951, and possessed very great influence in the Order. This Auberge was under the control of the Grand Hospitalier, who was in charge of the Hospital, appointing its Overseer and Prior and also ten writers to the council. The District Commissary General resides here, and the Military Treasury, the Pay, Supply, Transport and Barrack Departments are concentrated beneath its roof.

Descending a slope we see on the right the Commissariat Bakery, which gives the name of "Forni" or "the ovens" to this street. The knights

107

usually leased this bakery to a contractor. Fairbairns'
machinery driven by an engine of 16 horse power
nominal, grinds about 16 qrs. of wheat per diem,
but 35 qrs. could, if neecssary be ground within
24 hours. Mules formerly supplied the motive power.
The Bakery keeps three of its seven ovens constantly
at work, using daily about 5250 lbs. of flour, and
issuing an average of 6,700 lbs. of bread. English
malt and hops are used in the manufacture of yeast,
and the rate of production could easily be doubled.
The Ordnance Store Workshops are in this building.

Facing us are the Augustinian Church and Convent. The site was granted in 1572, the architect
being Gerolamo Cassar, and the Convent was rebuilt
between 1764 and 1794. The present church contains a picture of S. Nicola by Mattia Preti. Free
schools for 200 boys are connected with this convent.

The Bailiff Plata resided at No. 51. No. 94 was
the Palazzo Delicata, and at the Corner of Strada
Teatro was the residence of Hompesch before his
election as Grand Master. Morrell's Hotel was the
home of the Bailiff Rospiglioni, and No. 106 was
the Palazzo of the Portuguese Bailiff Cascaxares.
The children of Israel were formerly obliged to reside at the lower end of Strada Forni, in close
proximity to a powder mill, which cost £796
to build. From the Jews Sally Port, boats cross to
Fort Tigné and Sliema.

On the right is the Auberge de Bavière, a
handsome building overlooking the Quarantine Harbour and occupied by the officers of the infantry
regiment quartered at Lower St. Elmo. The Anglo
Bavarian Language established in 1784 at a cost of

108

£1,408, was united to the Priory of Poland and had an annual income of £877. Some curiously painted ceilings still exist.

The undulating Strada Zecca, (named from the Mint, which formerly belonged to the Language of France, and which was established at the present No. 3,) runs parallel to Strada Forni. L' Isle Adam before coming to Malta claimed the right to coin money. Nearly every Grand Master struck medals and eighteen at least of the Grand Master Pinto are in existence. The copper coinage of the Order was withdrawn from circulation on Novr. 20th 1827. For full particulars respecting the Mint see Furse's Medagliere Gerosolimitano. The official residence of the Officer in charge of the Ordnance Store Department is in this street.

The Ordnance Store office is in Strada Scozzese or "Scotch Street." Descending some steps, crossing Strada San Marco, and traversing Strada San Patrizio we reach the steep Strada Ponente or "West Street." No. 14 was the Palazzo Britto. It contains some old pictures, the bust and arms of the Grand Master Pinto, some interesting mural decorations, and frescoes of Belem Castle and "Black Horse Square" at Lisbon.

The Auberge of Germany stood close by, but was pulled down about forty years ago to make room for the English Church. The Language of Germany had an annual income of £4,095. Its chief was the Grand Bailiff who had jurisdiction over the fortifications of Città Vecchia and of Gozo. The Auberge of Germany was a plain massive building, with a central corridor from which rooms opened on either side.

109

The Anglican Church of St. Paul (see p. 57) is styled Collegiate, objections having been raised to the title of "Cathedral."

Its architecture is Grecian, and its detached tower and lofty spire are visible from afar. The church has 750 sittings, a fine peal of bells, a good organ, stalls for clergy, and a Bishop's throne. Beneath the spire is a valuable theological library for the use of the clergy. The Revd. E. A. Hardy resides at No. 32 Strada Marsamuscetto, and the clerk (R. Beck) lives close to the church. For church services see local papers. Church expenses are met by means of offertories.

On the opposite side of the square, which is called Piazza Gelsi from three old mulberry trees long since uprooted, stands the Auberge d'Aragon, the former residence of the Bishop of Gibraltar, but at present occupied by the General Commanding the Infantry Brigade. The head of the Language of Aragon, which had a yearly income of £11,505, was the Grand Conservator, who was in charge of the Conservatorio, and of clothing, and who purchased all necessaries for the troops and hospitals. The Priory of Aragon was the present Nos. 32. & 33. Strada Marsamuscetto.

In Strada Ponente is the church of Our Lady of Pilar the principal picture in which is said to be by Erardi. It was built in 1670 by the Language of Castile and Portugal to which it belonged, beautified in 1718 by the Grand Master Perellos, and restored in 1864. The Commander Felice Innignes d' Ayerbe, who was buried here in 1691, and Raymondo de Soler, Bailiff of Majorca, were great benefactors.

110

We turn to the left at the bottom of Strada Ponente, and skirt the San Sebastian Bastion, and the German Curtain, opposite to which is the Telegraph Office (p. 56.). On our left are numerous stables and storehouses, and high above us rises the graceful spire of the English Church.

Half a battery of artillery is stationed at the Marsamuscetto Barracks, close to which are the Marsamuscetto steps, at which P. & O. passengers land, and from whence boats ply to Sliema, Pietà, Forts Tigné and Manoel. Half way down these steps is the Marsamuscetto Gate, with its drawbridge, electric clock, and escutcheon with the date 1508. A tariff of boat fares is exhibited at the landing.

The road to the right leads to the Jews' Sally Port. The rocks hereabouts swarm with bathers on summer evenings, and boats and canoes can be hired. at moderate prices from Potts and others. The old Quarantine buildings on the left are now Public Baths (4d. per hour), and the Royal Laboratory. (Lighted cigars and red-hot pokers objected to, gunpowder being plentiful.)

A steep path beneath the lofty ramparts leads past the San Rocco Baths (4d per hour), and the San Rocco Chapel, (formerly assigned for the benefit of persons in quarantine) to the Hay Wharf, so named during the Crimean War, at which corn was landed in the days of quarantine. The conspirators who wished to seize Valletta during the siege of 1798 1800 were captured amongst these rocks. In yonder red painted boats the Royal Engineers conduct experiments in submarine mining.

Returning to the top of the Marsamuscetto Steps, we see before us the bustling Strada San Marco,

111

which leads into strada Forni and the heart of Valletta.
On the left is the entrance to the Manderaggio,
This name means "a place for cattle."
A number of the poor and needy here herd together in underground chambers originally intended
for an arsenal. It is in contemplation to erect good
houses in the suburbs for the denizens of the Manderaggio. On the right are the stables of the fine
Government mules which are shipped from Spain
to Malta and Cyprus, at a cost of about £ 25 each.
Climbing a street of stairs we reach the Barrack Department Stores with the date 1807 upon
them, but which are evidently far more ancient. On
St. Andrew's Bastion is the base of a column 70
feet in height, which was erected by Maltese subscribers, •in memory, of the Hon F. C. Ponsonby,
who was Governor of Malta from 1827 to 1836. This
column was greatly damaged by lightning in January 1864, and was taken down in consequence. On
the Spencer Bastion is the tomb of the Hon. Sir
Robert Cavendish Spencer, C. B. who died on board
and in command of H. M. S. Madagascar at Alexandria on November 4th, 1836.
These Bastions command fine views over the
open sea, the Quarantine Harbour, and the interior
of the island. Strada Molini a Vento which skirts
the ramparts, bordered by a triple row of trees,
derives its name from two wind mills on St. Michael's Bastion, one of which is in ruins. In a garden upon St. John's Bastion close' to St. John's
Cavalier, sleeps the Marquis of Hastings, who was
Governor from 1824 to 1826, and whose tomb for
six . months after his funeral was covered with choice
flowers and garlands by the unseen hands of the

112

peasants, bringing their farm produce to market ere the dawn.

St. John's Communication gives access to Floriana by means of a drawbridge, and the two neighbouring Cavaliers or elevated works styled respectively St. John and St. James, the former of which is at present used as a store, whilst the latter can accommodate 130 men, were amongst the first fortifications constructed in Valletta, and were respectively assigned to the Languages of Provence and France. Col. Porter quotes the words of General Marmont. "The Maltese were furious. We had at first much uneasiness as to the carrying into effect of the capitulation. These peasant soldiers were in possession of two inner works, very lofty cavaliers closed at the gorge, armed, and commanding the whole town, called St. John and St. James. They refused to surrender them, even after we had entered the gates and penetrated within the *enceinte*. It was by the merest chance that they did not continue their resistance; and, if they had, it is impossible to say what effect this one obstacle would have had in the position in which we then were." These Cavaliers were used as prisons, and were afterwards occupied by the Malta Fencibles.

We reach the Guard-house above Porta Reale, and must now briefly glance at a few objects of interest in the streets which cross Strada Reale at right angles.

Turning to the left opposite the Opera House into Strada Mezzodi or "South Street" we pass on the left some Ordnance Stores, and on the right the Scotch Church and the Auberge de France (see p. 106) No. 12 is the official residence of the Colonel of

113

Artillery on the Staff, and Admiralty House, the official residence of the Naval Commander in Chief, was the home of the Bailiff Don Raymondo Gonsalvi. Buonaparte gave this house to Bishop Labini, to be used as a seminary.

In a narrow street parallel to Strada Mezzodi called Strada Cavallere or the "Street of the knights" is the United Service Institute which provides shelter, welcome amusement and religious instruction for soldiers, sailors and marines. It is managed by a Committee and is doing good work in the garrison. Visitors to Malta should see for themselves what is being done, and contributions towards the funds will be gladly received by the Secretary.

Strada Britannica, the next cross street was formerly called the "Street of the Grand Falconer" who commanded the 300 falconieri, and who provided the falcons annually presented to the kings of France, Spain, and Portugal, and to the Viceroy of Sicily, at a cost of £103. This dignitary resided at No. 74, the present official residence of the Commanding Royal Engineer. There are still some pictures of Grand Masters and ecclesiastics in the house.

In Strada Teatro is the Teatro Manoel built by the Grand Master Manoel de Vilhena "for the honest recreation of the people." The building on the plan of the theatre at Palermo, was commenced on March 20th 1731, and completed during the following year, "Merope" by Maffei was the first performance. During the two years' siege, the French kept open this theatre to the last. It was restored by order of Gen. Sir H. Oakes, and re-opened on August 8th with the musical drama of Elisa. The actors had houses adjoining the theatre which is

8

114

said to be the oldest in Europe and can accomodate 770 persons. Vernacular performances, chiefly on Sundays. This theatre, in which operas were performed before the erection of the Opera House, is sometimes hired by the Amateurs of the Fleet and Garrison.

Just below the theatre are the Carmelite church and convent, founded by public subscription in 1573.. Gerolamo Cassar was the architect of the church which contains pictures by Mattia Preti, Raymondo di Domenici, &c. The two Oratories of San Giuseppe aud of our Lady of Carmel are connected with the church.

In Strada Vescovo or " Bishop's Street " are the Hotel de Verdelin, and the Palace of the Archbishop of Rhodes and Bishop of Malta, cómmenced in 1622 by Bishop Baldassare Cagliares. The Grand Master Alofio Wignacourt raised objections, saying that no one except the Grand Master ought to have jurisdiction in Valletta. On appeal to Rome it was decided that the palace should be completed, the Bishop's Prison still remaining in Vittoriosa. Bishop Cagliares left this palace to the Cathedral by will. The architect was the Maltese Tommaso Dingli. It has been the official residence of sixteen successive Bishops of Malta and is at present occupied by the Most Revd. Count D. Carmelo Scicluna D. D. who was consecrated in St. John's Church by the Archbishop of Reggio on April 11th 1875.

No. 138 Strada Cristoforo, now occupied by Mr. H. B. Bennett as a first class lodging house, is the Palazzo Cotoner. The Grand Master Nicholas Cotoner lived here before his elevation to supreme power. A subterranean "mina" or tunnel connects this Pa-

115

lazzo with that of the Governor, and there is a curious communication in the wall between the upper and lower rooms. A marble bust of the great Nicholas is still to be seen in his old home. No. 58 is the Palazzo Ximenes, the former residence of the Grand Master of that name, previous to his election. Having explored Western Valletta, let us return to Porta Reale, and start over again.

CHAPTER V.

STREETS AND BUILDINGS
(Continued).

St. James' Cavalier and the Auberge de Castile. — Upper Baracca, Church and Garden.—View from Upper Baracca.—Churches of Vittoria and Santa Caterina d' Italia.— Auberge d' Italia, Palazzo Parisio, and Church of San Giacomo. The Castellania, and Post Office.— Monte di Pietà, and Market.— Church of Our Lady of Damascus.—Jesuits' Church, University, and Lyceum. The Dominican, and Anime Purganti Churches.—Military Hospital and the Camerata.— Cemetery, Nibbia Church, Hospital for Incurables, and Orphan Asylum.—Strada San Paolo and the Church of St. Paul Shipwrecked.—Churches of the Minori Osservanti, San Rocco, and Santa Ursola.—Old Slave Prison and the Lower Baracca. —Strada Levante, and the Santa Barbara Bastion.—The Sultan's Garden, Nix Mangiare Stairs, Barriera, and Church of Santa Maria di Liesse.—The Mina Lascaris, Custom House, and Marina.

ON the ramparts to the right of Porta Reale is the Military Gymnasium erected in 1873, facing which is St. James' Cavalier, which was formerly called the Cavalier of Italy. The ancient Maltese standard was hoisted upon it by the insurgents in 1775, but, 50 carabineers having been posted on the roof of the adjacent Auberge de Castile, this important post was easily stormed by 100 knights, 120 French merchant seamen, and numerous volunteers. Their leader an Italian knight named Corio, was killed,

117

but a few days afterwards, the heads of three of the defenders were exhibited on the roof.

St. James communication here connects Valletta with Floriana, and facing us is the Auberge de Castile, on a site which was originally set apart for the palace of the Grand Master. This is the finest of all the Auberges. The architect was Gerolamo Cassar. The Language of Castile and Portugal was one of the most powerful, and possessed an annual income of £15,639. Rivalry between the French and Spanish Languages ran high. The Grand Chancellor who ruled this Auberge always presented the vice-chancellor to the Council, and was obliged to sign and witness the stamping of BULLS with the great seal. "Those who filled this office were required *to know how to read and write." This Auberge is occupied by the officers R. A. and R. E. The Senior Chaplain has also quarters here.

Over the entrance is a trophy of warlike weapons carved in marble, surmounted by a bust of the Portuguese Grand Master Pinto, who ruled for 32 years and died at the age of 92, greatly to the disgust of those who would fain have filled his place. The Grand staircase is much admired, and the corridors are delightfully cool when summer days are long. The rooms are lofty and spacious, and could formerly boast of beautifully painted ceilings which have been destroyed, the cost of restoration being too great. The left hand corner of the building bears the mark of a shot fired from Corradino during the siege of 1798-1800. Between the Auberge and St. Peter's Curtain are 15 Fosse containing 6,705 qrs. of corn, and near at hand is the Baracca School-Chapel, which is used as a Garrison

118

Church. It can accomodate 500 persons, and efforts are being made to make it a more filling soldiers church than it is at present.

Passing under an archway, we enter the pleasant garden of the upper Baracca, maintained by the Economico-Agrarian Society, which holds an annual flower show here. No smoking please, when the red flag is hoisted. There is powder not far off!

The tomb of Sir Thomas Maitland, who when Governor of Malta from 1813 to 1824, was generally known as "King Tom," is in the centre of the garden. Several other monuments are not far off, and a French author says that the "English have made the proud battlements of Valletta sepulchral!"

This Baracca was called the Porta d' Italia, being included in the station of that Language. Two half-obliterated inscriptions tell how Fra Balbiani Prior of Messina, roofed and greatly improved it at his own expense in 1661. The conspirators of 1775 assembled here, whereupon the Grand Master ordered the removal of the roof. The old pictures of Valletta at the Borsa represent the two Baraccas as roofed in 1715, the Duc de Vendôme, Grand Prior of France gave a great banquet at this Baracca to the knights who had assembled in force to repel a threatened Turkish invasion.

From the projecting gallery we look over the open sea. On the left is the entrance of the Great harbour overlooking which is the Lower Baracca, also the busy Marina, and the countless roofs of Valletta, above which rises the Torretta of the Palace, gay with signal flags. Immediately below us are

119

the garden called "the Sultan's," Fort Lascaris, in which the Royal Malta Fencible Artillery are quartered, the dome of the little church of Santa Maria di Liesse, the semicircular fish-market, and the Custom-house. A few feet below us is the Saluting Battery, the name of which explains itself.

Looking across to the other side of the harbour we note Fort Ricasoli, which, with Fort Sant Elmo protects the entrance. In the distance is Fort San Rocco on a hill-top. Rinella Creek almost washes the walls of Fort Ricasoli, and on the promontory of Bighi stands boldly out the Royal Naval Hospital, below which is Calcara Creek.

Fort St. Angelo,—which, in some shape or other, has existed for a thousand years—gives challenge to all hostile intruders, and sheltered beneath its protection are the houses of Vittoriosa, with the Naval Victualling Yard and Bakery. The Dockyard Creek runs far inland, and at its extremity are the suburb of Burmola and H. M. Dockyard. This Creek was formerly called the Port of the Galleys. The town of Senglea terminating in Isola Point separates the Dockyard Creek from the French Creek or Man of War Harbour, beyond which are the heights of Corradino on which we note an obelisk in memory of Captain Spencer, of H. M. S. Madagascar, and the Military and Civil Prisons. In the far distance are the massive fortifications of Cotonera and the Cotonera Military Hospital stands out against the sky-line.

Now let us walk to the other end of the Baracca and look down into the yawning gulf below! The Turkish captives who excavated that moat must have heartlily loathed their task! Beneath this arch was once a "huge and enormous" bronze gun. It

120

only weighed 20812 Italian lbs after all! The upper
portion of the harbour is crowded with sailing-craft,
and great additions have of late years been made
to its area. The pleasant, regularly built suburb of
Floriana with its fortifications is just in front of us,
whilst upon a distant hill are the domes and towers
of Città Vecchia, the ancient capital whereat St. Paul
probably sojourned for three months. The tower of
Verdala Palace is visible on the horizon, and several
populous villages are in sight. But we must proceed.

Leaving the Baracca, and re-passing the Auberge
de Castile we reach the head of Strada Mercanti,
where we must halt for awhile. On our left is the
Church of the Nativity of the B. V. M. commonly
called Della Vittoria.

The foundation stone of Valletta was laid on
this site (Malta and Its Knights p. p. 152-156) on
March 28th, 1566 amidst great public rejoicings. La
Vallette erected a chapel here dedicated to Our Lady
of Victory, which was used by the workmen and
others during the building of the city, and wherein
his remains rested from August 22nd 1568 until
their removal in the following year to St. John's
Church. In 1617 the Order made this church parochial, and it was restored and enlarged in 1752.
The paintings on the roof are by the Maltese artist
Enrico Arnaux, and the picture of the Good Shepherd
is by A. Falzon. The Venetian admiral Ems who
died in Malta on March 1st. 1792 is buried in this
church at which the annual blessing of the animals
takes place on January 17th and wherein the Malta
Fencibles, Artillery, and Roman Catholics sailors have
attended mass since 1837.

121

On the facade is a bronze bust of Pope Innocent XII. who settled certain differences between Bishop Palmieri, and the Prior of the Church. The G. M. Perellos was the donor.

Facing this church is another, Santa Caterina d' Italia, which was erected by the Language of Italy in 1576, from the designs of Gerolamo Cassar, and was attached to the adjacent Auberge d'Italia. The principal picture, representing the martyrdom of St. Catherine, is by Mattia Preti, who intended it for the church of Zurrico. It was however so much admired that the Italian knights retained it for their own church. The picture of Our Lady of Sorrows is the only work in Malta of the Bolognese artist Benedetto Luti.

Large numbers of children attend this church for religious instruction. Adjoining the church is the plain massive Auberge d' Italia. Over the entrance is a bronze bust of the G. M. Gregory Caraffa, with an inscription recording his two victories over the Turks at the Dardanelles, and a marble trophy of warlike weapons carved from one of the columns of the ruined temple of Proserpine on the heights of Emtarfa, near Città Vecchia. The head of the Language of Italy, which had an annual revenue of £23,533, was the Admiral of the Order, who also held military command, when the Grand Marshal was absent. Within the entrance gateway are two memorial tablets. Another tablet, affixed to the walls of a room gives an account in spirited Latin of the great victory over the Turks at the Dardanelles on June 26th 1656. Another inscription is "the accustomed place of the Congregation of the Galleys," or, in other words, the Admiralty of the Order. A handsome

122

arch above a well stands in the garden in the centre of the building. Each Auberge had its garden. In the Auberge. which is occupied. by the Royal Engineers, are preserved the archives of deceased notaries public.

Saliba's Livery Stables are opposite. Horses and carriages on hire. Four omnibusses daily to Città Vecchia. Fare 6d. Omnibusses daily at 7. 0. a. m. for Marfa and Gozo. Fare to Migiarro in Gozo, including ferry boat 2s. To St. Paul's Bay 1s.

This building, the old Palazzo Parisio, was offered by its owner, the Baron Paolo Parisio, a Maltese nobleman, to the First Napoleon, who made it his head-quarters. Here he treated the Grand Master Hompesch with cool contempt, and here assembled Bishop Labini and his clergy. Let Sigr. Ferris speak: "Buonaparte, turning to the ecclesiastical assembly, said in a loud voice, " Reverend sirs, preach the Gospel, respect, and cause to be respected, the constituted authorities, recommend to the people submsssion and obedience to the French laws. If you are good priests, I will protect you, but, if you are bad ones, I will chastise you ! ' " Summary certainly !

The church of San Giacomo or St. James is nearly opposite. Erected in 1612 at the expense of the Grand Chancellor Pietro Gonzales de Mendoza who enriched it with carvings, it belonged to the Language of Castile. The architect was a Maltese named Barbara. The church contains a picture of St. James by Paladini, and another of Our Lady of Sorrows, which has a curious history. The latter was presented by a Conventual Chaplain in 1646.

123

This church is the Oratory of the Institution of Catholic Education.

A handsome facade, with an inscription and marble statues of Justice and Truth, points out the old Castellania or prison which was rebuilt and enlarged, beautified by the Grand Master Pinto. The work was commenced in 1757, under the direction of the Civil Architect Francesco Zerafa, who however, died on April 21st 1758, and was succeeded by Giuseppe Bonnici, who completed the building in 1760. The Chapel was blessed by the Vice prior Mons. Constans on Nov. 15th of that year. Three days afterwards the prisoners were brought from "the tower of Porta Reale," and the Courts sat at 9. 0. a. m. The carvings on the facade and in the chapel are the work of Maestro Gian, a Sicilian imprisoned for homicide.

The President of the Castellania was a knight selected by the Grand Master every two years from the several Languages according to seniority, and styled the "Castellano." He was constantly followed by a page bearing a waud. The Castellania is now occupied by private families and the Gas Office At the top of the descent of Strada San Giovanni is a pillar on which those condemned to the punishment of the " strappado " used to stand. During the Carnival· a plank was placed across the street to shew that judicial punishment were in abeyance. This slope is called "the prisoners' Hill " because those in durance used to ask alms from passers by. From the door of the present Gas Office came forth criminals condemned to death, and those sentenced to be flogged through the streets mounted upon

124

an ass. Lord Cochrane escaped from the balcony over-head, by the aid of a rope ladder.

We pass St. John's Church (p. 80). The office of the P. and O. Co. with its electric clock, is at No. 41. On Sundays and festivals an open-air market is held in the Strada Mercanti, for the sale of odds and ends and "unconsidered trifles." The Post Office is at No. 197 (p. 56). Many efforts have been made to rebuild or remove it to a more convenient position. The building was erected in 1640, at the suggestion of the Commander Abela as a place of security for the Archives of deceased notaries public, and as the Banco dei Giurati or town Hall. The Giurati or Magistrates (see Ciantar's Malta Illustrata. Vol I. p. p. 66-7) sat here daily to regulate the price of provisions, and until 1818 the Grain Department was also under the same roof. The G. M. Zondadari made great improvements in 1721, and in 1798 Buonaparte had a bad fall on the stairs. An adjoining house having been given in 1611 by the Commander C. Bellot was restored in 1746 by the Assembly of Conventual Chaplains.

Opposite to the Post Office is the Monte di Pietà, or Government Pawnbroking Establishment. In 1598 the Portuguese knight Emanuele Couros (Luiros?) offered £200, and the Cav. Francesco Moleti also advanced £100 for five years without interest to start the Monte, which commenced operations under the name of Santa Anna, with the G. M. Garzes as patron.

In 1607 Fra Raffaele Maltese, Capuchin Friar, proposed from the pulpit of St. John's Church the formation of a Monte di Redenzione for the ransom of Maltese and Gozitans captured by the Turks. The

125

knights and Maltese eagerly subscribed, and in 1619 Caterina Vitale a Maltese of noble birth, endowed the Monte with all her property and jewels. Six years afterwards Dr. G. D. Felici gave £600 for the same purpose. On June 23rd 1787 the Grand Master De Rohan united these two charitable institutions. The French plundered the Monte of nearly £35000, but after the surrender of Valletta the English Government advanced £5,800 without interest, and the institution is again prosperous. It benefits others besides the poor, as advances are made to the amount of £600. Precious metals and jewellery are retained for three years, linen for two years, cloth and woolen goods for six months, after which time unclaimed pawns are disposed of, any profits of sale being handed over to the holders of the tickets. Interest 5 per cent. Open from 8. 0. a.m. till 3. 0. p.m. A Savings' Bank open on Saturdays and Mondays from noon till 1. 0. p. m. and which allows interest at the rate of 2 per cent on amounts below £100, is attached to the Monte. The number of depositors on December 31st 1878 was 3,407, with £217,287. 0. 9. placed to their credit. In the Gozo Branch Bank 241 depositors were credited with £9,120. 4. 7. The Committee of Charitable Institutions has managed the Monte since January 1st 1838.

The street is crowded. On one side is the Governor's Palace, and on the other the Market House which was commenced in 1859 and completed in 1861, a temporary Market being held meanwhile in the Lower Baracca. The old market House was very badly arranged. The new one, which Valletta owes to Sir Gaspard Le Marchant, is square in form, with stores below. Light and airy in appearance,

126

it is divided into five gas-lighted avenues, with six entrances, three in front, and three at the sides. An electric clock keeps time, meat and poultry are on the right, fish at either end, and fruit and vegetables are abundant and cheap. For weights see page 59.

Turning for a moment out of Strada Mercanti into Strada Vescovo, the next cross street, and passing a police-station, we enter the church of Our Lady of Damascus (Greek rite) built between 1576 and 1580 at the expense of Giovanni Calamia, a noble Rhodian who followed the Order to Malta. This church was made parochial for the Greeks in 1587, and contains a picture of the Blessed Virgin Mary which is said to have journeyed without human aid from Damascus to Rhodes, after *the capture of the former city by the Saracens. The picture of the Resurrection is by Stefano Erardi.

Returning to Strada Mercanti, we enter the church of the Jesuits, who were invited to Malta by Bishop Gargallo in 1593, and banished by the G. M. Pinto in 1768. The engineer Bonamici was the architect in 1592, and Bishop Gargallo, who is buried here, and whose portrait is in the sacristy, was a great benefactor. The church which consists of a choir, nave, and side aisles, was consecrated in 1731. The principal picture representing the Circumcision of Christ is by Baldassare Peruzzi, and in the second chapel from the entrance are three pictures by Mattia Preti. Two Oratories are connected with this church which is attached to the University. Roman Catholic soldiers attend mass here.

The adjacent College was under the control of the Jesuits from 1592 until their expulsion in 1768,

127

when the Pope transferred their property to the Grand Master with the obligation to found a University. Great changes were made after the arrival of the English in Malta, and also in 1839 in accordance with the report of the Royal Commissioners. The University has four Faculties, viz., of Law, Philosophy Arts, Medicine, and Theology. The Museum is rich in geological and natural history specimens. Admission free, on application to the Secretary. A Lyceum or preparatory school is connected with the University. Both the Univerity and Lyceum are under the superintendence of a Rector. For the names of professors, subjects of study, &c. see the Malta Almanacks. There are also Lyceums in the Three Cities and at Gozo.

Just below, on the left are the Dominican Church and Convent. The church which is also called Porto Salvo was originally designed by Gerolamo Cassar, and was rebuilt between 1804 and 1815. It consists of a choir, nave, side aisles, and side chapels. The decorations are rich, and the principal picture is by P. P. Caruana. The Oratory of the Rosario is attached to the church.

Nearly opposite is the church of the Anime Purganti or Souls in Purgatory. Originally dedicated to S. Nicola, it was built in 1580 as the first parochial church of the Greek Rite, and rebuilt between 1652 and 1658 by the Society of the Anime. Purganti. It was consecrated in 1782. The principal picture is by Mattia Preti, and there are two others in the sacristy by the Cav. Favray. The Grand Master Pinto appropriated a larger sum belonging to this church, and on being told that the souls would suffer in cousequence, replied "I am

128

very old, in a short time I shall join them, and I promise to settle with them!"

Below the church is the Military Hospital, built in 1575, with accomodation for about 200 patients. It is large and spacious one portion being assigned to the sick belonging to the Malta Fencible Artillery. There are three quadrangles, one of which is surrounded by wide corridors, also quarters for medical officers, and a detachment of the Army Hospital Corps, a medical library containing about 1200 volumes and a portrait of Dr. Henin, a celebrated anatomist, who died in 1754. In front of the library is a fountain with three stone pears, the arms of the Grand Master Perellos, carved upon it. The office of the Principal Medical Officer, and the Staff Dispensary are also here. In the Dispensary are a huge pestle and mortar of bell-metal, with the date 1710, and the arms of Perellos. Above the guarded gate within the quadrangle is a sundial and the date 1774 when £722 was spent in repairs. The basement walls are of enormous thickness, and one ward, at the extremity of which is a picture representing the gift of the right hand of St. John the Baptist to the Grand Master D' Aubusson by the Sultan Bajazet, is said to be the longest room in Europe unsupported by pillars. It is 185 ft. 5 in. long, 34 ft. 9 in. broad, and 30ft. 11 in. high.

Above a window is an unfinished inscription "Francisco Alle:" the bells of the clock, removed some time since, were cast in 1646, and at the postern gate is the date 1633. Successive Grand Hospitaliers ruled the hospital, emblazoning their arms upon its walls. They, as well as the Infirmarians whom they appointed, belonged to the Language of

France. The Infirmarian resided in the hospital, as did also at least one surgeon. In 1687 the physicians, surgeons, and students were numerous. The Hospital was a sanctuary, and all officers, except the Grand Hospitallers, were obliged to leave their badges of authority at the door. In 1712 the officials of the Inquisitors entered by surprise, but were instantly expelled. The Prior, Vice Prior, and other officers were appointed by the Grand Hospitaller. The Prior was a Conventual Chaplain, belonging to one of the three Languages of France, Auvergne or Provence. The Vice Prior was usually a Maltese. The other officers were, for the most part, Conventual Priests. The chapel was built by the Grand Master Perellos in 1712. Ten chaplains were attached to the hospital, in the centre of which was an altar. There were also altars in the various wards. This was the first hospital in Europe that admitted patients of various creeds. Patients who were not Roman catholics, and also those suffering from wounds and ulcers, had separate wards. The Great Hall contained 24 beds, which were reserved for the knights. There were usually 500 beds, with space for 2000. The annual average of patients was 2000, who were served on silver plate for the sake of cleanliness. This plate, which was afterwards melted down by the Order, or confiscated by the French, was on April 30th 1788 valued at £3,449. The knights of Provence took charge of the patients on Sundays, and were followed by the other Languages according to seniority, the Anglo-Bavarian and the German Languages being united. Illegitimate and destitute children were reared at an annual cost of £614, and Vertot estimates the whole yearly expense

130

of the hospital at 50,000 golden crowns. In 1788 the annual cost was £7,947, or a daily average of 10*d.* to 1*s.* per patient. The French, who lost at least 725 men between Sept. 1798 and August 1800, used the building as a Military Hospital, and it was subsequently used as a wine-store. The rope-walk of the Order, which cost in construction £542, was close by. John Howard gives a terrible account of this hospital in 1786, but on August 2nd, 1676, the Revd. H. Teonge, Chaplain of H. M. S. Bristol thus writes:—"The hospital is a vast structure, wherein their sick and wounded lye. 'Tis so broad that 12 men may with ease walke a brest up the midst of it: and the beds are on each syd, standing on 4 yron pillars, with white curtens, and vallands and covering, extreamly neate, and kept cleane and sweete: the sick served all in silver plate: and it containes above 200 bedds below, besyds many spatious roomes in other quadrangles with in; for the chiefe cavaliers and knights, with pleasant walkes and gardens; and a stately house for the chiefe doctor, and other his attendants."

The sick soldier here receives every care and attention. There are also wards for women and children. A Laboratory and Meteorological Observatory do useful scientific work.

Facing the Hospital is the Camerata, occupied by married soldiers and their families. On this site formerly stood a large building, erected in 1593, and restored in 1696 by a grant from the Treasury. The rooms on the right were occupied by the pious knights who lived in community, assembling at stated hours for purposes of devotion. Those on the left were called La Lingerie, and were in

131

fact the linen stores of the hospital, as well as a laundry for bedding and clothing. The College of St. Paul directed by the Jesuits was transferred from Città Vecchia and established here in 1852, but in 1859 Bishop Casolani erected on the old site the present building for the accommodation of poor families; it has since passed into the hands of the Government.

The Camerata formerly possessed a Library, which was founded by the Commander Sansedoni, and augmented by the Bailiff Chiurlia Cavaniglia. Most of the books are now in the Public Library.

Close to the hospital is its former cemetery. All Brethren of the Order were buried in their mantles à bec, i. e. with points, and with the white cross. "We order that the corpses of secular persons that die in our infirmary should be buried handsomely; that the chaplains shall walk before the corpse and pray for the soul of the deceased: that the four persons that carry the bier shall wear black robes which shall be made and kept for this particular purpose." No mourning was to be worn at funerals, even for the Grand Master. On a portion of the cemetery stands a semicircular building used as a dissecting room by the medical students of the University, and close by is a large charnel house the walls of which were ornamented with bones and skulls by a priest some years since.

Hard by stands the little church of Nibbia or the Holy Name of Mary, erected in 1619 at the expense of the Commander Giorgio Nibbia, who was interred here. The church was rebuilt in 1731.

The neighbouring Hospital for Incurables was formerly a female Hospital called La Cassetta, under

132

the charge of a Grand Cross and two Commissaries. It was endowed by a charitable lady named Caterina Scappi of Siena with all her property in 1642, which bequest was augmented by a legacy of Flamminia Valenti in 1717. The Hospital formerly contained 250 inmates, but at present accomodation is provided for 221. The chapel is dedicated to Santa Caterina, and the hospital was applied to its present use in 1850.

Facing the Hospital for Incurables was the Nunnery of Santa Maddalena, established here in 1609. The French marched out the sisterhood between files of soldiers in 1798, and converted the building into a hospital, the sisters retiring to the Nunnery of Santa Caterina. The church .was used as a ward for patients suffering from wounds and broken limbs. It was consecrated by Monsignor Alpheran on May 23rd 1748. The old Nunnery was in 1852 converted into an Orphan Asylum, attached to which are the Government Primary Normal Schools, the hospitals being removed to a new large building at Floriana.

In rear of the Military Hospital are St. Lazarus Curtain and the Castile Bastion, commanding a fine view of the open sea and of the Great Harbour.

Strada San Paolo runs parallel with Strada Mercanti. In this street are entrances to the University and Lyceum, and the Church of St. Paul Shipwrecked. It is said that an ancient chapel formerly stood on the site of Valletta, dedicated to St. Paul, which was almost destroyed during the Great Siege of 1565. The first church dedicated to St. Paul Shipwrecked was erected in 1677, at the expense

133

of the Cathedral, from the plans of Gerolamo Cassar. The parochial boundaries were settled in 1605, and in 1591 a synod ordered the church to be enlarged. The present church was commenced in 1639 and completed in 1679. It is chiefly of the Ionic order of architecture, and is in the form of a Latin cross, consisting of a nave with six side chapels, two large chapels, and a sacristy. The treasury of the church contains many valuables, and, at certain times of the year, marriages are not only celebrated gratis, but the bride even receives a present of £8. 6. 8.

This church claims to possess, amongst other relics, a portion of the column upon which St. Paul suffered martyrdom. The principal picture representing the shipwreck of St. Paul is by Paladini. It contains a portrait of Bishop Gargallo, at whose expense it was painted. The picture of The Last Supper is by Favray: that of St. Michael is by Mattia Preti, that of St. Martin by Stefano Erardi, and that of St. Omobomo by the Maltese artist Ceci. A won den statue in the choir was carved at Rome by se Melchiorre Gafà in 1657. The festival of the Shipwreck of St. Paul is celebrated annually on Feb. 10th.

We turn into Strada San Giovanni, which is here, in very deed, a "street of stairs," and enter the Church of the Minori Osservanti (Franciscans). The adjoining Convent was commenced in 1571 and completed four years afterwards. The Grand Master Manoel contributed towards its restoration, and additions were made in 1810. The church is large and of composite architecture, consisting of a nave with side aisles, which were ornamented by the Grand Masters N. Cotoner and Caraffa. Much of the painting in the church was executed as a labour of love by various

134

Maltese artists. Near the church is the Oratory of the Crucifixion. The present building dates from 1698. The principal picture in the church, representing the Betrothal of Santa Caterina is by Antonio Catalano and was painted in 1600. The picture of St. Carlo Borromeo and other saints is ascribed to Guido Reni: and that of Our Lady of Sorrows is by Erardi.

Turning to the left at the corner of the church we find ourselves in Strada Sant' Ursola, in which are the Church of San Rocco and the Church and Nunnery of Sant' Ursola. The former was founded in 1592 by the University of Malta in fulfilment of a vow on the cessation of the plague. After the plague of 1675-6 the Giurati of Valletta, making a vow in the name of the University rebuilt it in 1680. Lorenzo Gafà was the architect, and the Grand Master Carafa defrayed much of the cost. The church which contains two pictures by Erardi was solemnly blessed on August 12th 1681. An institution of Catholic Education for Children was established on March 25th 1863.

The Ursoline Nunnery was founded by the Grand Master Verdala in 1583, transferred from Vittoria to its present site in 1595, and enlarged by the Grand Master Pinto in 1759. The nuns belong to the Order of Saint John of Jerusalem, and still wear the cloak of that order. They received an annual pension from its funds of £594.

The church was restored by the Grand Master De Paola, whose arms are over the entrance. The roof was painted in 1717 by Alessio Erardi at the expense of the Grand Master Perellos. The principal picture representing the martyrdom of Santa

135

Ursola is by Mattia Preti. The silver group representing the Flagellation, was given to the Grand Master Pinto, by Monsignor Gregorio Salviati, on his arrival in Malta as Inquisitor in 1754.

Turning to the right into Strada Cristoforo, we pass on the right No. 12 the Palazzo Connidi, built as his escutcheon testifies, by the Grand Master Perellos (p. 57), and on the left the ancient Slave and Civil Prisons (see Howard's Hospitals and Lazarettoes of Europe). The slaves were about 4000 in number, obtained either by capture or purchase, and were employed in the construction of fortifications, the manufacture of cotton sail cloth, or as domestic servants. Their prisons maintained at a yearly cost of £3,826, were miserable places. The Order spent £449 per annum in purchasing slaves, whilst the ransom of these hapless captives brought in £1,661. Constant fears of a rising were entertained. Slaves who had been baptised, and Maltese convicts were kept separated from the rest. The Civil Prison had in the centre a large courtyard for exercise, intersected by four diagonal walls meeting in the centre. Government schools and stables, together with the vast wine stores of Messrs Woodhouse and Co. occupy the old prisons. This firm has been established here ever since the arrival of the English. We note that Sicilian wine is kept in casks of chestnut wood, but other wines in American oak.

Strada Cristoforo is behind us, and on our left is Strada Irlandese or "Irish Street" with numerous blacksmiths' shops, leading to St. Lazarus Curtain and the Military Hospital. On our right is Strada Levante. Immediately before us is the Lower Baracca, with a monument to the memory of Sir A.

136

J. Ball, "who seems to have been a good man all round," and who has found a grave at Fort St. Elmo, in the bastion which bears his name. The monument is a miniature reproduction of the Temple of Theseus at Athens, and is fast going to decay. This Baracca was, like the other, formerly roofed. The enclosure was converted into a market garden by the French during the siege of 1798-1800; and during the erection of the new Market-house in Strada Mercanti, a temporary market was held here under canvas. From hence we have a fine view of Valletta, the Great Harbour, the Three Cities, and Fort Ricasoli.

Returning to Strada Levante we note a large wooden shed, which is the centre of the wholesale vegetable market. Strada Levante, in which dwell marble cutters and ship-chandlers, has on the right the Ursuline Nunnery, and on the left the Castile Curtain, and the Bastion of Santa Barbara. From the broad terrace of the latter we have a fine view of the harbour. The old ice-house is here which, when snow from Sicily was scarce, reserved its stores for the use of the hospital. Facing the street of the same name is the Church of Santa Lucia, built in 1570, and originally dedicated to San Francesco di Paola. It was served by the Dominicans until the erection of their convent in 1771, and was rebuilt by the wine merchants of the marina with the dedication of Santa Lucia and San Vincenzo Ferreri.

At the Marina Gate is a fountain surmounted by a marble Baptism of Christ with the Latin inscription. "Amongst those born of women there

137

hath not risen a greater than John the Baptist," close to which is a standard barometer.

To the left of the drawbridge are bamboo-using basket makers, and on the right the "Sultan's Garden" laid out by the Grand Master Lascaris, who also built close by a house wherein the Grand Master and his knights might play cards, regaling themselves meanwhile with ices and sherbet. The word "Sultan" means in Maltese a "King" or "ruler." In this garden is a fountain with papyrus plants. The house was afterwards occupied by the Captain of the Port, but was pulled down a few years since, and its site occupied by Fort Lascaris, which is garrisoned by the Royal Malta Fencible Artillery.

On the left are the beggar haunted "Nix Mangiare" or "nothing to eat" Stairs, visited by Midshipman Easy, at the bottom of which is a landing place off which lie steamers and sailing craft. To the left is a range of stores built by the Grand Master Perellos, and the old Health Office over the door of which is a Latin inscription which means "Love of the People did this." The little church of SS. Salvatore formerly stood here, for the benefit of persons in quarantine. It has been demolished, and the bronze bust of Our Saviour is above the principal door of St. John's Church. On the quay are a number of stone pillars, connected when necessary by wooden bars, and called the Barriera. Here merchants and others were allowed to speak to their friends in quarantine. Two thousand persons could assemble here. The curious in ancient rules of quarantine at Malta are referred to M. Houel's Voyage Pittoresque (1687,) in the Public Library.

138

Either once more climbing the Stairs of Nix Mangiare, and descending a slope, or else following the shore we reach the semi-circular fish market, erected by the Grand Master Despuig. The fountain in the centre was formerly surmounted by a statue of Neptune which is now at the Palace.

On our right is the much venerated Church of Our Lady of Liesse with its legend of Ismaria and the three captive knights. It was first built in 1620 at the expense of the Bailiff d' Armenia, and belonged to the Language of France, by which it was rebuilt in 1740. The principal picture is by Enrico Arnaux, and refers to the legend above alluded to. The French knights were specially devoted to this church, and the Comte de Beaujolais, brother of Louis Philippe, directed that his heart should be interred here. The marble altar was given by a former rector, and the church contains an image of the Virgin, which was brought from Fort St. Elmo or, some say, from Liesse in Picardy.

We pass through a tunnel called the Mina Lascaris, it having been cut through a projecting rock by that Grand Master, as a Latin inscription above the entrance testifies. At the further extremity is the Dogana or Custom House. A portion of the site was formerly called "the bay of insects," this being the basking place of the slaves. The Custom House was built on piles by the civil and military architect Giuseppe Bonnici, a pupil of the Chev. Tigné, during the rule of the Grand Master Ximenes. Exports are free, and ships taking a cargo from the island pay no tonnage. For duties on imports see the Malta Almanacks. It was originally intended to accomodate exports here, but the

139

space designed for that purpose is now occupied by
the Port Department. Just within the entrance of
the Custom House is a monument to the Cavaliere
Giulio Amati, an Italian Knight and Admiral of
the Order, who, at his own expense, greatly improved the landing place in 1651 before the erection of the Custom House. This monument was
rescued from oblivion by the Hon, V. Inglott C. M. G.
Collector of Customs, who has most kindly given me
much valuable information. The Long Room is ornamented with a complete series of the escutcheons
of the Grand Masters, and there are in the building portraits both of the founder and architect, and
also a picture of the quay previous to the erection
of the Custom House.

The busy bustling Marina is always full of
interest to the traveller. On one side is the harbour with its numerous steamers, sailing craft, men
of war, speronaras and dghaisas, and on the other
are long ranges of stores erected by the Grand
Masters Lascaris, Pinto and Zondadari and also by
the Università of supplies, which provided Malta
not with learning, but with corn, meat, oil, and
charcoal, for 250 years until its abolition in 1818.
Some of these stores were for the supply of the
galleys and men of war. The Order intended to
establish its arsenal near the site of the present
Custom House, but the sparks from the pipe of an
idiot, who chanced to stand upon the Baracca, burnt
a new galley, and the design was abandoned as too
dangerous.

Calcara Gate, at which a guard is posted, and
which is reached by the steep ascent of the Cro-
cefisso from the Marina, is named from a kiln at

140

which all the lime was burnt for the public buildings of the Order. At the end of the nineteen Pinto stores is a small church erected by the same Grand Master in 1752, close to which is a fountain which supplies water to shipping. The old Naval Bakery was adjacent to the church, and is at present used as an oil store.

We pass through the Right Marina Gate. Above is the Capuchin Monastery, and around us are the Ordnance Wharf, Gas Works, Mortuary, a Flour Mill, and the Government Slaughter-house.

An obelisk marks the former termination of an avenue of poplars planted by the Grand Master Manoel de Vilhena. We have now completed our itinerary of Valletta.

141

CHAPTER VI.

FLORIANA.

Politeama Theatre.— The Suburb of Vilhena. — Gates and Fortifications.— The Maglio, and Pavillion. — Soldiers' and Sailors' Home. St. Francis' Barracks, Princess' Theatre, Capuchin Convent. — Wignacourt's Aqueducts, and Bouverie.— Churches of Sarria and Saint Publio.— The Argotti Garden, Casa di Manresa, and Central Civil Hospital. — Floriana Barracks, Charitable Institutions, and English Cemeteries.—Sa Maison and its Recreation Ground.

JUST outside Porta Reale is an obelisk with no inscription, and below us is the Politeama Theatre, open during the summer, for Italian performances at moderate prices. A winding road through the fortifications brings us to a large open space, commanding a fine view over the Great Harbour and the interior of the island. Before us is the suburb of Floriana, named after Col. Pietro Paolo Floriani, an Italian engineer in the service of the Pope, (by whom he was despatched to Malta at the request of the Grand Master, in the year 1635,) who designed the fortifications by which it is defended. It is also called the "Suburb of Vilhena," who ordered the erection of many of its buildings. It has four gates. The one giving access to the Quarantine harbour is called "della Marina," and also "under the gallows" as criminals were formerly executed close by.

142

Notre Dame Gate opening towards the country is called "the gate of pears," from the arms of the Grand Master Perellos, viz, three pears.

St. Ann's Gate, sometimes styled "Porter's Straits," (having been remodelled by Major Porter R. E.,) is the "Dog's Gate," from two pillars surmounted by dogs which formerly stood on either side.

The outer gate, called Porte des Bombes, which derives its name from some large stone shells, was erected in 1721, and has upon it the arms of the Grand Master Perellos. This gate and that of St. Ann were rebuilt in 1868.

The French were repulsed at this point in 1798 and marks of shot fired from the Maltese batteries, during the two years' siege, are still to be seen. By this gate the allied English, Maltese and Neapolitan troops entered Valletta in 1800.

The fortifications commenced in 1636 were discontinued two years afterwards, and not recommenced until 1716, the defences of Margarita Hill and the Cotonera Lines having been taken in hand meanwhile. Part of the cost was defrayed by a corntax of about 7*d*. per qr.

To the left is a large parade ground, sacred to drill and cricket, whilst directly facing us is the Maglio or Mall, which forms a pleasant and favourite walk. It was laid out in 1805, during the rule of Sir A♦ J. Ball, is maintained by the Government, and contains a bust of Dr. Luigi Pisani who died in 1865. This spot was formerly set apart for the game of hand-ball, and the Grand Master Lascaris ordered the erection of a Latin inscription to that effect.

143

To the left of the Maglio are numerous Fosse for grain, which contain many qrs. and form a large paved space known as "the granaries," a favourite public resort. Military and other bands often perform here. The Pavillion now occupied by the officers of the Infantry Regiment quartered at the Floriana Barracks was originally built by the University of Supplies as the Market of Floriana.

The houses in this suburb are arranged in blocks and the streets intersect at right angles. Through the centre runs Strada Sant' Anna, a broad street with arcades on either side.

In the Piazza Maggiore is the Soldiers' and Sailors' Home, of which the Revd. J. Webster, Wesleyan Minister to the Forces, is Secretary and Treasurer, and which is doing good work in our midst. It has a well furnished Library and Reading Room, Dining and Smoking Rooms, with ample smoking accomodotion. Charges very moderate. The Secretary will be glad to receive contributions.

At the end of the cross streets, we have a fine view of the Great Harbour, and near the outer defences are St. Francis' Barracks, the head quarters of the Royal Engineers.

Adjoining the Barracks is the Princess' Theatre in which the R. E. Dramatic Club and other amateurs tread the boards. A large wooden cross stands on St. Mark's Bastion, close to which are several Fosse for grain, and we reach the Capuchin Church and Convent. The former is dedicated to the Invention of the Holy Cross, and was consecrated in 1773. The principal picture was painted by Paladini, at the expense of the Grand Master Nicholas Cotoner. The picture of St. Francis is the work of Erardi.

144

An image of the B. V. Mary is kept here which some Christian slaves brought from Constantinople, having made themselves masters of a Turkish galley. A quaint picture commemorates this event. The Convent was founded in 1588, (the architect being Gerolamo Cassar,) but has since been restored and enlarged. It has a good library and the monks number about 60. They support themselves and a large number of the poor and afflicted by means of daily-collected charity. If you visit the Convent, do not forget to give alms! For many visitors come hither to see what are popularly called the "Baked Monks." The bodies of deceased monks are placed in niches, in a vault, dressed in the robes which they wore during life. They have not, however, been embalmed, baked, or otherwise prepared, but have simply been laid for at least twelve months in sloping graves. This is not a Maltese, but a Sicilian custom, introduced by the first Fathers who founded the Convents. Deceased brethren are now interred in the Addolorata Cemetery. The Church of Rome *tolerates* such exposition of the remains of the faithful simply as a check to human pride.

We pass St. Ann's Gate and fountain erected in 1728 by the Grand Master Vilhena, and skirting St. Ann's Curtain, reach a tower which serves as a drinking fountain supplied by the Grand Master Alofio Wignacourt's aqueduct, about which we must say a few words.

It was commenced in 1610 in order to supply Valletta with water, which was formerly brought with great labour from a spring called Ghain - Filep at the head of the Great Harbour. Several springs

145

amongst the Bingemma Hills were united by means of pipes, and their waters led into one channel. The principal spring is at Diar Ghandul about 9¾ miles distant from Valletta. The whole cost of the work was £15,480, of which £11,480 was defrayed by Wignacourt himself, the remaining £4000 being made up by a tax upon the Public Granaries and Bakery. The first architect was Padre Natale Tomasucci a Jesuit of Messina, who brought the water as far as Casal Attard. He then resigned, and the work was completed by Bontadino. On April 21st 1615 the water was admitted into a fountain in the centre of St. George's Square, amidst great public rejoicings. All praise to Wignacourt giver of water. The aqueduct supplies a daily average of 108,000 gallons to Valletta and Floriana.

To the slight detriment of rural gardens, but to the great benefit of the Three Cities of Burmola, Vittoriosa, and Senglea, which were formerly dependent upon the somewhat brackish water found at the head of the Great Harbour, Sir H. F. Bouverie constructed an aqueduct, which collects the waters of numerous springs at Fauara, Imtahleb, and in the neighbourhood of the Casals of Curmi and Dingli, &c. It runs underground to the Three Cities a distance of about seven miles, and supplies daily about 57.600 gallons.

Opposite the aqueduct tower is the circular Church of the Conception of the B. V. M., usually called Sarria, having been built at the expense of a Navarrese knight of that name in 1585. During the visitation of the plague in 1675-6 the Grand Master R. Cotoner and the Council vowed to build a church upon the site of this old chapel, which

10

146

was accordingly done in 1678. Several pictures by
Mattia Preti were placed here. The picture of Santa
Anna is by A. Falzon. In the sacristy are portraits
of the founder and of the Grand Master Cotoner,
together with an ancient picture, which, perhaps,
belonged to the old church.

Close by is the Parish Church, dedicated to
S. Pubblio. The first stone of the present structure
was laid in 1733 by Bishop Alpheran de Bussan,
but it was not completed until 1768. It was enlarged between 1856 and 1862, and now consists
of a choir, nave, two large chapels, and side aisles.
The principal picture representing the Martyrdom
of San Pubblio is by Favray. Near these churches
are large Infant and Primary Schools, and hard by
the end of the Maglio is the Argotti Garden, in
which was formerly the house of the Bailiff
Argotti. It is a pleasant place of resort, and was
much improved by the late Lieut. General Villettes,
to whose memory a monument has been erected
within it.

Nearly opposite are the Church and House of
San Calcedonio, which are also styled those of "Our
Lady of Manresa." This almshouse owes its origin
to Father Francesco Rosignoli, and was opened in
1751. It serves as a religious retreat for pious persons during the days of Carnival, for candidates
for ordination, and for pious ecclesiastics and lay-
men. In 1858 Bishop Pace Forno founded a seminary in this building at his own expense with
a chapel dedicated to Our Lady of Sorrow.

The chapel of this almshouse owes its origin
to Don Pietro Infante of Portugal, Grand Prior of

147

Crato, and was consecrated in 1786. It contains pictures by the Cav. Favray and other artists.

Facing the Casa di Manresa is the Central Civil Hospital originally built as a Conservatorio for Poor Girls by the Grand Master Manoel de Vilhena. In 1825 great reforms were introduced. The inmates, about 200 in number, were taught various trades and occupations. They could not go out without permission, but might become domestic servants under proper sanction. They might leave to be married, but could not return again.

The outbreak of cholera in 1837 checked the prosperity of the Institution, and about thirty years ago the building was appropriated to its present use. The girls were removed to the Aged Asylum and gradually dispersed.

The Hospital with accomodation for 250 patients has a daily average of 170, and its professional staff comprises, in addition to two Visiting Physicians and Surgeons, three resident professional men. The sick are tended by Sisters of Charity, and are visited by clergymen of their own faith. The removal of this hospital to another site is under consideration.

At the back of the Hospital are the Floriana Barracks, which are occupied by an infantry regiment.

Passing through the neighbouring Polverista Gate we see the Asylum for the Aged and Infirm, which was built for a powder mill by the Grand Master Pinto in 1762. Col. Porter says that the saltpetre was refined at another mill in Valletta, the process of manufacture being completed here. These two mills could produce 1408 lbs. weekly at

148

5½d. per lb. Further supplies were procured from France.

The building is now occupied by about 700 aged and infirm persons, and connected with it is the Female Prison (having on an average nineteen prisoners with light sentences), under the amiable custody of a Sister of Charity. Also, the Magdalen Asylum containing about fifteen voluntary inmates, and the Foundling Hospital, in which, in 1878, sixteen young children were being nursed.

Close to this Asylum a road leads to the cemeteries long since fiilled with English dead, which afford food for much quiet and profitable thought.

Passing the Asylum, and threading our way through a labyrinth of fortifications, we reach Sa Maison, the old home of a Bailiff of that name.

The Government house which formerly stood here is said to have been used for the meetings of the Masonic Lodge, founded in 1785 by the Bohemian Count Kollowart. Great numbers of knights were initiated, and the Grand Master Rohan only closed the Lodge in consequence of stringent orders from Rome.

The Malta General Recreation Club has established itself at Sa Maison. Family Tickets, 15s. per annum; 5s. per month. Single Ticket 10s per annum; 2s. 6d. per month. Full particulars on application to the Secretary. The gardens are tastefully laid out, and, we pass a curious well with quaint carvings. Fortifications are above us and around us. Connecting two bastions is the celebrated arch of Sa Maison thrown across a small ravine called Giorff Id-del, or the "Shady Precipice" which has since been filled in with stones and earth, and in which

149

formerly dwelt a hermit. This arch was constructed by the Maltese Architect and Superintendent Giovanni Barbara who assisted Col. Floriani in the erection of these works. It is intended for the passage of artillery, and curves obliquely for more than half its length. Its diameter is 42 feet 6 in., its thickness 35 feet, and it presents a different appearance according to the position of the spectator.

Amongst other monuments we remark one to "Rose" the favourite dog of the Band of the 74th Highlanders, with these lines:

> Of you my new comers,
> I humbly request
> This small spot of ground,
> Wherein I may rest.

The road to the left leads directly, and that to the right by a more circuitous route, back to Floriana and Valletta.

150

CHAPTER VII.

PEMBROKE CAMP, ST. JULIANS, AND SLIEMA.

The Wimbledon of Malta.—St. Julian's Bay, and the Forrest Hospital.—Fougasses.—Jesuit College.—The Forgotten Church.—Boat and carriage fares.—Cure for fever.—Sliema.—Officers' Bathing House, and Fort Tigné.—Churches of Sliema.—Fort Manoel and its Island.—The Lazaretto, Misida and the Hydraulic Dock.—Pietà and its Cemeteries.

AT a distance of about four and a half miles by road from Valletta is Pembroke Camp: Sliema, and St. Julians are not quite four miles away. But Sliema can be reached in a few minutes by boat from the Marsamuscetto Steps, Fare 3d, (or, in company with other passengers, $\frac{1}{2}d$), and from thence to St. Julians and Pembroke Camp is only a short walk or drive. Targets, firing-points, and the crack of rifles are the prevailing characteristics of Pembroke Camp, which is named after the late Lord Herbert of Lea. The first stone was laid by H. R. H. the Prince of Wales on June 6th 1862. The camp has accomodation for 1200 men, and was built at a cost of about £20 per man, or about one-fifth of the ordinary cost of barracks. Brawny arms which first gained pith and vigour on the shores of the English Channel, here love to breast the laughing sunlit waves with sturdy stroke, or to pull vigorously seawards, in some or other of the many boats

151

which lie moored within the land-locked bay. But Pembroke Camp is also a place for hard work, as every soldier in Malta is well aware, a place for acquiring skill in the use of the "Martini," and the scene of the Annual Malta Rifle Meeting. Pembroke Camp is our Maltese Wimbledon. The neighbouring St. George's Bay, to guard which a tower was built by the Grand Master Lascaris, is named, according to Ciantar, from a neighbouring church. The guard stationed at this point was called "the western look-out." The mansion of the Marchese Scicluna stands upon Dragonara Point, which is called by the natives Chark el Hamiem or "the doves' cleft," as wild doves found rest there. The noise of the waves gave rise to wild stories that this was the home of either a sea-monster or gigantic eels, and that the waters of this bay had a subterranean connection with those of the Great Harbour.

St. Julian's Bay was fortified at the expense of the Grand Master Pinto. Just outside are St. George's Bank, with from four to seven fathoms of water upon it, and the Spinola or Mercanti Reef, named after the Bailiff Spinola, who had a country house here, which is at present called the Forrest Hospital, from its originator Dr. Forrest, Inspector of Hospitals. It is a Military Hospital. The church which gave its name to the bay is now called Ta Lapsi or "the Ascension," possibly from a picture by Raffaele Caruana; it was founded in 1580, rebuilt in 1682, made vice-parochial in 1848; and enlarged between August 20th 1852 and Feb. 20th 1853, when it was re-blessed. The principal picture represents the assumption of the B. V. Mary, with S. S. Peter and Paul.

152

On the shore below the Forrest Hospital is a fougasse or mortar cut out of the rock, intended to hurl showers of stones upon hostile boats. These fougasses were formerly about fifty in number, the mouths of some being six feet across. Others may be seen at St. Paul's Bay and Marsa Scala. On the beach is a statue of St. Julian. In May 1768 abundance of alabaster was found near the shore, and used to beautify the Palace.

A Protestant College formerly existed at St. Julians, of which the late Dr. Gobat, afterwards Anglican Bishop of Jerusalem was the first principal. The grounds, which are planted with orange and other trees, slope down to the shores of the bay and command a fine view seaward. The Protestant College proved a failure, and the buildings were in April 1877 occupied by the Jesuits, who have purchased them, and are making great improvements. A new College chapel is in course of erection, also a dormitory 70 feet long, class rooms, and Professors' houses, &c. This College will probably do much to raise the standard of education in Malta.

Close to the shore in the district called Tal Ballut or "the oaks" is the pretty church of the Madonna del Carmelo, the foundation stone of which was laid on Nov. 21st 1858, and which was built at the expense of the Valletta confraternity "del Carmine." Sig. Gius. Bonavia was the architect, and it was solemnly blessed on Sept. 18th 1859. It is proposed to build a new Military Hospital on the hill-top above the bay. Not far from the intended site is the curious rock-hewn church of Minsia or "the forgotten," fashioned about four centuries ago. The priest who lives close by keeps the key, and we

153

descend a flight of steps. There are the usual votive offerings. One picture represents the burning of a line-of-battle ship about the year 1800, and another pourtrays a scene at Floriana during the Plague of 1813. Near the church is a picturesque valley.

Many English officers and residents live at Sliema and St. Julian's Bay, which is a favourite and rapidly increasing suburb of Valletta. Boat from Marsamuscetto steps to landing place at Sliema 3*d*. four-wheeler from thence to St. Julian 8*d*., go-cart 4*d*. Four-wheeler from Valietta round the head of the Quarantine Harbour 1*s*. 8*d*. Return 2*s*. 6*d*. Houses may be obtained at moderate rentals. Tariff changes proposed. The English church at Sliema, (Holy Trinity), is conveniently situated for residents at St. Julian's Bay. The situation is healthy, and sea-bathing very enjoyable, with a bottom of sand in some places.

Fever patients were formerly placed in the sand and mud at the head of the farther arm of the bay, and afterwards washed in a neighbouring spring. This was considered an almost certain cure. Along the shore are numerous salt-pans, which are Government property, and which used to be under the control of the Grand Master's Secretary. There is a heavily armed battery on Sliema Point and not far off another fort is in course of construction, yet one more link in that girdle of stone and iron which will ere long completely encircle " The Flower of the World," which is beyond all question one of the brightest jewels in the British crown. How many there are now scattered far and wide over the world's surface, who have, at some time or other, called Sliema or St. Julians " home ! "

154

and to whom the very mention of those names calls back pleasant memories of happy family life, memories which, perchance, cannot now be recalled without a certain huskiness of voice, and an unwonted dimness of vision.

Sliema derives its name from a church dedicated to our Lady of Safety, which Maltese sailors used to salute when entering or leaving port. Sliema is a Maltese word meaning "Hail" and is equivalent to the Latin "Ave." This church was built in the 17th century, restored in 1741, incorporated with a six-gun battery constructed in 1757 and 1760 by the Grand Master Pinto at Cala-ta-lembi or "Basin Bay," and finally destroyed by the fire of the Maltese batteries during the siege of 1798-1800. The magazine of Pinto's battery was called Santa Barbara, she being the patroness of guns and gunners. The magazine of a French man-of-war is called St. Barbe.

The rapidly increasing population of Sliema already numbers nearly 3000. During the last few years many new and handsome houses have been built, and numerous shops opened. The principal hotel is the Imperial (p. 55), and during the summer months a branch of the Union Club is opened in Sliema.

Along the shores of the Quarantine Harbour are numerous baths. Take a dip: only 4d an hour. Close to Fort Tigné an Officers' Bathing House has been erected, fitted up with every comfort, at which refreshments can be obtained. Admission is limited to Officers of the Fleet and Garrison, and to visitors introduced under certain restrictions.

Fort Tigné stands upon Dragut Point, off which is the Dragut Rock. Both the rock and the point

155

bear the name of the famous Algerine corsair who was second in command during the Great Siege of 1565, and "who had the wisest head and the bravest heart in all that mighty host." He erected a four-gun battery upon this point at the entrance of the Quarantine or Marsamuscetto Harbour. This harbour derives its name from the Arabic words "Marsa" "a port," and "nagh hus eiait" "not an open coast," meaning therefore "a harbour to winter in." It lies to the west of Valletta, and is principally used by vessels not admitted to free pratique, whence its name of the Quarantine Harbour. The P. and O. steamers are however always moored in it for convenience of coaling and easy access to their stores. The steamers belonging to the Telegraph Companies also lie here. It is defended on the East by Fort. St. Elmo and other batteries, and on the West by Forts Manoel and Tigné in conjunction with the coast dedefences of Sliema. Fort Tigné was constructed and solemnly dedicated in 1793 by the Grand Master Emanuel de Rohan and named after the Chevalier de Tigné who designed it under the direction of the Commander Stephen de Tousand. The latter caused solemn prayers to be offered "that the very good and great God would prosper the undertaking." Copper and silver coins were placed beneath the foundation stone, and the Grand Master sanctioned a contribution from the treasury. This small fort has been modernised and greatly strengthened and has a small garrison of artillerymen. Many cavities have been worn by the waves in the soft limestone cliffs. The fossil echinus or sea egg is found here, and the echinus sphœna is abundant all along the coast from E. to W. Gregales or

156

north easters have laid bare the hard crystalline lime stone, and saltpans are numerous. The Malta Gun Club meets at Fort Tigné, usually on Tuesdays. Entrance £1. Members pay 1s when taking part in the Shooting. The Royal Malta Yacht Squadron, of which the Admiral Superintendent is *ex officio* Commodore, often musters here.

To return to Sliema. The Eastern Telegraph Co. has a Branch Office at 3, Strada Ghar Illembi. The foundation stone of Holy Trinity Church (Anglican) was laid on Sept. 20th 1866, by the late Sir W. J. Ridley, then administering the Government of Malta, and the church was consecrated on April 23rd 1867, by the Right Revd. Dr. Trower, the late Bishop of Gibraltar, to whom its erection is due, and who defrayed much of the cost. The church is built in the Early English style, with about 200 sittings, on a commanding site overlooking the open sea and the Quarantine Harbour. The present chaplain is the Revd. J. Knight Law B. A. and the services are duly advertised in the local papers. Church expenses and other funds are provided for by means of offertories. The Parsonage is close to the church.

A large Roman Catholic Church is being built by voluntary labour, but at present the principal church of that faith in Sliema is dedicated to the B. V. Mary under the title of "the Star of the Sea." The first stone was laid on April 28th 1853. The 22nd Nov. 1854 saw the church completed, and it was blessed on August 11th 1855. The architect G. Bonavia drew the plans gratuitously, superintended the work for two years, and presented the church with a bell. It holds 600 persons, was built at a cost of £1200, and is of the Ionic style of archi-

157

tecture. The principal picture is by Raffaele Caruana, and the festival is on the Sunday after August 18th.

Sliema is connected with Valletta by a good road which is much used as a pleasant drive on summer evenings. Fare by four-wheeler about 2s. In the Quarantine harbour is Gezira or "the Island," generally known as Fort Manoel Island, and connected with the mainland by a bridge. This is a favourite spot, with the botanist and ornithologist (See Tallack's Malta under the Phœnicians, Knights and English" also Seddall's "Malta Past and Present"). On this island stands Fort Manoel built in 1726 by the Grand Master Manoel de Vilhena at his own expense. The estimated cost was only £2,500 but whether this amount was exceeded we know not. It was constructed for the protection of Valletta on the side of the Quarantine Harbour, which was previously almost defenceless. The whole design of Mons. de Tigné (who was NOT the engineer who built Fort Tigné) has never been carried out.

The Fort has accomodation for a garrison of 329 men, with officers' quarters, &c. Its founder not only provided it with all things necessary, but also endowed it with a yearly income of £1050 for the support of the Governor, his Lieutenant, Chaplain, and Garrison. The first Governor was the Bailiff F. D. Emanuele Sousa, a Portuguese, whose first Lieutenant was Fr. Giuseppe Coulon, a Frenchman who defrayed the cost of the chapel, of St. George in the church of the Fort. This church dedicated to St. Anthony of Padua is now used as a chapel school, and Divine Service is performed in it every Sunday by the Chaplains to the Forces. Its architecture, carvings, and monuments, deserve careful

158

preservation, and are worth a visit. Its first Rector was Fr. Mederico Attard, who erected four of the six altars which the church formerly contained, and established two pious Confraternities. In the centre of the square formerly stood a statue of the founder, the work of the Cav. Savasse, with a suitable inscription on the pedestal. This statue was removed by order of Sir Gaspard Le Marchant whilst Governor of Malta and placed in front of the Public Library. Over the principal entrance there is also an inscription in praise of the founder. Fort Manoel which still bears marks of the several bombardments to which it was subjected by the combined English and Maltese forces between 1798 and 1800 was formerly used as a Lazaretto, and enjoyed the reputation of being the best and the most confortable in the Mediterranean.

During the winter of 1856, an Italian Legion stationed in this fort, broke out into mutiny. The Bridge connecting the island with the mainland was at once secured, and H. M. S. Hannibal took up her station abreast of the fort, whereupon the mutineers submitted, were disarmed, deprived of their uniforms, disbanded, and left to shift for themselves. Boat fare to Fort Manoel $1\frac{1}{2}d.$ in company with others $\frac{1}{2}d.$

Close to Fort Manoel are the buildings of the Lazzaretto erected under the rule of the Grand Master Lascaris, the Cathedral receiving lands at Fiddeni in exchange for the island. Quarantine regulations were formerly very strict, and each Grand Master was bound by oath not to interfere with them. M. Houel, writing in 1687 gives a very graphic description of the precautions taken. The crew

159

and passengers of a ship were shut up in a room in which a quantity of straw was burnt, together with 14oz. of aromatic herbs. Those in quarantine were put upon oath as to their state of health both before and since their arrival in Malta: the health officers swore that they had faithfully discharged their duty: and if any one was detected in a falsehood he was hanged at once. The Lazaretto has been but little used of late and was occupied in 1878 by some of the officers and men belonging to the Indian Contingent, a portion of which was encamped near the Lazaretto.

The rocky headland of Tasbiesch with its coal stores and numerous coal barges belonging to the P. and O. and to the Telegraph Companies projects into the harbour. The steamers of these Companies lie off this point. Fare for passengers between a P. and O. steamer and the Marsamuscetto Steps 1s. per boat. Fare for others, going on board, 3d. The harbour here divides into two arms. The one to the right between Tasbiesch and the Public Baths built during the administration of Sir Alexander J. Ball, (4d. per hour) is called Misida Creek. This was formerly an unhealthy neighbourhood, but Sir A. Ball did much to improve it by the construction of a stone quay and wide road. There are some good houses at Misida which has a population of 2000. Misida is variously interpreted to mean "the valley of fishing" or "the fishers" or "The Mother of Our Lord." This latter title is derived from a tradition that the church dedicated to the B. V. Mary was erected in gratitude for deliverance from a Turkish invasion. This church is first mentioned in 1575, and was originally a rock-hewn crypt. It was rebuilt about 1640, en-

160

larged in 1670, and again enlarged between 1856 and 1859 at a cost of £250.

In the Misida Creek is situated the Hydraulic Dock, which was opened by Admiral Lord Clarence Paget on Jan. 23rd 1873. Ships of 3000 tons can have either hull or machinery repaired. · H. M. S. Cruiser was the first vessel lifted upon the pontoon. This dock is a great convenience to ship owners, is in constant requisition, and employs numerous workmen. At the head of the creek the straight road leads to the village of Birchircara two miles distant. The branch to the right ascends a slope, and passing Holy Trinity Church, Sliema, turns off to St. Julians and Pembroke Camp whilst the road which skirts the shore of the promontory of Tasbiesch is the route for Sliema landing place.

Returning to the Public Baths, and turning to the right we are in the suburb of Pietà, named from the church which is built on the site of a cemetery wherein many victims to the plague are interred, and which is dedicated to Our Lady of Sorrow or of Piety. Built in 1590 it is the most ancient within the district of Floriana. Its festival is on Sept. 17th. Mustapha Pasha resided at Pietà, and organized the Slaves Conspiracy in 1749. Annual races are held on the Pietà road on August 16th, which were instituted after a visitation of the plague.

A lane on the right leads from the head of the harbour to the Military Cemetery wherein sleeps in peace many a brave soldier, together with soldiers' wives and little children. To the right of the main road which here ascends a hill is the pretty Ta Braxia Cemetery, wherein rest many English

161

residents and visitors, together with others who have breathed their last in Malta. It is under the management of a Committee. All information can be obtained from Mr. Martin at the Garrison Library. The Jewish Cemetery, opened on January 19th 1836 through the exertions of Sig. Jacob Abeasis is close by. We re-enter Porte des Bombes, and return to Valletta.

CHAPTER VIII.

THE MARSA AND BURMOLA.

Out of Porte des Bombes.—Porto Nuovo.—The Marsa, and the Race Course.—Corradino, its Fortifications, and Prisons.—The French Creek and the Naval Canteen.—Burmola, its Fortifications, and Gates.—The Cotonera Hospital.—Churches and Convents.—The Dockyard and Marina.

LEAVING Floriana by the Porte des Bombes, we reach a place where the road forks. The right hand branch goes to Pietà, Misida, Sliemâ, and St. Julians, and that in the centre to the Ta Braxia Cemetery, whilst our road to the Marsa lies straight before us. On the left are the fortifications of Floriana, and we soon reach another division of the road. To the right the San Giuseppe Road goes to Città Vecchia and the interior of the island. Between the roads is a cemetery in which the poorer classes were interred from 1813 until just before the opening of the Addolorata Cemetery. Soldiers also lie here. No less than 15,000 are interred at this spot. We remark a monument to the men, women, and children of the 44th Regt who died in Malta between 1848 and 1851.

We incline to the left, and see below us numerous barges laden with " black diamonds " for the use and benefit of steamers. Two trees upon a slope mark the site of the ancient burial place of galley slaves and other Mahometans, which was granted

163

by the knights in 1674. The walls were pulled down a few years since, and the human remains transferred to the new Mahometan cemetery.

For some distance we have on the left Porto Nuovo or the New Harbour. The Romans embanked this portion of the harbour, and at a later period basins were constructed, but becoming silted up, an extensive marsh was formed. This whole neighbourhood, called the Marsa or port was most unhealthy, but about twenty years ago the upper part of the harbour was extended and deepened. Coal stores, quays and all possible conveniences for shipping are found here, including a telegraph office (p. 56).

On our right is the expanse of the Marsa, on which the Turkish army was encamped during the Great Siege. One day the garrison of Città Vecchia attacked the camp, slaying all the sick and wounded in hospital! Chivalrous times, truly!

The Government Laundry is on the right, and the Steam Flour Mills and Contractors' Cattle Store and Depot on the left. We note the Mahometan Cemetery, with its domes and minarets, and on a hillside the graceful spire of the Gothic Church of the Addolorata Cemetery. This Cemetery is constructed in terraces, connected by flights of steps. It is laid out on the plan of the Highgate Cemetery near London, was consecrated in November 1869, and is supplied with water from the aqueduct which passes down the road behind. The inhabitants of the four cities of Valletta, Vittoriosa, Cospicua, and Senglea, as well as Floriana are buried here. More than 1500 interments take place annually. The cemetery is well worth a visit. The Marsa is

164

the largest and most level plain in Malta. It collects the water from the high grounds, and is itself drained by a canal. The Malta Jockey Club holds two annual meetings here. The race course near which is a well cultivated market garden celebrated for its artichokes is a favourite riding ground. Season tickets 12s 6d. Quarterly tickets 5s. The Grand Stand is on the N. side of the oval course, which is about one mile and three quarters in circumference. The soil of the Marsa is deep and well watered. Beyond the flour mills is the Casal or village of Luca and on the right is Casal Curmi.

On the eastern side of the Grand Harbour are the heights of Corradino. This name means a promontory. The Phœnicians erected a temple here, which was unfortunately destroyed a few years since by the Royal Engineers, during the construction of some new works. A few traces may still be seen close to the moat. These heights on which were situated the *haras* or horse breeding establishments and the game-preserves of the Grand Masters, were fortified a few years since, and connected with the Cotonera Lines, of which we must say a few words. They were designed by Count Valperga, Chief Engineer to the Duke of Savoy in 1670 at the request of the Grand Master Nicholas Cotoner, enclosing the whole of the Margarita heights, and connecting with the fortifications of Senglea and Vittoriosa. The first stone was laid with much ceremony in the Bastion of St. Nicholas on August 28th, 1670. . The works were intended to afford a refuge for the population and their cattle in the event of a siege, and a poet, wishing to be complimentary, compared the Grand Master to Noah, since he had

165

provided shelter for all the animals. The Commander Blondel designed nine gates, only three of which have ever been used. After ten years labour and an enormous outlay, the lines were left unfinished, and it was not until 1716 that they were proceeded with and rendered defensible. Their extent aud magnitude excite the astonishment of even the most casual observer.

On the Corradino heights are situated the Military and Civil Prisons, the former of which has accomodation for 116 and the latter for 250 prisoners, also large water tanks for shipping, and a powder magazine. Not far from the Military Prison are the remains of a Maltese battery, constructed during the siege of 1798-1800, near to which is a monument to Capt. Spencer of H. M. S. Madagascar who is buried on St. Andrew's Bastion, Valletta. A flight of steps leads down to the water from this monument, and off this point men of war are allowed to ride out their quarantine. The Turks erected batteries on these heights during the Great Siege of 1565.

Near at hand at the water's edge is the Naval Canteen, which provides refreshment combined with amusement both for mind and body. A Library, racquet courts, reading room and theatre, are amongst the attractions of this deservedly popular institution. On the shores of the French Creek or Man of War Harbour are the Naval Barracks in which a ship's company is now and again quartered, the Admiralty coal stores, and the pumping station for the new drainage works. A spring called Ghain Dqieli or "the spring of vines" is very useful for washing purposes. Much ship building was formerly

166

carried on here in private yards, in which the Russian squadron was refitted after the battle of Navarino in 1827.

At the head of this creek is populous Burmola, which means either "the well of the Lord" or "the lofty place." It also received the name of Cospicua from the Grand Master Zondadari in 1721, on account of its massive fortifications, which connect with those of Vittoriosa and Senglea, and of which the first stone was laid on December 30th 1635. They were designed by P. Fr. Vincenzo Maculano da Firenzuola, a Dominican monk, who was one of the Pope's Engineers. The Grand Masters Perellos in 1716, and Zondadari in 1721 carried on the work which was completed by Manoel de Vilhena in 1736.

The gates are five in number, viz, the Upper and Lower Burmola Gates close to the Somerset Dock under the walls of Fort St. Michael, St. Helena Gate from the Old Market, one on the other side called the Rock Gate, and the Santa Margarita Gate. The Gates of the Cotonera Lines are those of St. Paul, St. John, St. Nicholas, St Clement, or Polverista, Notre Dame, St. James, Zabbar, St. Louis, and S. Salvatore only three of which are open, viz., St. Clement's or Polverista which gives access to the Casals of Zeitun, Tarxien, &c. Also St. Helena Gate above which is an inscription, and within which proceeding upwards we reach a large parade ground called St. Clement's Retrenchment which commands the entrances from the Polverista and Zabbar Gates by means of long curtains. Below are casemated batteries, and communications with Verdala Barracks.

167

The third open gate is that of Zabbar, a lofty structure visible. from afar, upon which is a bust of the Grand. Master Nicholas Cotoner, with a most eulogistic inscription An infantry detachment is stationed at this gate, and close by is the Military Hospital for the Cottonera District. Commenced in November 1870, it was not completed until July 1873. The building contains 4 large wards, each of which can accomodate 32 patients. Also 4 small wards for serious cases, and on the ground floor a ward for prisoners, and another for opthalmic cases. The ventilation is perfect, and nothing is forgotten that can conduce to the comfort of the sick soldier. Officers' wards have lately been opened. There is a very extensive view from the terrace, embracing a wide expanse of sea, and nearly half the island.

Between the Zabbar and Rock Gates is a hollow, in which is a garden. Here many victims of the plague are interred. There is a burial ground just outside the Rock Gate, and another close under the Cotonera Lines.

The southern extremity of Burmola is protected by Fort St. Francesco di Paola, which is garrisoned by English infantry. The Verdala Barracks are situated on the highest part of the city.

Burmola is partly low lying and partly on a slope. It is thickly populated, has narrow, steep, irregular streets, and is chiefly inhabited by artisans. On October 10th, 1869 the lower portion was flooded, and it was necessary to break down the Dockyard Gates to provide an outlet for the water. A tunnel has since been cut in the rock to prevent any similar disaster in future.

168

Though not requiring detailed description Burmola will repay a visit as it is much more Maltese in character than cosmopolitan Valletta. In 1575 the inhabitants numbered 1200, but the present population is about 13,000. The parish church dedicated to Our Lady of Succour or *della Concezione* was commenced in 1587, and rebuilt in 1637: various additions were made until 1690. It was consecrated by Mons Alpheran de Bussan, on July 26th 1732.

The principal picture is by P. P. Caruana, and in a side chapel is a picture of Our Lady of Grace by the Cav. Favray. There are numerous pictures and carvings by various artists. The Oratory of the Crucifixion, consecrated by Mons. Labini in 1793, adjoins the church. St. Paul's Church was first built in 1590. The present building was erected on the site of the old one in 1741, and the principal picture representing the Conversion of St. Paul is by Rocco Buhagiar. This church is in Strada San Paolo.

The Church of St. John the Almsgiver outside St. Helena Gate was pulled down in 1680 to make room for the Cotonera Lines, and was rebuilt on its present site in 1682 at the expense of Fra Pietro Viany.

The Church of San Francesco di Paolo is situated on the Corradino quay. It was built in 1747 together with an adjoining villa by the Bailiff Francesco de Sousa, the nephew of the Grand Master Manoel.

At the foot of Santa Margarita Hill are the Carmelite Church and Convent. The convent was founded in 1625, and in 1681, an Oratory for pious knights was added, the Grand Master Carafa contributing £50. The church consists of a nave with

169

six side chapels, and was consecrated in 1787. The principal picture, representing the Coronation of Santa Teresa is by Fra Luca Garnier. The picture in the Oratory of the Convent was left unfinished by Mattia Preti at his death.

On the hill of Santa Margarita just outside the entrance of Vittoriosa are the nunnery and church of the same name. This, the last nunnery established in Malta, was founded in 1726, and completed in 1730 by the Grand Master Manoel de Vilhena. The nuns belong to the Order of Santa Teresa. The church was consecrated in 1787 and the principal picture representing St. James is by Francesco Zahra.

The Conservatorio of San Giuseppe in Strada San Giórgio receives and educates poor girls. The old building is now used as the Primary Schools of Burmola. The present building was erected in 1810. The adjacent church of San Giuseppe has over the door the arms of the Bishops Labini and Mattei. The principal picture is by Sebastiano Conca.

On the hill of Santa Margarita is a School Chapel with accomodation for 500 persons, which is used as a Garrison Church, in which the Chaplains to the Forces officiate.

Burmola is intersected by the Port of the Galleys, now called Dockyard Creek, at the head of which was the old market of Burmola the site of which is now converted into spacious docks. Two new markets have been built close by.

The old Arsenal for the Galleys was constructed between 1776 and 1783 at a cost of £6,098, storehouses costing in addition £715. The Order spent yearly upon its navy £47,494. The Galleys, originally six

170

or seven iu number, were afterwards reduced to four. The seamen and galley-slaves were clad in French cloth, and were under the command of the Congregation of the Galleys. A proveditore superintended the rigging, and the Commandant of the Arsenal the refitting of the galleys.

The building of a galley cost £4,272. She had 26 oars on either side, with five men to each, and was 166 ft. long with 26ft 8½ in beam, 116ft. 6 in. being decked. When not in use the galleys were drawn on shore, and placed under covered arches, some of which stood on the site of the Naval Bakery, and others within the present Dockyard. Three ships of the line were first built in 1704, Their number was afterwards increased to four, but the fleet was eventually reduced to one sixty-gun ship and three frigates. The latter cost £11,834 each, and two men of war were sold in 1781 for £17,722. Cleansing the Port cost £468 per annum.

Fruitless efforts to construct a dock were made in 1815, but in 1841 operations were again commenced, and the first pile was driven in the spring of 1843 under the superintendence of Rear Admiral Sir George Lewis.

The first stone was laid on May 1st. 1843, at a depth of 43ft. 6 in. below sea-level, and the first stone of the Dockyard was laid by Sir Patrick Stuart, then Governor of Malta on Coronation Day, 1844. The first vessel docked was the Antelope, on Saturday, September 5th, 1848. There are now two docks in the Dockyard Creek, in which three ships were last year placed at once. Their whole length is 525 ft, with nearly 30 feet of water on the sill, and they can be pumped dry in about six hours.

171

The Dockyard possesses the usual ranges of store-houses and workshops, and also a chapel, which Admiral Inglefield did much to improve. The Dockyard Chaplain officiates and services are amounted in the local papers.

A tunnel leads to the Somerset Dock, which can receive the largest iron-clads. It was designed by Colonel Clarke, R. E., Admiralty Director of Works, constructed by C. Andrews Esq., C. E, and opened in 1870 by the Duke of Somerset then First Lord of the Admiralty, under the superintendence of Rear Admiral Sir Astley Cooper Key. Length 468 feet, at bottom 427 ft. Breadth 104 ft. Depth of water on sill 34 ft. It holds 7,000,000 gallons of water. and can, be pumped dry in four hours.

The offices of the Admiral Superintendent and of the principal officers of the Dockyard are situated in one of the bastions of Fort St. Michael upon the top of which are the Masting Shears. Passing the Workmen's Dining Hall we leave the Yard and find ourselves on the Anchor Wharf, so called because it was formerly covered with anchors, ranges of chain cables of every possible size, moorings &c. This wharf was also called La Sirena from the figure of a Siren carved in the rock within a small cave.

From hence boats cross to the St. Lorenzo Steps in Vittoriosa on the opposite side of the creek. Fare $\frac{1}{2}d$. On the site of the ancient dwelling of the Captains of the Galleys a row of handsome houses has been erected called Dockyard Terrace, which are occupied by various principal officers of the Dockyard.

. The Marina is before us, covered with boats and picturesque, but lined with too many grog

172

shops. Some of the smaller ships of war are generally moored in the Dockyard Creek. We mount a long flight of steps on the left, and speedily reach the principal street of Senglea.

173

CHAPTER IX.

SENGLEA,

VITTORIOSA, AND FORT RICASOLI.

Origin of Senglea,—Churches and Convents,—H. M.
S. Hibernia, Fort St. Angelo, and the Temple of Juno.—
The Victualling Yard, Slave Prison, and Naval Bakery.—
The Old Palace and Hospital.—Churches and Convents.—
San Lorenzo.—Soldier's Institute.—Column of Victory.—
Inquisitor's and Bishop's Palaces.—La Vallette's Obser-
vatory.—Salvadore Gate, and Calcara Bay.—Naval Cemetery
and Hospital.—Rinella Bay, and Fort Ricasoli,

THE site of Città Senglea was formerly called "St.
Julian's Hill" from an ancient chapel erected early
in the 14th century, It was also styled "Windmill
Hill" from some mill of early date. Projecting
as it does into the Great Harbour it bore in addition the name of *Chersones* or peninsula. The
Grand Masters had a menagerie here. It was fortified by the Grand Master d' Omedes between
1541 and 1552, and the guns of the principal fort
having been mounted on May 8th. 1552, the day
of the Apparition of St. Michael, the standard of
the Order was hoisted upon it, and it was named
St. Michael. How nearly both it and Senglea were
captured during the Great Siege of 1565, and how
gallantly they were defended, let Porter, Seddall,
and Townsend tell. Fort St. Michael commands
the entrance into the town, and also the harbours

174

on either side, and has quarters for about 300 men. The Masting Shears have been erected upon one of its bastions. Senglea was considerably strengthened by the Grand Master Claude de la Sengle, who also encouraged the erection of numerous buildings.

After the Great Siege it received the proud title of Invitta or "the Invincible," and its inhabitants were exempted from the payment of certain taxes. It is also called "St. Michael's Island" or briefly Isola, from its principal fortification. The works were strengthened in 1716, and in subsequent years.

The streets of Senglea contain many good houses, and much attention has of late been paid to sanitary measures.

In the principal street is a marble statue by Vincenzo Dimech, erected in gratitude for the exemption of Senglea from the plague in 1813, when 6000 persons perished.

The Collegiate and Parochial church in Str. Vittoria had its origin in the before mentioned Chapel of St. Julian. It was made parocchial in 1581, and rebuilt about 1650. It is of Doric architecture and consists of a choir, nave, and several side chapels. Length 142 ft., breath 46 ft., 6 in., breadth of nave 31 ft., The church was consecrated in 1743 and made Collegiate in 1785.

Notice the carved seats in the choir made in 1730, and two statues of the B. V. M. by Gerada and Bonnici. The principal picture, representing the Nativity of the B. V. M. was painted by Tommaso Madiona in 1850. There is also a picture of Santa Caterina by Erardi. A marble tablet records

175

the exemption from certain taxes of the people of Senglea after the Great Siege of 1565. Adjoining the church are two Oratories, and the Church of the Purification. The Oratory and Church of the Congregation of San Filippo Neri overlook the Great Harbour. The Oratory was completed in 1695, and rebuilt and enlarged in 1744. It possesses a good library bequeathed by Father S. Cassar in 1779. The present church was erected in 1662. The high altar was made in 1663 and the principal picture is by Erardi. St.Julian was formerly the patron saint of Senglea. The present church in Str. San Giuliano is the third built upon this site since 1311. It was finished in 1711. The Hospital of St. Anna is on the Marina of Senglea. It was founded by two wealthy Maltese • Nicola Dingli and Maria Cornelia 'in 1794. It is intended for the reception of female convalescents belonging to Senglea and Casal Siggieui. This hospital, the chapel of which is dedicated to Sant' Anna, was blessed in 1817. From hence we take boat and cross the Dockyard Creek to Fort St. Angelo in Vittoriosa, passing close to H. M. S. Hibernia, which does duty as receiving ship and on board which the crews of ships of war under repair are berthed. She is almost stationary now, only shifting her berth during the summer months from below Fort St. Angelo to the centre of the Dockyard Creek. Our idea in Malta of the Greek Kalends is "When the Hibernia goes to sea!"She has however been and still is most useful. The Hibernia fires a gun daily at sunrise, also at 8. 0. p. m. in winter, and at 9. 0. p. m. in summer. On the point below Fort St. Angelo may still be seen some links of the chain which, supported by

176

pieces of timber and empty wine casks, was used during the Great Siege to close this creek then called the Port of the Galleys.

Fort St. Angelo, formerly styled "the Castle on the Rock" was built according to Marmol by the Arabs in the year 828, but 973 is a more probable date. It was under the Spanish monarch the hereditary governorship of the Nava family and on the arrival of the Knights, Alvarez de Nava transferred the castle to them in consideration of an annual pension. The Commander Peter Piton, at the head of a company of foot first took possession. Its armament consisted of one small cannon, two falcons or three-pounders, and a few iron mortars.

L' Isle Adam stengthened it and in 1533 the Grand Prior of Toulouse added a bastion ' on the side towards Calcara Bay, then called the English harbour. In 1541 the Grand Master John d'Omedes by the advice of Caramolin the Emperor's chief engineer erected a Cavalier or elevated work, "that they might see what passed in the port of Marsamuscetto." A bastion still bears the name of Omedes. La Vallette erected a battery on the point below the fort almost on a level with the water, which did good service during the siege. In 1690 Don Carlos de Grunemberg the King of Spain's Engineer constructed "three great batteries which hinder the coming into the harbour." St. Angelo was the state prison of the Order, and corresponds to our English Tower of London. This fort, in common with the other fortifications of Malta, cannot be visited without an order from the military authorities. The arms of Naples and Sicily may still be traced upon a defaced escutcheon above an entrance to the Officers' Quarters. At the door

177

of the Commandant's Quarters are some interesting Norman capitals and carvings, and within are the arms of several Governors of the Castle between 1714 and 1792. A Norman arch has been built up, and in the garden are the arms of L'Isle Adam with the dates 1531 and 1533. A time gun is fired daily at noon, and at sunset. Beneath the bastion on which it is placed is an ancient slave prison. There are two chapels in the fort. The lower one dedicated to the B. V. M. is said to date from 1090, and within it the ancient confraternity of Bombardiers used to worship. The chaplain of the fort was independent of the parish priest of Vittoriosa. The upper chapel was built by the Nava family, who were hereditary governors of the castle, and is dedicated to Sant' Anna. The Grand Master L'Isle Adam rebuilt it in 1531, and was buried in it in 1534. Notice his monument. His remains together with those of succeeding Grand Masters were transferred to St. John's Church in 1519. The building is now used as a Chapel-school and its roof is supported by a column of red granite, (probably Egyptian) which is said to have originally formed part of Solomon's temple, and to have been brought hither from Rhodes. It seems more probable, however, that it is a relic of the temple of Juno which stood close by. Beneath four shady trees is the grave of those who fell in the siege of 1565 and of the victims of the plague of 1676.

Quitting Fort St. Angelo we cross the bridge which spans the moat. Here again we are on classic ground, for this was the site of the celebrated temple of Juno (see p. p. 15, 18,). We see on the

178

left the R. E. workshops, erected by the Giurati or Magistrates in 1665 as one of the granaries of the University of Supplies, in front of which are several subterranean receptacles for grain. This was the scene of Midshipman Easy's triangular duel. A covered portico extends along the adjoining quay on which are the official residences of the Admiral Superintendent, the Naval Storekeeper, and the Clerk in charge of the Victualling Yard, which were formerly occupied by the Captain General of the two squadrons of the Order, his Lieutenant, the Captain of the Galleys, and as the Court House of the Giurati. A long range of storehouses is filled with supplies for the Mediterranean Fleet, which is largely dependent upon the Malta Victualling Yard.

Immediately in rear is the large galley-slave prison cut out of the solid rock, above which is a ruinous building, now a carpenter's shop, which was formerly used for the same purpose. Permission to visit these ancient and curious prisons must be obtained from the Admiral Superintendent.

A short walk along the quay brings us to the Naval Bakery, on the site of which formerly stood three large arches beneath which the galleys were drawn up for repairs and refitting. The Bakery has fifteen ovens, of which only two are generally used, and which bake about 6,200 lbs of biscuit per diem. This quantity could of course be largely increased. Each biscuit is baked in about 25 minutes. The machinery is driven by steam power, and the rotary oven bakes 4,500 lbs of biscuit in about eight hours.

The old "Borgo del Castello," or "Town of the Castle" received the proud title of "Città Vit-

179

toriosa" or the Victorious City," together with the escutcheon of an armed hand grasping a drawn sword between two branches of palm and olive on a red ground, after the defeat of the Turks in 1565. The streets are narrow and uneven. Many old houses are to be seen here and there bearing traces of former magnificence. For an account of its fortifications and of its gallant defence in 1565 the reader is referred to "A History of the Fortress of Malta," and "Malta and its Knights," by Lieut. Col. Porter R. E.

The Bastion of Castile which was the scene of such fierce contention overlooks Calcara Bay. Being encircled by the Cotonera Lines the three Cities of Vittoriosa, Senglea, and Cospicua or Burmola are sometimes styled Città Cotonera. In Strada Antico Palazzo del Governatore formerly stood the old Governor's Palace which was adorned with stone medallion portraits of the Emperors. These were unfortunately destroyed when the old building was demolished a few years since. The old entrance still exists at No. 102.

In Strada Scolastica are the Nunnery and Church of the same name. This building erected in 1538 was formerly the Knights' Hospital. Above a handsome Lombard gateway are two defaced escutcheons with pomegranates the emblem of Granada at the corners. For this and many another interesting heraldic detail in Valletta and the Three Cities I am indebted to the Revd. W. K. R. Bedford author of the "Blazon of Episcopacy."

The Nunnery of Santa Scolastica was founded at Città Vecchia by Bishop Valguarnera, under the rule of St. Benedict in 1496. The nuns were trans-

180

ferred to Vittoriosa in 1603 by Bishop Gargallo, in spite of much popular opposition, and removed to their present home in 1652. The church was rebuilt in 1679, blessed in 1780, and consecrated in 1787. The principal picture is by Mattia Preti. The Church of S. Filippo Neri dedicated to the B. V. of the Angels, originated in the 15th century. The present structure was consecrated in 1788. A small picture of S. Girolamo Penitente is by Mattia Preti. An oratory adjoins the church. (Strada S. Filippo.)

The Church and Convent of Carmine near the Naval Bakery were built at the expense of the crews of the galleys in 1611. The convent was suppressed in 1652. This church was much frequented by the officers and crews of the galleys, and in 1670 Francesco Caraffa, General of the Galleys presented the picture of S. Francesco di Paola. The church of the SSma Trinità behind the Victualling Yard was erected in 1784 by Lucrezia Gauci Falzon whose portrait may be seen there.

The Dominican Monastery was founded in 1518. The church in Strada Porta Maggiore, is called the Annunziata. It was rebuilt in 1659, contains an ancient statue which was formerly preserved at Fort St. Angelo, and has a picture of St. Peter by Mattia Preti. The Capuchin Monastery was completed in 1743. The church was consecrated in 1747. The principal picture representing the Martyrdom of Santa Barbara is by A. Massucci. The Monastery possesses a portrait of the Grand Master Manoel.

"San Lorenzo by the sea" is the principal church and should be visited. The parish dates from 1090,

181

and on the arrival of the Order in 1530 S. Lorenzo became the Conventual Church. The present building was commenced in 1681 and consecrated in 1723. The principal picture is a master-piece by Mattia Preti, and there are some old Byzantine pictures in the sacristy. Some ancient vestments from Rhodes are very interesting, also the chasuble of Pope Alexander VII. when Inquisitor of Malta. The silver crosses, chalice, censer, &c. brought from Rhodes can be seen on application to the sacristan.

Adjoining the church is the Oratory of San Giuseppe, or the Church of "Santa Maria dei Greci," so called from having been assigned to the Greeks who accompanied the Knights from Rhodes. Here are preserved the hat and sword worn by La Vallette on the day of his triumph over the Turks. The Oratory of the Crucifixion stands upon a portion of the cemetery wherein those slain in 1565 are interred. This cemetery covers the whole paved slope to the north of the church.

Close to San Lorenzo are the San Lorenzo steps from which we may cross the Dockyard Creek to Senglea, (Fare ½d) or to Valletta (Fare 3d. or in company with other passengers ½d.)

To the right, and in the immediate neighbourhood of these steps is the "Soldiers' & Sailors' Institute," which is a centre of good and useful work. Subscriptions will be gladly received by the Revd G. Wisely, The Manse, 205, Strada Forni.

Returning to the church of San Lorenzo, and turning to the right we reach the Piazza Vittoriosa, in which stands a monument erected in 1705 and restored in 1760, surmounted by a figure of Victory in memory of the repulse of the Turks in

182

1565. This monument is now again under restoration. On the former centre of the square stands a tower the clock in which is said to have been brought from Rhodes. One of the bells was cast in 1513.

Leaving Piazza Vittoriosa by Strada della Porta Maggiore we see on the left a plain massive building at the door of which a sentry is posted. This is the old Inquisitor's Palace, and is now occupied by the officers of the regiment stationed in Vittoriosa and at Fort St. Michael in Senglea. Two inscriptions remain, which refer to the Popes Alexander VII. and Innocent VII. who were both former Inquisitors of Malta. Many of the dungeons have been walled up, but some years ago workmen whilst excavating a wine cellar discovered a rack. The Inquisition was first introduced into Malta in August 1574, in order to settle certain disputes between the Bishop of Malta and the Grand Master. In 1657 the Inquisitor Odi interfered to hinder, if possible, the election of De Redin as Grand Master, and in 1711 the Inquisitor Delci insolently demanded that the carriage of the Grand Master should stop on meeting his, and that the hospital of the Order should be under his jurisdiction. The Pope, however disallowed these lofty claims. The Inquisitors used to grant *patents* the holders of which exempt from all obedience except to the Inquisition. The French suppressed this tribunal, and confiscated its property. The Dominican Church and Convent are on the right side of the street.

In the Strada del Vescovo or "Bishop's Street" is the old Bishop's Palace, built by Bishop Çubelles in 1542. When Bishop Cagliares not without

183

much opposition from the Grand Master removed the episcopal residence to Valletta in 1622, the Bishop's prisons remained here. The building has been used as a government school since 1872. The arms of La Vallette are affixed to a house which faces the Palace, and at the end of the street are the Vittoriosa Barracks, which were formerly an armoury, and afterwards a hospital. Close by is a cavalier or elevated work, which is said to have been La Vallette's post of observation during the Great Siege. Returning to the main street and passing beneath St. John's Cavalier, we leave the ancient Borgo by the main gate above which is a defaced inscription, to the effect that Manoel de Vilhena restored and strengthened the fortifications in 1727 • and the text " Thou hast covered my head in the day of battle." The outer works have upon them the dates 1722 and 1723, having been taken in hand in 1716, by Mons. de Tigné a French engineer. Much valuable information concorning the Borgo has been most kindly given by the Revd. Canon Patiniott, Officiating Chaplain to the Forces.

We have now reached the hill of Margarita, (Chapter viii.) and turning to the left through the gate of the same name we cross a large open space. On our right are the Zabbar Gate and the Cotonera Hospital whilst close by is a hollow with gardens. This was also a plague burial ground. On the left are the San Salvador Barracks and we pass through the gate, of the same name. The fortifications on this height which commands Vittoriosa were constructed by the Grand Master Manoel de Vilhena in 1724. A path to the right leads to the Capuchin Convent.

184

Descending a slope we reach the head of Calcara Bay, named from some ancient lime-kiln. Gas works and a boat-slip may be noted. Turning to the left, we see on our right hand the entrance to the old Jewish Cemetery, which dates from 1784. A narrow lane leads up the hill past the "Milking Cow" grogshop, and on reaching some cross roads we turn to the left. The Naval Cemetery, which is kept in admirable order, is on our right. Admission by application to the Deputy Inspector General at Bighi Hospital. Want of space forbids the insertion of several quaint and touching epitaphs.

We are at the entrance of the Royal Naval Hospital. To the right is the ancient church of S. Salvador. Destroyed during the siege of 1565, it was rebuilt by La Vallette, and afterwards in 1651 by Prior Giovanni Bichi, from whom the whole promontory on which the hospital stands derives the name of Bighi. Prior Bichi built a country house here, died of the plague in 1676, and is buried in the church. Long before his day the Phœnicians knew this headland, as inscriptions found here which are now in the British Museum clearly prove.

Prior Bichi's home afterwards belonged to the Cavalier Frisari, but was nearly destroyed during the siege of 1798-80. In 1830 it was converted into this noble institution. King William the Fourth was greatly interested in the matter, and the works were under the superintendence of Admiral Sir Pulteney Malcolm. There are residences for the medical officers and others connected with the hospital. The grounds are tastefully laid out and accomodation is provided for 50 officers and 224 men in 24 cabins and 16 wards. The hospital library,

185

and officers' quarters occupy the central building, on which is the date 1832, and the wards, cabins, offices, &c. are on either side. A long flight of steps at the entrance gate leads to the water, close to which are the Dockyard Chaplain's Quarters and the Infectious Hospital. Boats ply from these steps to Valletta, and also cross to the opposite sally-port in Vittoriosa.

Retracing our steps from the Naval Hospital past the Naval Cemetery to the cross roads we turn to the left and descend the hill. On the right in the distance is Fort San Rocco upon an eminence, and a lane also on the right leads to the Military Cemetery. We pass on the right a carefully guarded powder magazine, and leaving Rinella Bay on our left reach Fort Ricasoli. This large fort stands upon a promontory, and, in conjunction with Fort St. Elmo, defends the entrance to the Great Harbour. The Turks constructed a battery here during the Great Siege, and on Jan. 15th 1629, a fort to prevent the escape of the slaves was completed on this site which was afterwards called Point L'Orso from the Cavalier Alessandro Orsi, a Bolognese knight who superintended the works. In 1670 the Commander Gio. Fran. Ricasoli expended £3,000 on the erection of the present fort, endowing it with all his property, to the amount of £300 per annum. For this act of generosity he was publicly thanked by the Grand Master and the Council, and it was ordered that the fort should in future bear his name. The Grand Master Nicolas Cotoner also gave an endowment for the maintenance of the garrison, and the Grand Master Perellos strengthened the defences in 1698 and following years. On April 3rd 1807

186

the celebrated Froberg Mutiny broke out in this fort, for an account of which see "Malta and its Knights." Beneath the flagstaff is an inscription commemorating the heroic death of Gunner John Johnston who was killed on this occasion whilst defending the magazine. His grave is in the little cemetery attached to the fort, and greatly needs restoration. In 1837 the inmates of the Poor House and of the Hospital for Incurables were removed to this spot, as cholera had appeared amongst them. They almost all fell victims to its ravages. A lighthouse shewing two perpendicular red lights guides sailors into port. The point below the fort from which a shoal runs out, is called Gibbet point, as pirates were formerly hung in chains there. Fort Ricasoli is usually garrisoned by infantry and artillery, and in the officers' mess is a marble bust of the founder. The chapel dedicated to St. Nicholas contains a picture by Mattia Preti, painted at the expense of the Grand Master Nicholas Cotoner, also some old paintings of the Byzantine School.

Descending the steps at the entrance of the fort we shout "Dghaisa, Joe!" and for the sum of 3d. are speedily conveyed to Valletta.

PART THIRD.

CHAPTER I.

ROUND THE COAST.

Naval Rifle Range, and Grazia Tower.—Geological Formations.—Marsa Scala, S. Tommaso Bay, and Delimara.—Marsa Scirocco, and St. Lucian's Tower.—Fossæ, Melcarte's Temple, and the Cave of Darkness.—Bir Zebbugia and its Fortifications.—Benghisa, and Hassan's Cave. The Southern Shore.—Fauara and Filfla.—Ruts at Fom-er-Rieh.—Marfa.—Melleha, Its Church and Bay.—Palace of Selmoon.—St. Paul's Bay and Island. — Shipwreck of St. Paul.—Neighbourhood of the Bay.— Saline Bay, Ghallis Rock, Maddalena Bay, and Casal Gargur.

CLOSE to Fort Ricasoli is a wave worn hollow in the cliffs called the "Grotto of the Mattress-makers" from some poor fellows who were drowned there. The coast trends S. E. by S., and we reach the Naval Rifle Range, used also by the Army, and kept in order by Marine markers from H. M. S. Hibernia. Above on the hill-top is Fort San Rocco and further away is Fort San Leonardo. Many salt pans are cut in the rocks, and fisher-men with rod and line contrive to fill their baskets. The surf beats fiercely upon the shore, but a line of defence which was either not completed or else has crumbled to decay, eight feet thick, with a

188

shallow ditch before it, is evidently intended to keep off hostile boats. Our road is not passable for carriages, and many branching lanes lead to fields and detached storehouses. A practicable road, however, leads from the beach to the village of Zabbar past the ruined tower of the Madonna della Grazia, named from the church of the village aforesaid, for the defence of which it was erected in 1620 by the engineer and architect Vittorio Cassar. He was a Maltese, a serving brother of the Order, succeeded his father Gerolamo Cassar as the Knights' Engineer, and in 1618 built the Tower of Comino. The tower was formerly approached by means of a drawbridge thrown across to a massive buttress upon which was a staircase. The drawbridge has disappeared, and the tower is inaccessible except to cats, monkeys, blue-jackets or other species of the natural order of climbers. The Grand Master de Redin, (1657-60) erected fourteen of these watch-towers along the shore at his own expense. In this neighbourhood are the detached "Blata el Bayda," or "White Rock" and several caves known as the "drawing-rooms" and frequented by pleasure-seekers. The rocks are very hard, reddish like porous marble, and this district is called "el zonkor" or "hard stone." Imbedded in the rocks are small stones of various colours called "serpents' eyes," which in common with the *Terra Melitensis*, and the *Terra sigillata Melitae* are said to be specifics against venomous bites and pains in the side. Mr. Ritchie says: "Keeping the sea-beach, we pass over rugged heaps of stones, displaced by the wash of the sea, some measuring twelve or fourteen feet in length, eight to ten feet in breadth, and two feet to two

189

feet six inches in thickness, of yellow sandstone, uncovering the hard underlying strata of limestone." (See Geology of Malta by Capt. Spratt, C. B.) The Zonkor or "Hard Stone" Tower is a landmark, and is painted with red and white bands. These coast-towers were formerly lettered, Zoncor being "Z."

We reach Marsa Scala or the "Ladder Port," from whence a road leads inland to Zeitun, Zabbar, and the Three Cities. Many of the inhabitants of these places resort hither in spring time, as the walk through Zabbar is pleasant. Marsa Scala is also called "Biskallin" or the "Sons of Sicily" from the landing here of Sicilian traders or emigrants. A church dedicated to St. Catherine was founded in the 12th century. The shallow bay is only suited for small craft, and fisher folk dwell on its shores. On the eastern promontory is S. Thomas' Tower, built in 1614, after the fleet of the Order had caused 60 Turkish galleys which landed troops on July 6th of that year to beat a retreat. St. Thomas' Bay, between which and Marsa Scala is a huge rock-hewn mortar, derives its name from a neighbouring church, and is surrounded by extensive, terraced, and gentle slopes. We pass another fishing hamlet. This coast was defended by a fort erected in 1715 at his own expense by the Duke de Vendôme, Grand Prior of France. The rocky spur of the Monsoiar Reef a mile and a half in length with from five feet to six fathoms water upon it, runs out below a white cliff. Prudent captains give it a wide berth. The coast is very picturesque before we reach the long promontory which terminates in Cape Delimara, at the mouth of the great inlet of Marsa Scirocco. Delimara means "the home

190

at the mooring place" or, perhaps " the shadow of the woman." Close to it is the islet of Ittactia, or the "broken off spot." Upon the cape is a lighthouse 151 ft. above sea level, with a red and white light, revolving every 30 seconds, and visible at a distance of 15 miles. Hard by are a new and powerful fort, and a telegraph station from whence the approach of ships is signalled to Valletta. A tunny fishery has until lately been carried on below the fort, but its continuance is doubtful, as the profits are not large. The bay of Marsa Scirocco is a safe harbour, but is exposed to the southerly winds, whence its name, the S. E. wind being known in Malta under the name of "Scirocco." There is good holding ground, but a sandy reef of shoal water fringes the shores. Marsa Scirocco Bay resembles in shape the harbours of Valletta, having in the centre a tongue of land called Marnisi. On the evening of May 18th 1565, the Turkish fleet entered this harbour, to commence the great siege of the Borgo, and on June 10th 1798 General Dessaix effected a landing, under the orders of the First Napoleon. A tower now used as a police barrack on the northern shore still bears the name of the French Fort, and at the head of the bay is the fishing village of the same name. This is a favourite resort for pleasure seekers from Zeitun on the afternoon of the procession of San Gregorio which takes place, weather permitting, on the first Wednesday after Easter. There is a statue of St. Andrew near the shore, and a spring, a little above sea level is very useful as a washing place. The sea gently bathes the shore washing up large quantities of weed which is used as manure. On the northern shore of the

191

bay are fishponds in which are kept fish of various sorts and of all sizes especially mullet to be sent hereafter to market. Vegetation thrives down to the water's edge. Fishing boats arrive, depart, or are drawn up on the shore. Nets are being made, repaired, or dried. The Lampuca is a welcome finny visitant to the fishermen in the autumn. A walk round the promontory known as Marnisi will bring the pedestrian to several crumbling fortifications, one of which as appears by an inscription on a marble slab was restored by the Congregazione di Guerra or the Knights' War Department, in 1795, and named after the Grand Master de Redin who did so much to strengthen the defences of the island. In another fort pierced for fourteen guns, ten cannon without carriages are rusting to decay. Crossing the base of the above named promontory by a field path we pass a building with nine or ten massive stone buttresses. This is a stable for cavalry built in 1711 by the Grand Master Alofio Wignacourt. The roof is arched. A stone manger for 25 horses on one side, and fastenings for as many steeds on the other, are still to be seen. Not far distant is St. Lucian's Tower built in 1611. The Grand Master Alofio Wignacourt named it St. Lucian's Tower from the church in France in which he had been baptised, and attended by numerous knights both of high and low degree, went down on board the flagship and galleys of the Order to superintend the mounting of the guns which were all of bronze. When the French landed on June 10th 1798, St. Lucian's Tower was one of the few posts that offered any resistance, and it only surrendered after the garrison had been for 36 hours without food or water.

192

It has lately been considerably strengthened and adapted for heavy modern artillery. Following the shore we reach the little bay of San Giorgio which is full of interest. There is a little church of great antiquity here, dedicated to St. George which was demolished in 1659 and restored in 1693, in which the crews of the galleys were wont to hear mass before starting on expeditions to Barbary or the Levant. A procession comes hither from Zurrico on Ascension Day. Close to the church is a small battery and on the shore are 70 or 80 caldron shaped fossæ from two to eight feet in depth, some of which are of considerable size. Some are below sea level, and all are more or less inundated when a scirocco is blowing. Several were evidently destroyed when the fort was erected. They are much wider at the bottom than at the mouth, all shew marks of intense heat, are calcined to the depth of two inches, and seem to have been originally coated with bitumen. Some authorities think that oil from the neighbouring district of Zeitun was stored in them previous to shipment, whilst others are of opinion that in them were kindled the bonfires lighted by the worshippers of Melcarte the Tyrian Hercules whose temple stood about 700 feet distant on the hill above the bay. Similar cavities were discovered in 1864 during the construction of a road to the Citadel of Rabato in Gozo, another of considerable size may be seen to the eastward of the temple of Melcarte, and one or two other cavities possibly of the same character exist on the hill top above the Boschetto, on the opposite side of the valley to Mount Verdala. Across these excavations run ancient deeply worn cart tracks which are visible

193

on the western side of the little bay which they
cross, again emerging on the small peninsula on
which are the fossæ and then disappearing once
more beneath the waves. What traffic wore these
deep ruts, which passing as they do over the
mouths of some of these cavities shew that the
latter must have been formed since this ancient
coast road was in use? Do these submerged ruts
indicate a local depression of the land during the
historic period, or are the phenomena due, as Dr.
Adams supposes, to the action of the waves upon
soft strata? The temple of Melcarte or the Tyrian
Hercules which stood on the hill top 700 feet to
the north of the church of San Giorgio was formerly held in great veneration. From its situation
it, could be seen from afar, and Quintinus somewhat credulously asserts its circumference to have
been not less than three miles! Ciantar speaks of
seeing a portion of the pavement which was partly formed of native marble, and partly composed
of mosaic work of one colour (monochromato) of
Roman workmanship, of such hardness as to resist
the long continued passage of carts, animals, and
foot passengers. Round stones like stone shot, broken
columns,&c. have been dug up, and a huge bronze
hinge belonging to one of the gates was presented
to the church of San Lorenzo in Vittoriosa, and
now forms part of one of its bells. The only remains at present to be seen consist of a stone wall
some 33 feet in length composed of very massive
stones uniting two others of semicircular shape.
Half way between the temple and the shore are
three huge monoliths arranged in the form of a
chamber or cromlech. The stone which serves as

13

194

architrave and roof is as usual somewhat slanting, and measures fifteen feet nine inches in length: the two vertical stones are respectively eleven feet three inches, and ten feet seven inches in height. The largest blocks forming Kit's Coty House in England are twelve feet long and those of the famous Lion's Gate at Mycenæ are but eleven feet in length. Dr. Vassallo thinks that this was the sacred boundary beyond which no woman was permitted to pass, and which was united to the temple by walls giving a total area of 300 feet.

Vases of coarse workmanship are sometimes met with and broken pottery is abundant, but Melcarte's temple with its fire worship is literally nothing but a heap of stones, of which it is impossible to trace the original outline. A cavity similar to those on the beach exists in an adjacent field, and not far off are the remains of a large reservoir which seems to have had some connection with the temple. It is about thirty three feet square, and apparently thirteen feet in depth. Like the temple it is much blocked up with stones. The roof is supported by twelve massive isolated pillars, without capitals and arranged in three rows. Some of these pillars are formed each by two blocks of stone 8 ft. 8 in. thick, and others by three blocks, without the aid of mortar. Pieces of bitumen still adhere to the walls; the roof is flat, and tho structure is known as the Ghar-el-Giganti, "the Giants' Cave" and also "Gigantja" the "Giants' Land." On the opposite side of the valley to the west of the temple of Melcarte is the cave of El Dalam or "the darkness" which runs a long way through the limestone rock, and is worthy the attention of explor-

195

ers. Ciantar even supposes it to extend as far as Burmola, and to have its exit near the ancient church of Sant' Elena. Proceeding eastward past the church of San Giorgio we speedily reach Ramla ta Bir-Zebbugia which means "the sandy space by the olive-well," on which stands a little village, much frequented during the summer by residents in Valletta and the Three Cities several of whom have country houses here.

At the top of the hill just before the houses are reached, there is a remarkable echo which, though not equal to the famous Irish one which when asked "How do you do Paddy Blake," replies "Very well, thank you!" is yet capable of repeating six or seven words distinctly in any language whatever! From Bir-zebbugia extend for some considerable distance extensive fortifications near the shore, which were erected by the Grand Master Emanuel Pinto in 1764 under the following circumstances as recorded in the Annual Register of that year.

"The Town of Malta was surprised on October 6th, (1760) at the near approach of a large ship of Turkish construction, having a white flag with a crucifix at her mizen-top and a Turkish pendant embroidered with gold that reached to the very sea. Boats were immediately sent off, which were informed that it was a ship of the Grand Signor's commanded by his admiral, and called the Ottoman Crown, that she sailed the 2nd of last June with two frigates, five galleys, and other small vessels from the Dardanelles, that the above mentioned Admiral had been with this ship only to Smyrna, Scio, and Trio, and at length anchored in the channel of Strangie, when he and his retinue, to the

196

number of 300 persons went on shore. The whole ship's complement was 700 men, but 400 being on shore on the 19th of September the remaining 300 were attacked and overpowered by 70 Christian slaves armed only with a knife each, part being killed, part obliged to jump overboard, and the rest to sue for mercy. The heroes, now no longer slaves, bore away immediately for Malta, but were soon pursued by the two frigates and a Ragusian ship, which, by crowding sail, they escaped. On the 8th this ship, mounting 68 fine brass guns, and bored for 74, was brought safe into the harbour of Valletta, amidst the acclamations of the people. The Order of Malta, as an encouragement to such brave fellows, have made them the sole proprietors of the ship and slaves, as well as all the contribution money which latter is said to amount to a million and a half of florins, and other effects on board. The Grand Signor was on this occasion so highly offended with the conduct of his admiral that he dismissed him from the command of the fleet." Prize money must have been plentiful in Malta just then! The Knights feared an attack in force, and erected these works besides making other preparations, but a compromise was effected. A reef runs out from Benghisa Point which serves as a breakwater when the wind blows strongly from the N. W. In the year 1761 a tomb was discovered in this neighbourhood with an inscription in memory of a certain Hannibal (see p. 14).

In a gorge in this neighbourhood five miles distant from the Mnaidra Gap, is a cove or inlet up which the sea penetrates for 700 feet, in which Dr. Adams made many important geological discov-

197

eries. (Notes of a Naturalist in the Nile Valley and Malta. pp. 189-196).

Hassan's Cave is not far off, named, accord ing to Dr. Badger, from a certain Saracen who made his home in it for some time after the expulsion of the rest of his countrymen from the island. He must have been a brave man, and chose a worthy home for a true lover of freedom. Ghar Hassan or Hassan's Cave is about 200 feet above the sea and is a favourite spot for naval picnics. Crowds of sea birds know it well, and after sundown the noises which they make are extremely curious, reminding the listener of the dulcet tones of Punch and Judy.

The entrance is somewhat difficult, along a narrow path, but is not dangerous if ordinary care be used. Those however who easily become dizzy should not attempt the task. Within the cave which branches out in various directions forming a labyrinth of passages abounding in petrifactions, cool, fresh water is continually dropping. The view over the sea from the entrance is very pleasant. Wild doves haunt this cavern and the neighbouring cliffs. Ghar Hassan commands a fine view of the singular detached rock known as "The Lady." An Italian author wrote a Canto in 1846 on Ghar Hassan which well deserves perusal. In a field a little to the north of the cave is an erect monolith with no remains around it.

The most interesting natural formations in Malta are in this neighbourhood, much of the rock having a calcined appearance. The cliffs rise higher and higher until they reach an attitude of from three to four hundred feet, broken here and there by some

198

Uied or ravine, such as those of Zurrico and Malak. Near Ghar Hassan are also apparently some remains of ancient buildings or rock tombs, which might repay the scientific excavator. The neighbouring district is called Kabar el gharib or "the strangers' grave." Who were these strangers? Phœnicians? Perhaps so!

Close to the pretty Uied or ravine of Zurrico where cliffs rise high in air, are the curious rocky mass called from its shape "Monkar" or "the beak" and Il Kneia or "the arch" the latter forming a sea-bridge of truly noble proportions. Notice Ghar Cattus or "Cat Cave."

Fauara formerly called "Megira Serba," or the "place of joy and gladness" overlooks the sea and is a pleasant spot. The ground is very fertile and rises in cultivated terraces. The direct road to it from Valletta is through Casals Zebbug and Siggieui but it can be reached by means of a rocky path from the Inquisitor's Palace some two miles distant. Fauara was a favourite resort for pleasure seekers, until it was called upon to furnish the water supply of the Bouverie Aqueduct.

A small island near the shore named Hagra Seuda or the "Black Rock," is said to have formerly been inhabited. Close by are Joseph's Rock (Hagra ta Usif,) and the fountain of the servant of God (Aaynghliem Alla), and about three miles from the mainland is the small anvil shaped island of Filfla or "Piper" whereon all the lizards are of a beautiful bronze black colour, none of their relatives on the mainland resembling them in hue. The stormy petrel, Manx, and the cinerous shearwater breed here. The eggs of the latter are pure white.

199

The only bird indigenous to Malta, the Thalassidroma Melitensis also builds its nest at Filfla. Both birds and lizards are exceedingly tame. A little church, dedicated to the B. V. M. since demolished and incorporated with the church of Bubakra near Zurrico, formerly stood on the eastern extremity. Landing is only possible in calm weather. The ascent to the top is difficult for ladies. Half way up the cliff is a natural shed, formed by a prodigious mass of fallen rock, the very place for a picnic. Men of war use the island as a target, and fragments of shot and shell are plentiful. The other day the remark was made, by a lady of course, that "the ships would be much more usefully employed in giving dances in Valletta Harbour than in firing at Filfla." Fishing boats cruise off the island, going thither occasionally to collect shell-fish. Boat from the small creek a little to the right of Wied Zurrico to Filfla and back 2s. 6d. Now and again sportsmen visit it in quest of pigeons and rabbits, but for the most part Filfla is left to solitude and desolation.

There is a Maltese proverb "See Filfla and die." It derives its name from "filfel" which means a "peppercorn;" at its western extremity are the rocks of Santa Maria.

All along this coast coral is to be found and the fishery was formerly worked but has of late years been abandoned as unprofitable. A coral fishing boat is sometimes manned by more than 20 hands; the labour is excessive, and the expense great. One who knows full well what are the hardships of the fishermen, says "Slavery is a joke to it." A heavy iron cross, covered with swabs, is flung over-

200

board and dragged along the bottom, breaking off
the branches and stems of coral in its course. It
is then hauled up and stripped of its gathered spoils.
The poor fellows who toil so hard live on the very
poorest and plainest fare, subsisting when times are
bad, as they but too often are, on little besides
bread and water. Ladies! as you admire the beautiful ornaments fashioned at the cost of so much
labour, spare now and again a kindly thought for
these poor "toilers of the sea!"

From this point onwards we pass a succession
of headlands and indentations which call for no special; remark; all bear Arabic names, and the cliffs
are boldly picturesque.

The most remarkable spots are Ghar Lapsi or
the Grotto of the Ascension, a favourite spot for
sea bathing on Ascension Day, the Ras el Raheb or
the Cape of the Monk, so called from its appearance from the sea, and the Bay of Fom-er-Rieh or
"the mouth of the wind." The district called Re-
dum Pellegrino or the Pellegrino Rocks derives its
name from a noble family of the same name. On
the edge of the cliff to the north of the Bay of
Fom-er-Rieh are ruts which terminate abruptly on
the brink of a precipice 80 or 100 feet high, prov-
ing that the coast has been much washed away during the historic period. Traces of Roman or Grecian buildings are to be seen close by.

Here and there a narrow ravine runs inland
from the sea, and we pass the strongly-fortified hills
of Bingemma, famous for their Phœnician tombs,
along the northern face of which runs the great
geological *fault*, which stretches across the island
to the bays of Maddalena and St. Marco. Below

201

are the sandy Bay of Gineyna tal Migiarro or the "Garden at the carting place," from whence stone was formerly exported to Barbary, the headland of Karraba or "the decanter" so called from its appearance, and Aayn Toffieha or the "fountain of the apple." Cape Majesa is called after an Arab of that name. The whole district of Melleha which we next reach, derives its name according to general opinion from the numerous salt pans which have been constructed on the shore, but the Revd. Dr. Camilleri thinks that the word Melleha is a corruption of the name Mellea applied to this district by the Greeks about the year 700 A. D. on account of the abundance of honey produced here. The Revd Dr. says that the salt pans only date from the 16th century. On the southern shore is the Tower of St. Agata, which was built and armed in the year 1649. Ras-el-Kammieh means the "hill of corn," and Uied-el-Musa is the "valley of Musa" named from a deceased Saracen. But here we are at Marfa where passengers for Gozo who have come by omnibus from Valletta, take boat to cross the Straits of Flieghi four miles in breadth, the southern portion of which is known as the Roadstead of Frioul. Fare for omnibus and ferry-boat 2s. There is a police barrack at Marfa and a house built by the late Marquis of Hastings when Governor of Malta nominally as a country house, but in reality as a shelter in bad weather for travellers, to and from Gozo.

The hills above Marfa are called Guedet-el-Rum or "the hills of the Christian Greeks." The cliffs rise sheer from the water's edge as we pass Cape Lahrash and Ras Lahrash the headlands which

202

mark the western extremity of Malta, where a tunny fishery has been long established. They are named from the rugged and barren nature of the soil. About three miles seaward is Ball's Bank sometimes called St. Paul's Shoal 3½ miles long by one broad with from 7 to 14 fathoms water. The Bay of Melleha opens out to the right. Here the tardy succours landed on Sept. 7th 1565 to relieve the hardly pressed knights after the famous siege of the Borgo, as did also General Baraguay d'Hilliers at the head of a French force on June 10th 1798.

In the sides of the ravine below the village of Melleha are numerous caves of various sizes, both natural and artificial. Some of these may have been Phœnician tombs, as lamps and lachrymatories have been discovered. Niches for lamps exist as well as smaller recesses in the larger chambers, which have carefully smoothed floors. These caves were formerly, as some of them are still, inhabited, or used as storehouses. In and near one of them close to the church Captain Spratt C. B. and Dr. Adams discovered fossil remains of the Hippopotamus Pentlandi, as they did also at Malak &c. near Crendi. Calypso, the fair goddess with whom we were all so well acquainted in the days when we used to study our " Aventures de Télémaque," is popularly supposed to have resided at Melleha. Homer in the Fifth Book of the Odyssey gives a glowing description of her grotto, which is in truth a miserable cave. There is however a fine view from the hill side and from the grotto wells forth abundance of clear spring water which fertilises a large garden below. Some hermits lived here early in the 17th century. The honey of Melleha

203

has been compared to that of Hyblà but since
wild thyme has been less abundant in the district, the honey has lost its flavour. The Bay is
broader than that of St. Paul, with excellent anchorage but exposed to the N. E. winds. There is
a rocky bank in the centre with shoal water, but
on either side there is a depth of five or six
fathoms. The Village of Melleha which is only a
short distance from the landing place has a church
much venerated by the Maltese. It is partly excavated in the solid rock, is hung with numerous
votive offerings, and the crypt below is variously said to have been consecrated by St. Paul, by
St. Publius, by some bishops on their way to the council of Milevo in Africa in 402 A. D., by the
bishops·who accompanied Belisarius from Syracuse
to Numidia in 540 A. D, or by those prelates who
followed Count Roger hither in 1090 A. D. Many
pilgrimages and penitential processions have been
made to this church which contains a very ancient
picture of the B. V. M. which is said to have been
painted on the wall by St. Luke, and the village
festival is held on Sep. 8th (Nativity of B. V. M.).
There is a square with a fountain in the centre in
front of the church for the reception of pilgrims
and picnic parties. In the Grotta della Madonna
below the church is a statue of the B. V. M., and
also several headless figures which are said to have
been decapitated by the French. Travellers will find
moderate accomodation at several village hostelries.

On the hill top near the village of Melleha is
the massive square tower known as Selmoon or Sa-
lamone Palace, which commands a very extensive
view over Malta and Gozo. Permission to visit it

204

must be obtained at the Palace, Valletta. In 1607 Fra Emanuele, a Maltese Capuchin Friar proposed from the pulpit of St. John's Church the formation of a "Monte di Redenzione" for the purpose of ransoming Maltese and Gozitan slaves from the Turks. The Grand Master Wignacourt became the patron of the "Monte," subscriptions flowed in, and in 1619 Caterina Vitale a Maltese lady left all her property including the estate of Selmoon to this charity. In 1625 Dr. Gio. Domenico Felice bequeathed 6000 scudi for the same purpose, and numerous liberated slaves took part yearly in the solemnities of Easter. This charity was under the control of one of the Grand Crosses of the Order, and prospered exceedingly. Over the entrance to Selmoon Palace is an escutcheon with a large "R" and three mountains upon it. The latter emblem symbolises the Monte di Pietà (p. 124). The Palace was erected as some say by the four commissioners who managed the property as a shooting box, whilst others ascribe its erection to the Grand Master Verdala as a defence against the Turks. From what funds the cost of construction was defrayed is uncertain. Leaving Selmoon Palace we soon reach the shore close to the island of the same name, so called from an ancient Maltese family which afterwards emigrated to Sicily. It is also known as Gzeier or the "islands." The channel which separates it from the mainland is shallow and the water is beautifully clear, reflecting objects at the bottom with the utmost distinctness. Rainbow tints of every hue, such as no artist in delirium ever had the faintest hope of imitating are below and at either side of us, whilst above us tower high the cliffs, here verdure clad, and there rugged,

205

bare, and forbidding, at the foot of which that ill-fated vessel which bore St. Paul went to pieces. Look about you, and say if yonder Bay of Mistra be not "a creek with a shore," and if this be not "a place where two seas meet." Think of all the other evidence in favour of this being the scene of the shipwreck, and you cannot fail to feel that you are on classic and sacred ground. And, moreover, you will hardly leave the island astern, marked as it is by a white statue of the Apostle, erected in 1845 at the expense of Sig. S. Borg and by public subscription with a commemorative inscription, and visible far to seaward, without a warm feeling of admiration for the manly courage displayed by that grand old man who, standing on the wet and slippery deck of a stranded ship, which might go to pieces at any moment, was more calm and self-possessed than any experienced mariner or veteran soldier of that shipwrecked company.

The island of Selmoon was also the scene of another heroic deed. Marco di Maria, Royal Pilot of the Galleys of the Order was one day returning from an expedition to the coast of Barbary, and when off Gozo fell in with the squadron of the Turkish Admiral Biserta. Being hotly pursued, he adopted the desperate expedient of running through the shallow channel between the island of Selmoon and the mainland. In this he succeeded by shifting his crew fore and aft, and from side to side, according to the varying depth of the water, without checking the speed of his galley. The Turkish pursuer followed but took the ground. In recognition of his skill and courage the island was granted to the bold sailor and his descendants in perpetuity. John and Narduccio his

206

son and grandson, equally skilful pilots with himself, succeeded him as owners, but the latter being killed by a musket-ball at the capture of a Turkish flag-ship, the island reverted to the Order. We may briefly sum up the controversy as to whether St. Paul was wrecked close to this island. Some have laid stress on St. Luke's words "we were driven up and down in Adria" to prove that Meleda in the Adriatic and not Malta was the scene of the wreck. But Procopius whose words agree with other authors says that "Adria" included the whole of the Ionian, Cretan, and Sicilian seas. "The islands of Gozo and Malta separate the Adriatic and the Tuscan sea." Euroclydon seems to have been a N. E. wind which would drive the ship towards Malta and not towards Meleda. A ship of the size of that which had St. Paul on board would drift at the rate of about 36 miles in 24 hours, or 468 miles in 13 days. Now the island of Clauda is 480 miles distant from Malta, and it was "on the 14th night" that "the shipmen deemed that they drew nigh to some country." The soundings in the bay agree with those given by St. Luke, and the little bay Mistra or "the North West" is just such "a creek with a shore" as a ship in distress would make for. The term "barbarous" that is, "not Greek speaking" people applies to the inhabitants of Malta but not to those of Meleda. The viper may easily have been brought in a bundle of firewood. in St. Paul's own ship, or may since have become extinct. . The disease from which the father of Publius was suffering is not uncommon during the autumn amongst strangers to the island, as the father of the Roman Publius was. Lastly

207

the course of "the ship of Alexandria" bound for Rome as described by St. Luke tallies completely and exactly with that taken now-a-days by vessels from Malta bound in the same direction, whereas from Meleda such a course is unintelligible. It therefore appears, to say the least, probable that the traditional site of the wreck is the true one, although the exact spot is most likely now submerged, as the crumbling cliffs shew plainly that the waves have been doing a work of destruction for many centuries. The following is a description of the opposite shore of this world famous inlet.

ST. PAUL'S BAY.

Here we are at last! A broad and sunlit bay, with an entrance nearly two miles wide, and running inland between two and three miles with from 18 to 24 fathoms of water at the mouth, and gradually shoaling towards its upper extremity, bears the name of the great Apostle St. Paul. The first object that attracts our notice is a square-built tower. This was erected in 1610 by the Grand Master Alofio Wignacourt, who laid the foundation stone on February 10th, the supposed anniversary of the shipwreck. There were great doings on these shores that day. The Grand Master rode down on horseback from Valletta, attended by grand crosses, commanders, and knights, galore. The clergy from Città Vecchia the ancient capital, mustered in full force, litanies were sung, solemn prayers were said, and then the Grand Master duly laid the first stone of the tower, of which the cost of erection was defrayed by himself. Close by the tower is a little church, also erected in 1610, on the site of a more

208

ancient edifice. It contains several frescoes representing the shipwreck, the preaching of the Apostle, and his miracles of healing. But the chief interest connected with it is the fact that it is said to stand on the very spot whereon, according to ancient tradition, the fire was lighted by the barbarous people who showed no little kindness to the shipwrecked mariners. Nor is this unlikely, for it is evident at a glance that no other spot on the shores of the bay could be more suitable than this for a fishing village, such as then existed and still does exist here. The creek just below the church is still the refuge for fishing boats during a gregale, as Euroclydons are termed in modern days, and is called "The Bay of the Idle" or "Take it Easy Creek." Near the tower is a stone table with seats which picnic parties find very convenient. The Marchese Scicluna has a mansion here and refreshments for travellers of frugal minds may be obtained at several modest hostelries. Boats to St. Paul's Island, from near the tower. Fare, about 6d. each person. This excursion should be made by those who wish to understand the locality.

Skirting the shores towards Kaura Point at the eastern entrance of the bay, we note a ruined battery and line of defence, erected some century since for the defence of the coast. Where are the soldiers now who once manned these works and drew water from yonder well? This district is called by the natives Buleben, or "The Father of Milk," although methinks to the eyes of an English grazier it would present a somewhat desolate appearance. Passing a tower for coast defence, built on a spot called Bugebba, by the Grand Master Las-

209

caris, we reach Kaura Point, lashed without ceasing by the ever sounding waves. Here it was that St. Paul and his friends heard the road of breakers as the "shipmen deemed that drew nigh to some country," and it is no slight confirmation of St. Luke's account that modern soundings exactly agree with those which he records. Just off Kaura Point, to perceive which at night the ship must have approached within a quarter of a mile, the depth of water is from 20 to 21 fathoms, whilst a little farther within the bay 15 fathoms are found. Close to this point is a district called "Benuarrat" or "The Possessions of the Heir," so called because the possessions of Publius, which the Ethiopic version says consisted of lands, houses, and gardens, are said to have been situated here. Retracing our steps and passing the Tower of St. Paul, we soon reach a roadside spring called Ghain Rasul, or "the Fountain of the Apostle." Tradition asserts that St. Paul and his companions being tormented by thirst, the Apostle caused this spring to burst forth. The probability is that he drank of its waters, and hence the name. Above on the hill top is Uardia, or "The Look-out Station," from whence it is said that the wreck was first descried by the watchers on duty. It may well have been so, for see yonder is a dghaisa bound for Gozo, close to the traditional scene of the wreck. How distinctly in this clear air can her every movement be distinguished! A winding road ascends the hill to Selmoon Palace and the village of Melleha from the bottom of the bay from whence a plain called Uied-in-nahlia or "the valley of bees" extends across the island. Leaving St. Paul's Bay, we reach the inlet of

14

the Saline or "the saltworks," where large and numerous saltpans earn money for the Government. The stream which during the rainy season flows in considerable volume down the Uied-el-Ghasel or "Valley of Honey" near Musta, here finds its way to the sea. This bay was protected by a fort before the year 1494, and sportsmen find amusement here during the autumn migration or Grand Passage which lasts from September 10th till the end of the year in pursuit of plover, woodcock, and aquatic birds.

Close in shore is the Ghallis Rock, wave-beaten for evermore, We pass the tower of Babar-e-Ciaac or "the pebbly sea" and the little bay of San Marco, defended by "the tower on the ridge," square and stone built. Maddalena Bay fortified by the Grand Master Lascaris, was the scene of a French landing on June 10th 1798. The church of St. John the Evangelist just below the northern extremity of the great geological "fault" which intersects the island, was built about 150 years since in gratitude for an unexpected escape from Turkish corsairs.

On the hill-top is the village of Gargur, and there are several caves in this neighbourhood. Maddalena Fort crowns the height, supported by Pembroke Fort. Both these forts are heavily armed. Crossing the Rifle Ranges we reach Pembroke Camp (p. 150.)

211

CHAPTER II.

COUNTRY EXCURSIONS.

ROUTE I.—*To and from St. Paul's Bay.*

The San Giuseppe Road.—Villages of Curmi, Birchircara, Lia, and Nasoiar.—Syndics and Villages.—The "Great
Fault."—The Valley of Honey.—St. Paul el Milki. — Musta Church.—Palace and Gardens of Sant' Antonio.

LEAVING Floriana by the Porte des Bombes we
soon reach the head of the Great Harbour (p.
162), and take the right hand road.

The San Giuseppe Road, along which our route
now lies, traverses a very populous suburb, inhabited by industrious working people. They toil hard
but they have labour to spare in the cause of religion. Witness yonder large and well-built church
on our left, which is by no means the only one
in the district. It was erected by the voluntary
labour of those who dwell around it. Would the
residents in many English parishes do likewise?
Close at hand is the Franklin cigar factory, the
courteous manager of which declares that he has but
one fault to find with the ladies, "They smoke, but
not enough." To our left is Casal Curmi (Casal is
the Maltese name for a village), which was formerly
the residence of nearly all the bakers who supplied
the tables of the knights. The church is dedicated
to St. George, of whom we in England know some-

212

thing, and claims to possess a piece of the standard carried by him as a Roman military tribune. We pass the cattle market, from whence comes much of our beef and mutton, and the arches of the aqueduct (p. 144). Just at the spot on which we now are a memorable skirmish took place. The French by their indiscriminate spoliation of churches and public buildings, had goaded the Maltese to madness, until at last they rose in insurrection and massacred the garrison of Città Vecchia. Ignorant of this disaster General Vaubois, who commanded in Valletta, despatched a detachment of 200 men to the relief of Città Vecchia. The Maltese met them at this point, and, armed only with stones, farm implements, and a few rusty muskets, and profiting by the shelter afforded by the numerous stone walls to be found everywhere in Malta, completely routed the detachment and compelled it to retire to Valletta.

On the right is the Conservatorio Bugeja, a noble almshouse built by a Maltese gentleman named Bugeja at his own expense. It was opened a short time since, and is under the control of Sisters of Charity. It provides a home for orphans. The cost is estimated at £50,000.

We here part company with the aqueduct, and turn to the right, passing through the village of Birchircara the name of which means "the flowing spring" with on the right its noble church dedicated to Sant' Elena, and on the left the ruins of another. Turning to the right in the village we soon reach Casal Lia sheltered by hills and with its church dedicated to S. Salvador. Here grow some of the sweetest oranges of which the Mediterranean can

213

boast, and the Villa Paris Hotel kept by G. B. Mallia has numerous visitors.

For purposes of police Malta is divided into seven districts, each containing several casals or villages. Each district is under the charge of a Syndic or Country Magistrate. These "Sindaci" were first appointed in 1839 as successors in legal, though not in military matters of the "luogo-tenenti" or "Capi dei Casali" who date from 1798. They have jurisdiction in civil cases below the value of £5., and in minor police cases, do various kind offices for the villagers, and are most useful as "Fathers of the People."

One Maltese village is very much like another. The streets are narrow, so narrow, indeed, that in many places two vehicles can scarcely if at all pass one another, but they have the great advantage of excluding the burning rays of the summer sun.

In the middle of the village there is always a noble church. In Malta church building seems to have been carried on to a great extent at two separate periods. The first was at the time when Englishmen were fighting hand-to-hand at Basing house, Marston Moor, and Naseby, and the other was in the days of the Second George. There are the usual statues of saints, a few stately houses, formerly the homes of foreign knights or native nobles, and numerous dwellings, all filled to overflowing with a busy, industrious, Arab dialect speaking population. The people look up pleasantly as we pass, and return our "Buon giorno," or "Sahha ghalicom" ("Health be to you") with right good will. The women especially, like all races of eastern origin, are exceedingly fond of in-door life, and the streets

214

are solitary indeed compared with those of any village in England. The ever-barking dog, the chirping sparrow, and the cicala, which, like Tennyson's "Brook," "goes on for ever," are often the only sounds to be heard. And the cicalas *do* make a noise. The other day a lady said "I must apologize for calling when you are just going to dinner. I can hear the frying of the fish." It was only the cicalas in the garden.

We climb a steep hill and reach the rock-perched village of Naxaro or Nasciar. Let us look for a moment at the fair and wide-spread prospect at our feet. Yonder, perched upon its hilltop, is Città Vecchia, a city of decaying palaces and crumbling ramparts, almost seeming a city of the dead. Yet it is has a stirring history of its own" to tell. Built, according to an intelligent compositor in a certain Maltese printing office, 1404 years before, instead of after the flood, Carthaginians, Greeks, Romans, and men of Tyre have alike toiled to strengthen it or called it "home." Cicero speaks of its cotton cloth, and—but stop a bit, is not its history told in each and all of the encyclopædias? Breaking the sky-line is the palace tower of Verdala, built by a certain Cardinal Verdala, Grand Master in Malta in the days when Good Queen Bess held sway in "Merrie England." Afar in the distance are the towers of Zeitun, a name which means "abundance of oil," and of Zurrico, where most of the people have blue eyes, and many a village more. All Valletta seems to lie at our very feet, although in reality some miles distant, whilst nearer, and rising amidst groves of golden orange and sombre cypress, is Sant' Antonio, some time the residence of their

215

Royal and Imperial Highnesses the Duke and Duchess of Edinburgh. Many another object of interest is there in that broad, fair, and highly cultivated plain, but "Forward" is the cry, and we enter Nasciar, which is a very good type of an ordinary Maltese village. The church was commenced in 1616, completed in 1630 and consecrated in 1742.

Just outside the village is a statue of St. Paul, who is said to have preached on this spot. The people of Nasciar claim to have been the first to receive Christian baptism, and it is somewhat singular that the Maltese still call themselves Nazarenes. But it is probable that Nasciar derives its name from an Arabic word, which means "separated," standing, as it does, on the top of the great geological "fault" which runs completely across the island and has here lowered the strata some 400 feet. We cannot better describe this "fault," which is one of the most characteristic features of Malta, than by quoting the Rev. H. H. Seddall:—"To the existence of this fault is due one of the most picturesque features of Malta. Often on a fine spring morning have I stood on the ridge of the Nasciar heights, the whole plain below glowing with the blossoms of the purple sulla or clover, the inlets of the bays of the Saline, and St. Paul and the Straits of Frieghi reposing like gems of deepest blue in their setting of white rock, which the sun irradiated into a dazzling lustre, enjoying the first cool breath of the maestrale, as it dimpled the azure of the lazy deep, and mapping out the course of present or future excursions with gun, hammer, or botanical box."

216

To the right is the village of Gargur, and we pass through the ruinous Nasciar Lines. Descending the hill we see the Great Fault towering high above us. To the left is the village of Musta with its wide spreading dome, nearly as large as that of St. Paul's Cathedral, and closer at hand is the Uied el Ghasel, or Valley of Honey, down the rocks of which, according to tradition, once literally flowed in a luscious stream the produce of the toil of the honey bees. But that was "once upon a time," and truth to tell, this deponent hath never been witness to any thing of the kind. The Uied el Ghasel is a rocky gorge, with lofty cliffs on either side, which during the winter rains, when a wild torrent fills the whole bottom of the ravine, might almost be mistaken for a mountain glen in Wales or bonnie Scotland. Within its recesses is a little chapel dedicated to St. Paul the Hermit, close to which is a spring, the water of which is so cool and delicious that some of the Grand Masters would drink no other. Tradition has it that a certain saint formerly dwelt in this secluded spot, and often had occasion to reprove the people of Musta for their wickedness. They laid a snare for him, hoping to convict him either of want of charity or immorality. The saint was more than a match for his persecutors, and walking down to the shore spread his cloak upon the waves and sailed away to Gozo. The people of Musta were, like Lord Ullin, "left lamenting."

On the heights is a strong fort, during the construction of which many antiquities were discovered. Close to the highway side is a little shrine which is interesting as recording the fact that so

217

lately as the last century the Bishop of Malta bore also the proud title of Archbishop of Damietta, a touching instance of the tenacity with which the Knights of St. John clung to the ancient traditions of the Crusades, wherein Damietta, the key of Egypt, on the side of Syria, played no unimportant part.

The plain of Nasciar is rich and fertile. One glance at its broad acres is sufficient to dispel for ever the myth that the soil of Malta was originally imported from Sicily. Why, whole fleets of *Great Easterns* kept chartered for an indefinite period would never have accomplished so Herculean an undertaking.

Here we are at length on the track of the great Apostle of the Gentiles. To the left, on the hillside above the road, is a little chapel, reared upon a spot which has for many centuries borne the traditional name of San Paul el Milki or "St. Paul received," whereon it has always been said that Publius, who was governing the island during the illness of his father, received the shipwrecked voyagers. Nor is it by any means improbable that such was the case. But no direct confirmation of the tradition existed until lately, when excavations, which are still going on, brought to light on this very spot the remains of a large and ancient oil mill, which, from various indications, is clearly proved to be contemporaneous with the visit of St. Paul to the island. Remains of a dwelling-house or villa are close by. The oil-vats and millstones, worked by mules or slave labour, are *in situ.* Fragments of tesselated pavement, a votive altar, partition walls, subterranean constructions, and in short, all the ac-

218

cessories of the country residence of an opulent Roman exist here. It is a great pity that this almost solitary and priceless relic of Roman occupation, and which is moreover connected by tradition with one of the most stirring incidents in the life of St. Paul, is not more carefully preserved.

From San Paul el Milki it is but a short distance to St. Paul's Bay, (p. 204).

We may advantageously vary our route by returning viâ Musta, to visit its noble church, the dome of which is one of the largest in the world. That of the Pantheon is 143 feet, St. Peter's is 139 feet, and St. Paul's Cathedral 107 ft. in diameter.

The first stone was laid on the 30th of May 1833. No scaffolding was used, and the new church was erected over the old one which was afterwards removed. The architect was Sig. G. Grongnet de Vassé, and the cost in money was £21,000, supplemented by the voluntary labour of the people on Sundays and festivals. The new church was consecrated in 1864, the old one being entirely demolished in eight days. A staircase leads to the summit of the dome.

En route for Valletta we pass through Casals Lia and Balzan, the latter name meaning "the place of paying toll." In Casal Lia are the Palace and Gardens of Sant' Antonio. The Palace was built in 1625 by the Grand Master De Paula, and was used as a country house by his successors. The gardens are well worthy of a visit. A permit must be obtained at the Palace in Valletta to visit the private gardens.

219

From hence we return to Valletta from which Sant' Antonio is about four miles distant by the highroad connecting Valletta with Città Vecchia, passing the Rose, Shamrock, and Thistle Hotel kept by J. Sheppard, opposite to which a portion of the Indian Contingent was encamped in 1878.

220

Route II.—*Città Vecchia and its neighbourhood.*

Casal Attard, and the Lunatic Asylum.—Città Vecchia, its Sanatorium and Cathedral.--St. Paul's Grotto, and the Catacombs.—Bingemma, Nadur, and Imtarfa.—Mount Verdala, and the Boschetto. — The Inquisitor's Palace.—Casals Siggieui and Zebbug.

AFTER passing Sant' Antonio Palace and Gardens (p. 218) we soon reach Casal Attard, "the village of roses" which has a fine church dating from 1613, consecrated in 1830, and dedicated to the Assumption of the B. V. M. The principal picture is by Pasquale Buhagiar. Between Casal Attard and Città Vecchia is the new Lunatic Asylum on the left of the road, in the Wied Incita.

It contains about 400 inmates, and was completed during the administration of Sir Gaspard Le Marchant. The old Lunatic Asylum was situated at Floriana.

A long ascent brings us to Città Vecchia the ancient capital. (For its history see Part I. Chap. ii.) In the time of the Order the city was governed by a Hakem or Ruler, chosen yearly by the Grand Master, from the principal Maltese citizens. He was called "the Captain of the Rod," and his jurisdiction usually extended over the civil and criminal cases of all the villages in the island. The Magistracy of the city consisted of three officers, called Giurati, who were also chosen annually by the Grand Master. The Civil Court was composed of three Judges one of whom decided lawsuits, whilst the

221

remaining two, called Idioti, only settled cases of small moment.

Over the gates of the city are inscriptions recording the strengthening of the fortifications by the Grand Master Manoel de Vilhena in 1724 and 1727. Under the principal gateway stands a battered statue of Juno, with peacocks on her breast, and just within the gate is the site of the ancient Temple of Apollo and a Theatre, some remains of which were discovered in 1747. On the right as we enter is the old Palace of the Giurati which was converted into a Military Sanatorium by Sir Gaspard le Marchant. Numerous dungeons in one of which is a block of stone on which criminals were beheaded, and the justice room of the Giurati are still in existence.

The Cathedral occupies the traditional site of the house of Publius, who entertained St. Paul, and is said to have been consecrated by him as first Bishop of Malta. The old Cathedral built about 1090, was destroyed by an earthquake in 1693. The first stone of the present structure was laid on May 21st 1697, and it was consecrated on October 8th 1702. The architect was Lorenzo Gafà.

On the west front are the arms of the Grand Master Perellos, of Bishop Palmieri, who consecrated the Cathedral, and of the city. The two bell towers 126 ft. high contain six bells, one of which belonged to the old church. The length of the church is 170 ft, extreme breadth 97 ft. 3 in. breadth of nave 36 ft. 2 in.

The paintings on the roof the work of Vincenzo Manno a Sicilian artist in 1794, representing the life of

222

St. Paul, the Apostles, and Prophets are very fine. Notice the marble mosaic tombstones in the pavement.

In St. Luke's Chapel the Evangelist is depicted as painting the portrait of the B. V. M. In the Chapel of S. Gaetano the saint is represented as receiving in his arms the Infant Jesus. The Chapel of San Publio contains pictures of his baptism and martyrdom. The Reliquary Chapel contains numerous relics and a curious Byzantine portrait of St. Paul covered with silver. The Choir has two beautiful mosaic pictures of S. S. Peter and Paul. The ancient wood work brought from Catania in 1480, the silver cross from Rhodes, and the music books five centuries old, are worthy of attention. The high altar is formed of costly marbles, and the altar stone is said to have formerly covered the grave of the father of Publius. In the Chapel of the Blessed Sacrament are interred the Bishops of Malta, and it contains a portrait of the B. V. M. said to be by St. Luke. In the Chapel of the Annunciation is a picture representing St. Paul routing 18,000 Moors who besieged the city in 1470. The font and the doors of the sacristy belonged to the old cathedral. In the sacristy is a portrait of Count Roger who freed Malta from Arab dominion in 1090. The treasury contains many objects of value and there is a fine view from the windows of the Chapter Room.

Near the Cathedral is the Bishop's Palace in which is a series of episcopal portraits. The Seminary was built in 1733. The chapel contains some pictures by the Cav. Favray. The heart of Bishop Alpheran is interred here. •

223

Passing the Cathedral the main street leads to a bastion from which there is a fine view. In Str. Magazzini may be seen the last calesse or Maltese carriage in the island.

We proceed to the populous suburb of Rabato. Beneath the church of San Publio is a grotto in which it is said that St. Paul lived during his three months' residence in the island. The stone of this grotto is asserted to be of great efficacy in the cure of fevers, poisonous bites &c, and tradition affirms that the size of the grotto never alters, however much stone is taken from it. Close to the church of the Shipwreck of St. Paul is a cemetery in which many natives and foreigners are interred. Also a statue of St. Paul preaching, it being said that he preached on this spot and planted the cross on the place on which now stands a cross of stone. On this occasion his voice is said to have been audible in Gozo. There are several churches and monasteries in Città Vecchia and Rabato, also two hospitals. The first of these dedicated to the Holy Ghost dates from at least 1370 but was modernised in the 17th century. It is under the control of the local government. The other hospital is called ta Saura, having been founded in 1654 by a Maltese doctor who endowed it with all his property. Numerous other benefactors have also contributed to its funds.

Close to St. Paul's Church are some large catacombs, which are variously said to be of Phœnician, Roman, and Christian origin. Admission and a guide are readily procurable. Long passages lead now and again to spacious chambers, supported by rudely formed columns. Sepulchral niches

224

for men, women, and children are to be seen in
vast numbers, some still containing human remains
whilst other tombs are closed by a large stone.
These catacombs cover a large area, and tradition
tells of a schoolmaster and his pupils who lost
their way, and perished miserably. Ladies should
put on shawls on coming out as the air of the
catacombs is cold. Some very interesting catacombs
were discovered in 1878 not far from those of S.
Paul, and similar excavations have been met with
in various parts of the island. They all contain
circular stones with raised rims, the use of which
is as yet undetermined.

Leaving Città Vecchia in a westerly direction
we pass the fountain of Ghain Clieb (see p. 22).
The road to the right leads to Bingemma where a whole
hillside is covered with tombs, apparently of Phœnician origin, some of which are used as storehouses
and even as dwellings. For a full account of these
tombs see Boisgelin's Ancient and Modern Malta.
Extensive is the view over land and sea from
that breezy hill-top. Good walkers who do not
object to scaling an occasional stone wall will
enjoy a walk along the cliffs to the new fort at
Bingemma to which carriages may be sent, and
from which a good road leads to Valletta. An
order from the Commanding Royal Engineer is
required to visit this fort.

Nadur is a pleasant spot upon the slope of
the Bingemma Hills, about two miles to the S. W.
of which is the rock fortress of Kalaa tal Bahria
(see p. 22.) At Imtarfa formerly stood the temple of Proserpine which was restored by the Roman
Procurator Chrestion. Imtahleb which means the

225

"father of milk" near the shore, and about three miles to the S. W. of Città Vecchia is a favourite spot for picnic parties. Wild strawberries abound, gardens are highly cultivated, water and shade are obtainable, and there is an extensive view from the neighbouring heights. Springs supply the Three Cities with water.

About two miles to the S. of Città Vecchia is Mount Verdala on which stands the fortress palace of the same name. Square built, it owes its erection to the Grand Master Cardinal Verdala. Notice the Latin inscription. "The dew and rain of Mount Verdala 1586." Permission to visit Verdala Palace may be obtained at the Palace, Valletta. Some frescoes by the Florentine artist Filippo Paladini represent the principal events in the life of the founder. H. E. the Governor sometimes resides at Verdala Palace during the summer months. Verdala being too far distant from Valletta from which, however, it is distinctly visible, the Grand Master De Paula built the Palace of Sant' Antonio as a country house. Unsuccessful attempts were made some years since to make Verdala Palace the centre of the manufacture of silk.

Descending the hill, either by the road or by a walk from the Palace we reach the garden called the Boschetto the country seat of the Grand Masters previous to the erection of Verdala Palace, attached to which was an extensive deer park. The orange gardens are pleasant, and an artificial grotto with abundant water, and furnished with a stone table and seats attracts numerous picnic parties.

The Economico-Agrarian Society holds an annual Agricultural Show in these gardens on June

15

226

29th (SS. Peter and Paul), on which day from time immemorial a popular festival has been held at this spot.

A pleasant walk through a fertile valley to the left of the Boschetto brings us to the Inquisitor's Palace. This country house is government property. It has a desolate garden, and a slope leads down to a spring called Ghain el Kbira or the "Great Fountain." This whole district produces quantities of fruit. To the E. of the Inquisitor's Palace is the district of Gorghenti, (see p. 16), watered by springs one of which has its source beneath an old building called Ta Durrensi. The Torre tal Fulia an ancient building is in this neighbourhood. To the E. of the Palace are also several enorm- ous stones in a wall above some caves, of the inhabitants of which there is an interesting account in Ciantar's *Malta Illustrata*. The neighbouring village of Siggieui or "Lord of air" so called from its commanding position has a fine church, but need not detain the traveller. It is called Città Ferdinanda. From the Inquisitor's Palace we may either return direct to the Boschetto, or enjoy a somewhat longer but most enjoyable walk along the lofty cliffs which form Malta's southern shore. Casal Dingli near the Boschetto named from an ancient Maltese family need not detain us. We may return from Verdala through Casals Zebbug "the village "of olives" which is also styled Città Rohan, and Casal Curmi. This latter name means either "the vineyard", "the head", or the waters'-meet." Casal Curmi bears the title of Città Pinto. The present church dedicated to S. Giorgio dates from 1584,

227

and was consecrated in 1731. The principal picture and the small one above it are by Mattia Preti.

Many cart builders, wheelwrights, millwrights, blacksmiths, and house carpenters dwell at Casal Curmi. We speedily reach Valletta.

228

ROUTE III.—*The Southern and Eastern Villages.*

Casals Luca, Micabiba, and Crendi.—The Macluba.—
Hagiar Khem.—Casals Zurrico, Safi and Chircop.—Casal Zeitun,
and its Procession.—Casals Tarxien, Paola, and Zabbar.

CROSSING the Marsa (p.163.) we ascend a slope and enter Casal Luca or the "village of poplars" inhabited by stone masons and quarrymen. The church dedicated to St. Andrew was rebuilt in 1650, consecrated in 1783, and contains three pictures by Mattia Preti. The whole of this district is one vast quarry. After the stone has been removed, the virgin soil found in the fissures is formed into fertile gardens. The first turn to the right leads to Micabiba and Crendi. Note the stone threshing floors on which muzzled oxen tread out the corn. Micabiba is distinguished by its square tower and mounds of quarry refuse. Its inhabitants are stone-cutters, and many of them attain a great age. Micabiba "the pleasant place" has a church dedicated to the Assumption of the B. V. M. which was completed in 1689; and consecrated in 1750. Casal Crendi, 6 miles distant from Valletta "the place of destruction" is a small agricultural village, wherein beggars abound. Its church was commenced in 1685 and finished in 1712. The principal picture is by Rocco Buhagiar. About half a mile from the village is the extraordinary chasm of the Macluba or " ruined place." This is an immense oval depression said to measure 350 feet by 200, with a depth of 130 feet. Obtain the key, and descend

229

by a rugged staircase to the garden below. The remains of a cistern are visible. The subsidence of a cave caused by an earthquake shock may account for this remarkable depression. Tradition says that a village formerly stood here, which was swallowed up on account of the wickedness of the dwellers therein. The Macluba is the very place for a picnic. A rural policeman will be found useful to keep the beggars in check. Close by stands a little chapel dedicated to St. Matthew.

A quarter of an hour's drive from the Macluba brings us to Hagiar Khem or the "Stones of Worship," one of the ancient high places of Baal which resembles the famous structures of Mycenæ. Several altars are *in situ* and broken fragments of others strew the ground. Many of the stones are pitted with small punctures, the well known Phœnician sacred emblem. Excavations were made here a few years since and seven Phœnician deities were brought to light, which are now in the Public Museum. (See the Guide to the Museum, by Dr. C. Vassallo, F. S. A.)

The various chambers of the temples were formerly separated by doors secured by bolts working in grooves. Ropes seem to have run through holes cut in the stones, and the mortice and tenon fastening was evidently in use. A mile distant from Hagiar Khem are the ruins of another temple called Mnaidra "the sheep fold" said to have been dedicated to Esculapius. It stands on the cliff nearer the sea to the W. of Hagiar Khem, is in a much better state of preservation, and should be visited.

Let us return through Casal Zurrico. This is a large village with some good houses. There is

230

a small inn near the church, recommended to travellers of modest requirements kept by Felice Ferraro. The present church is dedicated to St. Catherine, was commenced in 1634, completed in 1656, and consecrated in 1731. There are several pictures by Mattia Preti. Zurrico means "blue" and strange to say, many of the people have blue eyes. Others derive the name from a neighbouring creek called "the blue sea," whilst a third derivation is from a word meaning "east" on account of its position.

In a street near the church are some huge stones forming part of a house. These are of either Phœnician or Greek workmanship, and are fully described in M. Houel's Voyage Pittoresque (1687) in the Public Library. In the adjoining hamlet of Bubakra "the Father of cows" is a large square tower, and in the church of San Leone is a triptych formerly belonging to the now demolished church on the islet rock of Filfla. (p. 198.)

Between Zurrico and the next village Safi are to be seen in Str. S. Andrea some huge stones forming part of a wall similar to those at Zurrico. In an adjoining field on the right are large tanks, probably Phœnician, empty during the summer only. The word Safi means "clear, serene," and it is said that its inhabitants have never suffered from the plague. It is a small agricultural village. The church commenced in 1726, was completed in 1740, and consecrated in 1754.

Between Safi and Casal Chircop are the ruins of the Torre ta Giauhar, " the tower of jewels or treasure," built of immense stones and circular in form. Many Phœnician tombs exist hereabouts, and this tower which needs careful clearing out.

231

was probably erected by these hardy sailors, though some think that Arab masons reared it. The tower is somewhat difficult to find without a guide.

Chircop a small agricultural village named from an ancient Maltese family, has a church built in 1500, enlarged in 1706, and consecrated in 1782. The principal picture is by R. Caruana. Casal Gudia may be recognised by its tall spire 102 ft high ercted by subscription in 1860. The architect was W. Baker, Esqre. The word Gudia means "the lofty hill." The church with the dedication of the Assumption of the B. V. M. dates from 1656. To our right is Casal Luca, but we incline to the left and enter Casal Asciach, a quiet secluded village on the highest ground in this part of the island. The signal tower has conveyed much intelligence between Valletta and Marsa Scirocco. The word Asciach means "delight." Tha church was built between 1733 and 1756.

We soon reach the large village of Zeitun wherein much lace is manufactured. Its name means "abundance of olive oil" The old parish church was commonly called Biskallin or "the sons of Sicily" from an ancient chapel erected near Marsa Scala in the 12fth century. The present church was commenced in 1692 and consecrated in 1742. On the Wednesday after Easter there is a solemn procession in this village: that of Our Lady of Piety. This procession is variously said to have originated after a deliverance from locusts, from the plague of 1675-6, or from a Turkish fleet which was wrecked near Marsa Scirocco. Maltese brides used formerly to stipulate that their husbands should take them to the next festival at Zeitun, seat them

232

upon a wall, and buy them a piece of hemp-seed sweetmeat. To our left is Casal Tarxien through which pass all the most direct roads to the east of the island. The Bouverie Aqueduct constructed in 1844-5 which brings water from Fauara, Imtahlep, &c, to the Three Cities, passes near Casals Crendi, Luca, and Tarxien. The name Tarxien (pronounced Tarshien), recalls the fact that the Carthaginians had a settlement here in days of old. The church was built between 1610 and 1618. Casal Paola farther to the west than Tarxien was founded in 1626 by the Grand Master Antonio de Paola. Being only two centuries old, Casal Paola is also called Casal Nuova or "the new village." The Civil Prison is near this casal. The church dedicated to S. Ubaldesca was built in 1626 by the Grand Master Antonio de Paula. Vittorio Cassar was the architect, but the church is still unfinished, and the village has never been densely populated.

A straight road lined with trees leads to Casal Zabbar, the inhabitants of which are employed in cotton weaving and agriculture. The word Zabbar means "the drinker" and in 1797 it received from the last Grand Master the name of Cittá Hompesch, as Casal Siggieui did that of Cittá Ferdinanda. The French made a desperate sortie in 1798, but were unable to capture this village. In the neighbourhood are the remains of an amphitheatre. The church dedicated to our Lady of Favour was commenced in 1641, completed in 1696, and consecrated in 1784. The principal picture is by Stefano Erardi. This church is much frequented on Tuesdays, especially in Lent, and is held in high esteem by seamen.

233

Less than a mile distant is Zabbar Gate protected by a lunette. An infantry detachment is quartered at this gate upon which is a bust of the Grand Master Nicholas Cotoner with the date 1675. The inscription below the bust ends somewhat as follows:

On the gate his name,
In the city, world, his fame.

We re-enter the Cotonera Lines, and return to Valletta.

CHAPTER III.

Gozo and Comino.

GOZO, our sister island is decidedly greener than the mass of heated stones commonly styled Malta. Some shooting is occasionally to be had there, it can boast of noble cliffs, and of some relics of remote antiquity, and it has occasionally been selected as the very place to spend a honey-moon.

Gozo may be reached from Valletta by an omnibus to Marfa starting daily at 7. 0. a. m. from Saliba's stables in the Strada Mercanti. From Marfa a ferry boat crosses to Migiarro in Gozo. Fare from Valletta to Migiarro 2s. Those who prefer a voyage varying in length from two to six hours may take passage in one of the sailing craft which ply between the islands. Fare about 1s. For a description of the Overland Route to Gozo see Part III. Chaps. 1 and 2.

Midway between Malta and Gozo which are separated by the straits of Flieghi is

THE ISLAND OF COMINO.

This small island, or rather islands, for though fragmentary it is yet further subdivided into Comino and Cominotto was anciently known as Hephœstia or Phœstia, that is the island of Hephœstos or Vulcan, and Cluverius speaks of it under the name of Lampas or "the Lamp." Its present name seems to be an Arabic corruption of the Greek word "Xi-

235

meni" which means "adjacent." Its length from N. E. to S. W. is two miles, its breadth one mile, and its circumference about five miles. The channel to the west is called the Passage of Gozo, and that to the east the Passage of Malta. Both are good and safe, with from twelve to thirty fathoms water and a sandy bottom. The straits of Flieghi with the islands of Comino and Cominotto have been depressed by geological disturbances to a depth of about 400 feet which has brought the marl into juxtaposition with the crystalline limestone. Commino is partially cultivated and is famous for watermelons. Rabbits are plentiful and the pheasant was formerly to be met with, but is now rare or extinct. In the middle ages Comino was a lair of Saracens. and in order to deprive the enemy of this retreat, the Grand Master A. Wignacourt in the year 1618 ordered the erection of a tower which is still standing. The architect was Vittorio Cassar, the son of the celebrated Gerolamo Cassar. The profits derived from the cultivation of oats on this island were formerly applied in accordance with a Decree of Council passed in 1618 to the maintenance of this fort, and to the general expenses of government. King Alfonso at the request of the University of Malta imposed in 1419 a duty upon wine for the defence of Comino. An ancient tomb and leaden pipes found here from time to time together with remains of buildings and of a church dedicated to St. Nicholas, seem to prove that this island had formerly more than its present number of thirty inhabitants. A very ancient chapel dedicated to the B. V. Mary desecrated in 1667 and restored in 1716 stands near the bay of the same. name, and there

236

are also a large government house, and a few peasants' dwellings. The island may be easily reached by boat from Migiarro in Gozo. It possesses several lovely caves, some of which can be entered in a boat, and several cliffs on the southern shore resemble at a distance the figures of animals. Still we hesitate to endorse the sentiments of Giovanni Fratta who in the 14th Canto of the Malteide sings the praises of Comino as being

"An ample, rich, and lovely land."

The Bay of Migiarro the name of which means "the carting place," is the principal commercial port in Gozo. The Grand Master Garzes erected a tower for its defence, some remains of which are still visible upon the heights, but the guns lie buried in the beach below, loved by bathers for its firm hard sand. The cliff of Ras et Taffal 150 feet in height is crowned by Fort Chambray which was captured by the French in 1798, only to be again surrendered ere long. Like many of the other forts in Malta and Gozo, it owes its existence to the liberality of one of the members of the Order of St. John. It was commenced in 1749 by the Bailiff Francesco de Chambray, a Norman knight, who expended a great deal of money upon it. He died whilst the works were in progress but left one fifth of his estate to ensure their completion. Even this proved insufficient, and the Order made up the deficiency, calling the stronghold "Fort Chambray." If you have any regard

237

for personal beauty, we will leave Migiarro at once,
for, as the Maltese policeman on duty at the landing place remarks, there are "plenty of mosquitoes on this station." But it is worth while, if
you belong to the pachydermata, have as little
sensibility as a rhinoceros or an alligator, and
have ruined your complexion (if you ever possessed one) in early youth, to linger at Migiarro
to examine the baskets of fish brought in by the
boats. All I know is that Mr. Frank Buckland
would be ready, desirous, and eager to let sandflies
and mosquitoes do their worst, if only he might
watch the ever-changing hues and multiform phases
of finny life here to be seen in abundance. But
our car is waiting. Our triumphal chariot is drawn
by a mule, and can boast of only a couple of wheels.
Our "Joe" takes his seat beneath the white awn-
ing which shields us from the sun, and up the
long hill we go. Every native of Malta is addressed as "Joe," by Thomas Atkins, even as West
Indian negroes one and all answer to the appellation of "Jim." For three miles we drive between
low stone walls, getting lovely glimpses of the Straits
of Flieghi, which look, from our point of view,
more like one of those fair lakes which nestle amid
the hills of Cumberland or Wales. The fields are
well cultivated, but what skulls the population of
Gozo must be possessed of! Any ordinary English-
man would infallibly suffer from sun-stroke if he were
to attempt to do half a day's work where these
patient, enduring, sun-browned, and it is to be
feared miserably under-paid peasants, toil uncomplain-
ingly month after month. What a pace we are
going at! "Joe" and his mule are evidently in

238

haste to get home, and the stone walls fly past us at a marvellous rate.

Ere long we breast a slope, and enter Rabato the quiet old world capital of Gozo. Lace making is the staple occupation of its inhabitants, and from every open door you hear the ceaseless clicking of the bobbins, which fly quickly to and fro, apparently bent upon solving the problem of perpetual motion. Very eastern are the faces of the workers, very lustrous are their eyes, and very guttural is their speech, for here in Gozo the language of the people is far more akin to the original Arabic, than is the dialect in common use in Malta. In Roman days Gozo was a municipality, and in the last century the attacks of the Algerine pirates were so fierce and frequent, that no Gozitan dared remain in the open country after sunset. *Mais nous Anglais avons changé tout cela.* There are plenty of flies and mosquitoes at Rabato, and if you kill one all his acquaintances are certain to attend the funeral. A comfortable little hotel, the "Imperial" by name, receives the traveller within its hospitable doors, and Peppina, the hostess, is one of the most motherly natives of these islands that I have as yet discovered. Take up that universally to be found volume, "The Visitors' Book," and there shall you read alike in prose and rhyme the praises of Peppina. Suffice it to say that you will be well lodged and fed, and, a word in your ear! for most moderate cost, at this hotel. •There is also the Calypso Hotel nearly opposite the "Imperial."

Wheat sufficient for home consumption is grown in Gozo, barley and cotton are exported, fruit and vegetables are sent to Malta, as are also grapes,

239

honey, poultry, fish, and apples, as well as small and large cheeses, made from the milk of the long-legged, long-necked sheep which are everywhere to be seen. In their funeral ceremonies the Gozitans resemble Eastern nations, and the male survivors sometimes allow their hair to remain uncut for several months after the death of a relative. But come along, let us climb to the summit of the citadel! What a grand view we have from these half-ruined and crumbling battlements. Almost all Gozo and half the island of Malta lie stretched at our feet. This must have been a formidable stronghold in bygone days of chivalry, but now the works are crumbling piece-meal. They are utterly useless, being commanded by high ground on several sides. This old citadel of Rabato will, however, always have an interest for Englishmen, for in 1551, after an unsuccessful attempt upon Malta, Sinam Pasha cruelly ravaged Gozo. Gelatian de Sessa the Governor made but a feeble defence, leaving the inhabitants to protect themselves. An English knight put himself at their head, until a shot from the Turkish batteries struck him down, and Gozo was taken, the Governor and 6,000 captives being carried into hopeless slavery. Close to the Augustinian convent are a number of monumental stones which the Gozitans gravely assure you were erected in memory of a number of African bishops, who died in the island on their way to attend a general council. Horror of horrors, what would be the result, if an attack of measles were to break out amongst the Lords Spiritual on their way to some Pan Anglican synod? The walk from Rabato to the lighthouse at

240

Guirdan is very pleasant, and the view over sea and land is very fine.

But we have lingered long enough at Rabato. We must take a hasty glance at the Giants' Tower. Bidding farewell to Peppina, we again mount a country car and off we go. The pace is, if possible, swifter than before, for our road lies down hill and Jehu is reckless. At length we slacken speed and begin to climb a long hill, at the summit of which is the Giants' Tower. Permission to visit it must be obtained either from the owner (24 Strada Mercanti Valletta, Malta) or from his agent at Rabato. It is always freely given, but application must be made, or admission will be refused by the tenant. A short walk brings us to this remarkable ruin, which was formerly the Temple of Astarte, the Phœnician Venus. We shall quote Dr. Badger: "The enclosure is of a circular form, and measures twenty five paces in diameter. It is formed by a wall of enormous masses of rock, piled up one upon another, without mortar or cement. It is entered by two massive doorways, constructed of four stones 18 feet high and five feet wide. These lead into separate ranges of rooms, each range laid out in the same order, and only differing in extent. At the extremity of the building, opposite the entrance is a semi-circular area, the floor of which rises higher than any other part, and is paved at the threshold with very large hewn stones." These are pitted with Phœnician sacred marks. " Besides these, there are two oblong chambers in each range, which cross the area at right angles, and which are separated by a thick wall, except along the nave, which is left open, and forms a second entrance into the inner room. There exist also the

241

remains of an oven, and a conical stone about 2½ feet in height and one foot in diameter, which was doubtless one of the deities of the temple. "To the right of the second apartment is a shallow circular concavity imbedded in the floor, with a raised rim resembling those which are met with in the Catacombs of Città Vecchia. In the doorways are holes for bolts and loops cut in the stone as fastenings for the ropes with which victims were bound. The figure of a serpent is roughly carved on a stone close by the entrance of the second apartment of the smaller temple." Leaving this most interesting relic of Phœnician idolatry with reluctance, we have the village of Nadur on our left hand, and learn that from thence come most of the apples with which Malta and Gozo are supplied. On reaching the little port of Migiarro once more, we are fortunate enough to meet with a friend who has run down in one of the "Mosquito Fleet," as the Royal Malta Yacht Squadron is often styled. Not much persuasion is necessary on his part to induce us to circumnavigate Gozo, and ere long we are standing out of the Bay of Migiarro with a fresh breeze. There is a coral fishery on this coast and soon the Bay of Shlendi opens out from which a ravine stretches inland for a mile. Cape Bombardo towers high in air, and we must not hug the iron-bound shore too closely. The Bays of Shlendi and Duejra offer opportunities for a hostile landing, but are of course guarded by fortifications. In the Bay of Duejra rises the General's Rock, about 150 feet from the shore on which grows the famous Fungus Melitensis formerly sent by the Grand Master to crowned heads. It grows to the height of five inches and blossoms in April

16

242

or May. When fresh it is of a dark red colour and rather soft, but when dried it is nearly black and becomes hard and solid. It was formerly much used in the cure of dysentery, hæmorrhage, and cutaneous diseases, also of syphilis, when given in broth or wine. A similar fungus is found at Tunis, and near Trapani. Also in the islands of Lampedusa, Favigliana and Ronciglio, on the coasts of Leghorn, and in the neighbourhood of Pisa, and some say, also in Jamaica.

Tieka Zerka or the "Azure Window" near the General's Rock is a great curiosity easily accessible from Rabato. It is a natural arch, the grandeur of which must be seen to be appreciated.

As we round Cape Demetri the breeze freshens and ere long we are abreast of the lighthouse at Guirdan which stands 400 feet above the sea level and is visible at a distance of 24 miles. It shows a revolving light once every minute. From this point news of the coming of steamers is telegraphed to Valletta, giving timely warning to traders and friends alike. Marsa el Forn, from which a remarkably good road leads to Rabato through a highly cultivated district, is a favourite summer resort. There is a safe anchorage here, as well as abundant water. If the position were not so isolated, Marsa el Forn would have been the metropolis of the island, as the Council of the Order of St. John had almost determined to remove the city to this spot. As we come abreast of Ras el Cala the eastern extremity of Gozo, we go under the stern of a P. and O. steamer. We wish her a prosperous voyage, as she departs homeward bound, whilst, running

243

before a favouring breeze, we are not long in reaching Valletta, having thoroughly enjoyed our visit to Gozo.

The Author will be much obliged for fuller information or suggestions for the improvement and correction of this Guide.

ADDENDA.

In April 1880 the Word Rate Tariff composed of the rate applicable to the actual number of words, plus an additional rate or grundtax of five words per telegram was adopted by the Telegraph Companies. A telegram of eleven words to Great Britain costs 5s. 6d. plus the initial or grundtax of 2s. 6d., or a total of 8s. Rates for other places may be ascertained on application at the various telegraph offices (p. 56.).

Attached to the Public Library is a small Museum originated by De Rohan, and arranged during the rule of Sir W. Reid which is well worthy of a visit. Description is needless as an admirable catalogue by Dr. Vassallo is lent to visitors on application. Admission free during the hours that the Library is open. This Museum deserves to be more known and appreciated than it is at present.

The price of Boxes at the Opera per month varies from £1 to £5.

The Revd W. K. R. Bedford says "I was fortunate enough to find in the Academy at Marseilles the design of the tapestry in the Council Chamber, Valletta. It is by Desportes, and is rendered with wonderful faithfulness in the tapestry." (See p. 96.)

246

On April 23rd 1880 a new Tariff for Carriages came into operation.

Fares by time at a speed of five miles an hour.

One horse carriage for not more than 15 minutes 6d. Under half an hour 1s. Under one hour 1s. 6d. For every quarter of an hour beyond the first hour 4d.

Two horse carriages a fare and a half.

Fares by distance.—One horse carriage for any distance not exceeding half a mile 3d. Not exceeding one mile 6d. For every half mile beyond the first mile 2d.

Two horse carriages for one-mile 1s. For every half mile beyond the first mile 6d.

Between one hour after sunset and one hour before sunrise these fares are increased one half.

Fares from one place to another within Valletta, Floriana, Sliema, or St. Julian's 3d.

From Valletta to Floriana 4d.

From Valletta to the San Giuseppe Road, Pietà, Misida, or Ta Braxia Cemetery 10d. To Casal Paola, the Addolorata Cemetery, or to Birchircara, Curmi, Tarxien, Luca, and Sliema 1s. 2d. To Zabbar, Zeitun, Gudia, Asciach, Zebbug, Balzan, Attard, Lia, or St. Julian's 1s. 8d. To Musta, Naxaro, Gargur, Siggieui, and Pembroke Camp 2s. To Città Vecchia, Rabato, Zurrico, and Crendi 2s. 6d. To the Boschetto or Inquisitor's Palace 3s. To Gebel Kim and Mnaidra, or St. Paul's Bay 4s. From Sliema to St. Julian's 5d. From Sliema to Pembroke Camp 8d. From Valletta to Cospicua, Senglea, or Vittoriosa 1s. 8d.

Some say that the two Baraccas (p.p. 118, 135.) were unroofed in consequence of the Priests' Re-

247

volution in 1775. Others state that the French garrison being in want of firewood during the two years' siege, reduced these buildings to their present condition.

The Turkish Fleet in 1565 did not assemble in the port of Migiarro in Gozo, but in that of Gineyna tal Migiarro in Malta (p. 201).

Sig. Rosario Denaro has lately been appointed Agent for the Florio and Rubattino Lines of Steamers (p. 58.). Office, No. 35 Marina. Weekly departures for Tunis. For Tripoli direct every Wednesday.

The Author's thanks are due to Major Ewing, Staff Paymaster, for his kind correction of a portion of the proof sheets.

CORRIGENDA.

Please read Page 7, line 6, 50 leagues.
,, 11, ,, 23, and p. 14 line 1, Marsa Scirocco.
,, 47, ,, 3, omit the word Esq.
,, 58, ,, 16, 173 D.
,, 76, ,, 17, from £1 to £5. For one night
from 6s. 3d. to £1.
,, 84, ,, 16, Blessed.
,, 90, ,, 9, De Rohan.
,, 99, ,, 34, guests.
,, 106, ,, 16, Manse.
,, 108, ,, 14, Gerosolmitano.
,, 115, ,, 8, once again.
,, 118, ,, 2, fitting.
,, 118, ,, 25, roofed. In 1715.
,, 120, ,, 32, Fencible Artillery and Roman
Catholic.
,, 122, ,, 2, Each Auberge formerly had.
,, 122, ,, 3, this Auberge.
,, 123, ,, 5, rebuilt, enlarged, and beautified.
,, 123, ,, 28, punishments.
,, 124, ,, 13, Town Hall.
,, 124. ,, 31, a Maltese Capuchin Friar.
,, 127, ,, 31, large.
,, 130, ,, 3, from 10d.
,, 133, ,, 20, St. Omobono.
,, 141, ,, 2, and p. 143 line 5, Pavilion.
,, 141, ,, 4, Wignacourt and Bouverie Aqueducts.
,, 143, ,, 18, sleeping accomodation.
,, 144, ,, 20, Convent.
,, 159, ,, 11, close by.
,, 162, ,, 20, 15,000 persons.
,, 171, ,, 4, announced.
,, 188, ,, 1, was.

INDEX.

Dedication and Preface. ... ... p. 3

PART FIRST.

CHAPTER I.

THE MALTESE ISLANDS.—Situation. Bays and Inlets. Population. Wages. Food. Greatest elevation of the islands. Appearance from the sea. The ancient Athalantis. Evidences of diminution of area. 7

CHAPTER II.

HISTORICAL OUTLINE.—Malta in the days of the Giants. The Phœnicians, Greeks, Carthaginians, and Romans. Arab Rule. Arrival of Count Roger. French and German Sovereigns. The Knights of St. John and the Great Siege. Decay of the Order. Malta surrenders to Buonaparte. Capitulation of General Vaubois. English Governors in Malta. 12

List of Grand Masters. 50

PART SECOND.

CHAPTER I.

THE CITY OF VALLETTA.—Situation of Valletta. Foundation of the city. Streets of stairs. Arrangement of streets. Houses, Lodgings and Hotels. Boat and Carriage fares. Postal in-

252

formation. Telegraph Companies. Medical Men, and Merchants. Lines of Steamers, and Steam Ship Agents. Consuls. Weights and Measures. 51

CHAPTER II.

CLIMATE.—Mild in winter. Prevailing winds. Gregale and Scirocco. Sultry in summer. Winter attractions for invalids. 60

CHAPTER III.

THE MONTHS IN MALTA.— 64

CHAPTER IV.

STREETS AND BUILDINGS.—Porta Reale. Strada Reale. Opera House. Union Club. Church of St. John. Courts of Justice. Public Library. Governor's Palace. St. George's Square. The Borsa, and Fort St. Elmo. Strada Stretta, the old duelling ground. Strada Forni. Auberge de France, the Bakery, and the Auberge de Baviere. Strada Zecca and the Mint. St. Paul's Church, and the Auberge d' Aragon. Marsamuscetto Steps and neighbourhood. Walk round the ramparts. ... 74

CHAPTER V.

STREETS AND BUILDINGS (Continued).—St. James' Cavalier, and the Auberge d'Italia. Upper Baracca, Church and Garden. View from Upper Baracca. Churches of Vittoria, and Sta Caterina d'Italia. Auberge d'Italia, Palazzo Parisio, and Church of S. Giacomo. The Castellania, and Post Office. Monte di Pietà, and Market. Church of Our Lady of Damascus. Jesuits' Church, University, and Lyceum. The Dominican and Anime Purganti Churches. Military Hospital, and the Camerata. Cem-

253

etery, Nibbia Church, Hospital for Incurables, and Orphan Asylum. Strada S. Paolo, and the Church of St. Paul Shipwrecked. Churches of the Minori Osservanti, S. Rocco, and St. Ursola. Old Slave Prison, and the Lower Baracca. Strada Levante, and the Santa Barbara Bastion. The Sultan's Garden, Nix Mangiare Stairs, Barriera, and Church of Sta Maria di Liesse. The Mina Lascaris, Custom House, and Marina.   116

CHAPTER VI.

FLORIANA.—The Suburb of Vilhena. Gates and Fortifications. The Maglio and Pavilion. Soldiers' and Sailors' Home. St. Francis' Barracks, Princess Theatre, and Capuchin Convent. Wignacourt and Bouverie Aqueducts. Churches of Sarria, and St. Publio. The Argotti Garden, Casa di Manresa, and Central Civil Hospital. Floriana Barracks, Charitable Institutions, and English Cemeteries. Sa Maison and its Recreation Ground.   141

CHAPTER VII.

PEMBROKE CAMP, ST. JULIAN'S, AND SLIEMA.—The Wimbledon of Malta. St. Julian's Bay, and the Forrest Hospital. Fougasses. Jesuit College. The Forgotten Church. Boat and Carriage fares. Cure for fever. Sliema. Officers' Bathing House, and Fort Tigné. Churches of Sliema. Fort Manoel and its island. The Lazaretto, Misida, and Hydraulic Doek. Pietà and its Cemeteries.   150

CHAPTER VIII. .

THE MARSA AND BURMOLA.—Out of Porte des Bombes. Porto Nuovo. The Marsa and the Race Course. Corradino, its fortifications and prisons. The French Creek and the Naval Canteen. Burmola, its fortifications and gates. The Coto-

254

nera Hospital. Churches and Convents. The Dockyard and
Marina. 162

CHAPTER IX.

SENGLEA, VITTORIOSA AND FORT RICASOLI.—Origin of Senglea.
Churches and Convents. H. M. S. Hibernia, Fort St. Angelo,
and the Temple of Juno. The Victualling Yard, Slave Prison,
and Naval Bakery. The Old Palace and Hospital. Churches
and Convents. San Lorenzo. Soldiers' Institute. Column of
Victory. Inquisitor's and Bishop's Palaces. La Vallette's Observatory. Salvadore Gate, and Calcara Bay. Naval Cemetery and Hospital. Rinella Bay and Fort Ricasoli. ... 173

PART THIRD.

CHAPTER I.

ROUND THE COAST.—Naval Rifle Range and Grazia Tower.
Geological Formations. Marsa Scala, S. Tommaso Bay, and
Delimara. Marsa Scirocco, and St. Lucian's Tower. Fossæ,
Melcarte's Temple, and the Cave of Darkness. Bir Zebbugia
and its fortifications. Benghisa and Hassan's Cave. The
Southern Shore. Fauara and Filfla. Ruts at Fom-er-Rieh.
Marfa. Melleha, its church and bay. Palace of Selmoon. St
Paul's Bay and Island. Shipwreck of St. Paul. Neighbour-
hood of the Bay. Saline Bay, Ghallis Rock, Maddalena Bay,
and Casal Gargur. 187

CHAPTER II.

COUNTRY EXCURSIONS.—ROUTE I. — *To and from St. Paul's
Bay.*—The San Giuseppe Road. Villages of Curmi, Birchircara, Lia, and Nasciar. Syndics and Villages. The "Great
Fault." The Valley of Honey. St. Paul el Milki. Musta Church. Palace and Gardens of Sant' Antonio. ... 216

255

Route II —*Città Vecchia and Neighbourhood.*—Casal Attard and the Lunatic Asylum. Città Vecchia, its Sanatorium and Cathedral. St. Paul's Grotto and the Catacombs. Bingemma, Nadur, and Imtarfa. Mount Verdala and the Boschetto. The Inquisitor's Palace. Casals Siggieui and Zebbug. ... 220

Route III.—*The Southern and Eastern Villages.*—Casals Luca, Micabiba, and Crendi. The Macluba. Hagiar Khem. Casals Zurrico, Safi, and Chircop. Casal Zeitun and its Procession. Casals Tarxien, Paola, and Zabbar. 228

Gozo and Comino.— 234
Addenda. 245
Corrigenda. 249
Index. 251

THE END.

J. E. Mortimer & Co.

" GIBRALTAR SHERRY "
SHIPPERS,
GIBRALTAR.

BRANCHES:
MALTA, and 21, Water Lane, LONDON.

———o———

SOLE PROPRIETORS AND SHIPPERS OF
THE CELEBRATED
"GIBRALTAR SHERRY"
"FRONTERA"

The finest Natural Pale Dry Sherry ever produced
in Spain.—Free from acidity and heat,
and with fine dietetic qualities.

PRICE FREE ON BOARD, GIBRALTAR,
£ 14 per Qr. Cask of 13 doz.
£ 7 „ 10 per Octave of 6½ doz.
28/- per doz. bottles duty paid•in Malta.

ALSO SHIPPERS OF THE CELEBRATED GIBRALTAR

"MANZANILLA"
(See Next Page.)

II.

NAVAL AND MILITARY

Co - Operative Stores,

282, STRADA REALE,

J. E. Mortimer & Co.

Every description of Provisions, Groceries, Wines,
Spirits and Beers, can be obtained at about
10 per cent above the prices published
by the Service Co-operative Stores in London.
The difference in price is necessary to cover Pack-
ing, Shipping, and Freight Charges, which at the
lowest estimate amount to about 14 per cent. All
Goods Guaranteed of best quality and sold at English weight 16 oz. to the lb., the Maltese lb. having
only 14 oz.

N. B.—MILITARY AND NAVAL CANTEENS,
HOSPITALS, ETC., SUPPLIED.

III.

W. B. WHITTINGHAM & CO.

WHOLESALE AND EXPORT

BOOKSELLERS & PUBLISHERS,

Manufacturing & Export Stationers,

ACCOUNT BOOK MAKERS,

Law, Commercial, & General Printers,

LITHOGRAPHERS & ENGRAVERS.

NEWSPAPERS AND PERIODICALS
Despatched with regularity to any
part of the World.

ESTIMATES FOR PRINTING
CATALOGUES,
PAMPHLETS, TRADE CIRCULARS,
AND BOOKS
PROMPTLY SUPPLIED.

Printing Works: **4,** White Hart Court,
Bishopsgate Church.

· **91, GRACECHURCH STREET, LONDON.**

iv.

BY APPOINTMENT TO
H. R. H. THE DUKE OF EDINBURGH.

L. CRITIEN

BOOKSELLER,
STATIONER, & PRINTER,
28, *Strada San Giovanni*,
VALLETTA - MALTA.

C. CARUANA,
GROCER,
AND
WINE MERCHANT,
31 & 32, *Strada Nuova, Marina*,
VALLETTA—MALTA.

Ship Supplier, Dead and Live Stock.
Orders executed on the shortest notice.
Bills on London Cashed
at the Lowest Rate of Exchange. ·

v.

TO PASSENGERS, CAPTAINS, & OFFICERS
OF VESSELS CALLING AT MALTA.

THE WINDSOR CASTLE
HOTEL,
REFRESHMENT ROOMS,
TEA GARDENS,
AND MUSEUM OF CURIOSITIES

IS SITUATE

22, *Strada Zaccaria*,

which is directly opposite the principal
entrance to St. John's Church.

Refreshments Furnished At all Hours.

Ale, Stout, Wines, Spirits, and Liqueurs of
finest quality only.

AMERICAN FANCY DRINKS.

CLEANLINESS, COMFORT, AND

MODERATE CHARGES.

EDWARD HARRIS, *Proprietor*,

Late of London, Melbourne, & New York.

VI.

Wᵐ WATSON

[LATE G. MUIR]

BOOKSELLER AND STATIONER,

248, *Strada Reale.*

A LARGE ASSORTMENT OF PLAIN
AND FANCY STATIONERY.

Tauchnitz Edition of British Authors.

PERFUMERY, FANCY GOODS, CUTLERY,
TOILET SOAPS, BRUSHES & COMBS.

PHOTOGRAPHIC VIEWS,

Orders taken for Periodicals, Newspapers, &c.

Printing and Binding.

CRICKETING WAREHOUSE.—FENCING
GLOVES, BALLS, GAMES, &c. &c. &c.

VII.

H. P. Truefitt,
HAIR-DRESSER,
HATTER,
Hosier, Perfumer, & Glover.

308 & 309 STRADA-REALE, MALTA.

Exactly Opposite the Opera House.

Branch of the well known firm of 20 & 21 Burlington Arcade, London. Brighton, Aldershot, Sandhurst, &c.

An order given at this establishment will be completed and delivered to any address in England before arrival of steamers.

PARCELS FORWARDED TO ENGLAND

At ONE SHILLING per cubic foot or under.

Baggage, Oranges, &c., forwarded to any address in England or the Colonies.

GOODS OBTAINABLE

from all the London Co-operative Stores at $2\frac{1}{2}$ per cent advance on their Price Lists.

Freight not included.

TEN PER CENT DISCOUNT ALLOWED FOR CASH,

and Fifteen per Cent to Members of Co-operative Stores and Subscribers to H. P. TRUEFITT'S Toilet Club. Agency transactions, attendances, and subscriptions excepted.

VIII.

M. A. CROCKFORD & SON,

General Drapers,

SILK MERCERS,

MILLINERS,

DRESSMAKERS,

UPHOLSTERERS, CABINET MAKERS,

AND

General House Furnishers,

AGENTS FOR MAPPIN BROTHERS'
CELEBRATED CUTLERY

AND

ELECTRO PLATED GOODS.

257, 258, Strada Reale, and

28, STRADA ST. LUCIA,

AND

86, STRADA PONENTE,

Valletta–Malta.

IX.

HOSKIN & CO.

DRAPERS,

Milliners & Dress-makers,

FANCY GOODS, UNDER CLOTHING, &c.

292D, Strada Reale,

Valletta = Malta.

HOSKIN & CO.

Wholesale & Retail

GROCERS,

WINE & SPIRIT MERCHANTS,

288, Strada Reale,

Valletta = Malta.

BILLS CASHED.

x.

BY APPOINTMENT TO H. R. H. THE PRINCE OF WALES.

V. MARICH & CO
TOBACCONISTS
44, Palace Square,
MALTA.

Established A. D. 1838.

ALSO REFRESHMENTS TO BE HAD.

F. BLACKLEY,
ENGLISH
BREAD & BISCUIT BAKER,
CONFECTIONER, &c.

By Appointment to H. R. H. the Duke of Edinburgh.

No, 21 Strada Reale,
VALLETTA-MALTA.

ALLSOPS'S & BASS'S ALES ON DRAUGHT.

GENUINE GUINNESS' STOUT
AND
BASS' ALE,

In Bottles at the usual low prices;
Viz: Stout at 3s. and 6s. per dozen.
Ale at 4s. and 7s. 6d. per do.

NOW IN EXCELLENT CONDITION AT

R. KIND'S,

287, Strada Reale, Valletta.

☞ Orders left at the above Depôt, will receive prompt and careful attention. Carriage Free.

XII.

LONDON STUDIO
Malta.

DAVISON & CIANTAR PREZIOSI
PHOTOGRAPHERS.
PALACE SQUARE ENTRANCE
133 Strada Teatro, and
134 Strada Stretta.

VIEWS OF MALTA.

This is the only House in Malta employing a Complete Staff of London Artists where every description of work is executed the same as in London, from the delicate Miniature on ivory, to the beautiful life size in Monochrome, Oil or Water Colour. On Carbon,— Opal — Ivory — Paper — Canvas &c. Specimens to be seen at the

SHOW ROOMS.

A. DIACONO

ARMY & NAVY
TAILOR & OUTFITTER

LADIES' RIDING HABITS.

GREAT STOCK OF CLOTHING &c.

Hats, Caps, Scarfs, and other Articles Supplied.

295, & 296, STRADA REALE,
Between the Union Club and the Opera House
Valletta, - Malta.

xiv.

E. N. ARCHER,

303/7, STR. REALE, & 46/8, STR. MEZZODI, VALLETTA-MALTA.

Opposite the New Opera House.

Draper, Hosier, and Haberdasher,

MILLINER,

DRESS & MANTLE MAKER

FAMILY MOURNING,

TOY & CRICKET WAREHOUSE,

LADIES' AND CHILDREN'S BOOT AND SHOE DEPOT,
LADIES' AND GENTLEMEN'S OUTFITTING,
GLOVES, PERFUMERY, CORSETS, ETC.
BILLS AND BANK NOTES EXCHANGED.

SOLE AGENT FOR THE UNDERSIGNED.

HINK's *Patent Triple Action Extinguisher Duplex Lamps.*

ANGLO - BAVARIAN BREWERY COMPANY,
In Wood and Bottles.

INDIAN CO-OPERATIVE AGENCY.

Constantine's Cooking Ranges.
Horniman's Pure Tea.
Prof: Hermann's Vermin Destroyer.

CURTISS & SONS, PORTSMOUTH,
General Carriers and Forwarding Agents.

xv.

CURTISS & SONS
RAILWAY & SHIPPING AGENTS
BROAD STREET
PORTSMOUTH.

———o———

AGENTS FOR
THE UNION S. S. CO. ROYAL
MAIL STEAMERS.

ALLAN LINE OF AMERICAN STEAMERS.

LONDON BRIGHTON & SOUTH COAST AND MIDLAND RAILWAY COMPANIES.

OFFICERS BAGGAGE, ETC. WAREHOUSED, SHIPPED,
CLEARED AND FORWARDED
TO ALL PARTS OF THE WORLD.

AGENTS ABROAD;
MADDEN & Co.—*Elphinstone Circle,* BOMBAY.
J. SACCONE, — GIBRALTAR.
E. N. ARCHER,—*Str. Reale,* VALLETTA-MALTA.

XVI.

JOSEPH AZZOPARDI & Co.

Ship Chandlers,

AND GENERAL AGENTS.

PROVISIONS, BONDED AND SHIP STORES

OF EVERY DESCRIPTION.

CANVAS, HEMP, AND MANILLA ROPE

OF ALL SIZES.

WIRE RIGGING, &C.

DIVER and Diving Apparatus always ready
for use on immediate demand,
at Moderate Charges.

———

AGENTS FOR THE

BRITISH SHIP-MASTERS' & OFFICERS' PROTECTION

SOCIETY,

SUNDERLAND

———

No. 12, *MARINA, close to the Custom House*

MALTA.

XVII.

COOK'S

EXCURSIONS, TOURS,

AND

GENERAL TRAVELLING ARRANGEMENTS.

THOMAS COOK & SON,

Pioneers, Inaugurators, and Promoters of the principal systems of Tours established in Great Britain and Ireland, and on the Continent of Europe, are now giving increased attention to Ordinary Travelling Arrangements, with a view to rendering them as easy, practicable, and economical as circumstances will allow. During 38 years more than SIX MILLIONS of travellers have visited near and distant places under their arrangements; and their system of Tickets now provides for visiting the chief points of interest in the Four Quarters of the Globe.

Owing to the large number of officers of the Army and Navy and others who are continually travelling to and from Malta and all parts of the Universe Messrs. COOK & SONS have opened an office at 280, Strada Reale, Valletta, for giving information and issuing tickets by any route to all parts of Central Europe, the United States, Canada, Australia, &c. They have placed Mr. C. AQUILINA in charge of the new office, who is well known in connection with their Egypt and Palestine business.

Office opened on 1st July, 1880.

XVIII.

SMITH & CO.
STEAM SHIP AGENTS
MALTA.

SOLE AGENTS FOR
HARRIS' NAVIGATION COALS,
LARGE STOCK OF THE
BEST WELSH,
And North Country Coals always on hand.
Steamers supplied on the shortest notice
at very moderate prices.

AGENTS FOR
BRITISH INDIA STEAM NAVIGATION COMPANY.
Messrs. MACGREGOR GOW & Co. *London.*
The Moss Steam Ship Co. *Liverpool.*
The Ocean Steam Ship Co.   do.
Messrs Lamport Holt. & Co.   do.

LONDON AGENTS
MESSRS LAMBERT Brothers
85 Gracechurch St.
MESSRS HENRY CLARKE & Co.
17 GRACECHURCH St.

XIX.

ITALIAN POSTAL LINE
OF STEAMERS OF I. & V. FLORIO & CO.
OF PALERMO.

DEPARTURE FROM MALTA,
EVERY MONDAY, THURSDAY, & SATURDAY,
At 6 o'clock, p. m.

For Italy &c. in Postal Service.

Monday, For Syracuse, Catania, Messina, Naples, Genoa and Marseilles. Coincidence for the North Coast of Sicily, to Palermo, and for the Piræus, Smyrna, Salonica, Constantinople and Odessa.

Thursday. For Syracuse, Catania, Messina, and Naples. Coincidence at Catania, for Taranto, Gallipoli, Brindisi, and ports of the Adriatic.

Saturday (direct). For Messina and Naples, Legghorn, Genoa, Nizza, and Marseilles. Coincidence at Messina, for Palermo and Tunis.

On the direct voyages the fastest steamers (probably paddle) will be employed.

For freight or passage apply to
ROSARIO DENARO, *Agent.*
No. 35 Fuori la Mina.

FOR TUNIS.

Taking goods and passengers for Susa, Monastier, Mehdia, Sfax, and Gerbi, Cagliari, Leghorn, Genoa, and Marseilles.

Weekly Departures For Tripoli (Direct.)

The Italian Steamer Sardegna, Captain Canepa, will start for the above mentioned ports every Wednesday at 3 p. m. precisely.

For freight or passage apply to
ROSARIO DENARO *Agent.*
No. 35, Fuori la Mina.

xx.

O. F. GOLLCHER
STEAM SHIP AGENT
AND
General Commission Merchant
21, STRADA ZACCARIA, MALTA.

*The best Welsh, and Newcastle Coals always
ready on Lighters.*
Agents in London: Messrs. BURNESS & SONS,
138, Leadenhall Street.
Agent for the HALL LINE between Liverpool
and Bombay, calling regularly at Malta.
Also for the *Anchor Line of Peninsular and
Mediterranean First Class Steam Packets.*
Communication
between Glasgow, Liverpool, Gibraltar, Tunis,
Malta, and Alexandria.
F. HENDERSON AND COMPANY'S
Line of Steamers between London, Liverpool,
and Rangoon.
Royal Netherlands Steam Navigation Company.
Communication between Holland and the East.
Line of Steamers
between London, the Levant, and the Black Sea.
Steam Communication
Between Malta and Tunis. (Weekly departures.)

Cunard Line
BURNS & MAC IVER'S
FIRST CLASS SCREW STEAMERS
BETWEEN
Liverpool & Constantinople, Smyrna, & Alexandria,
CALLING AT
GIBRALTAR, MALTA, AND SYRA.

For rates of freight or passage apply to

CHARLES LOWE,
Agent.

XXII.

MALTA
IMPERIAL HOTEL
VALLETTA
91, Strada Santa Lucia,

BY

G. ELLUL.

———

IMPERIAL HOTEL
SLIEMA

BY

G. ELLUL.

This Establishment is situated in the highest part of Sliema and commands an uninterrupted view of Valletta, the sea and country. The apartments, suites and single, are more than usually lofty, well ventilated and elegantly furnished.

TABLE D' HOTE.

TERMS MODERATE.

DUNSFORD'S CLARENCE HOTEL

254, *Strada Reale,*

Valletta=Malta.

ESTABLISHED 1824.

For Families and Gentlemen.

TABLE D'HOTE.

WARM AND COLD BATHS.

MODERATE CHARGES.

F. DINNING PROPRIETOR.

XXIV.

GREAT BRITAIN HOTEL

42, STRADA MEZZODI

(*Near the Opera House.*)

———o———

This First Class Family Hotel is situated
in the best part of the Town.

LARGE & SMALL
SUITES OF APARTMENTS
AND BEDROOMS,

Commanding a view of the Street.
Visitors to Malta will find Home Comforts
combined with Moderate Charges.

EXCELLENT TABLE D'HOTE.

WARM AND COLD BATHS.

This Hotel which has the personal Superintendence of the Proprietor,

(C. LAWRENCE)

IS HIGHLY RECOMMENDED BY
ENGLISH FAMILIES.

xxv.

Sᵀ· GEORGE

BY

VINCENT ZAMMIT
PRIVATE LODGINGS
OPPOSITE THE OLD OPERA.

Strada Teatro No. 74.

Valletta = Malta.

HOTEL D'ANGLÉTERRE
BY

JOHN BELLUTI

Strada Sta. Lucia. Entrance No. 34, Strada Stretta.

Every accomodation for Families & Gentlemen
visiting the island.
Well Furnished Rooms. Excellent
Table d' Hôte.

(ESTABLISHED 1856).

Valletta = Malta.

XXVI.

AN UNKNOWN POEM ON A WELL KNOWN SPOT.

Now as the Sun gains height and strength,
And days are stretching out their length,
'Tis well to know some shelter'd spot,
To cool our thirst when 'tis so hot.
A shady place I would suggest,
Where weary, parched, or "peckish" guest,
May calm enjoy, 'mong trees and shrubbery,
The blessings of a quiet snuggery.
Within the WINDSOR CASTLE's walls,
Are fresh and green embower'd stalls,
Hid from the throng'd and busy street,
Affording all a cool retreat.
Near, and in front, St. John's Church door,
The street's direct and straight before,
Call'd Zaccaria, Twenty Two,
But at the front there's nought to view:
'Tis when the house we enter in
Our int'rest and delight begin.
There ease and quiet reign sublime,
Choice Drinks, made antidote to clime.
Refresh and cheer our drooping "sprites,"
Aud stimulate our appetites.
The cheapest Lunches have such zest,
We bless OLD HARRIS and the rest,

XXVII.

For his cheap bills of fare I think,
Exhaust the lists of food and drink.
He caters well, just go see him,
And his Museum kept so trim,
Cocktails, grins, and *smiles* preparing
Prairie Oysters so ensnaring;
Pleasing all with well spun "cuffers,"
Anecdotes of "ancient buffers,"
And yarns both truthful and polite
For HARRIS is "Cosmopolite;"
Treats all his friends as they desire,
His suavity you must admire.
He loves to please, but not for "pelf,"
For pleasing *us,* he's pleased *himself;*
But call on him and then decide,
From St. John's Church 'tis but a stride,
Call morning, noon, or e'en at night,
He'll welcome you with much delight.

THE WINDSOR CASTLE

REFRESHMENT ROOMS & GARDENS,

Cleanliness, Dispatch, Comfort and Moderate Charges.

HARRIS, *(Cosmopolite)*

PROPRIETOR,

Late of London, Melbourne and New York.

XXVIII.

V. FALZON

LATE

J. BUCKLER & Co.

NAVAL & MILITARY TAILOR,

HABIT MAKER &c. &c.

No. 19. *Strada Reale*

MALTA.

BY APPOINTMENT TO H. R H. THE PRINCE OF WALES

SALVATORE ZARB & CO.

ARMY AND NAVY TAILORS AND OUTFITTERS

50, Strada Reale &

97, STRADA SANTA LUCIA.

.BILLS CASHED.

ESTABLISHED 1840.

HABIT MAKERS.

VALLETTA-MALTA.

XXIX.

PAUL BONAVIA,
General Printer,
23, STR. CRISTOFORO,
VALLETTA, - MALTA.

Every description of Printing executed with taste and accuracy, at very moderate charges.

THOMAS CERAVOLO
Book - Binding
In all its branches.

———o———

82, *Strada Teatro*,
VALLETTA—MALTA.

xxx.

BY APPOINTMENT TO H. R. H. THE DUKE OF EDINBURGH.

CHARLES SHAW DALZEL & CO.

AUCTIONEERS

AND

APPRAISERS.

283, *Strada Reale.*

[AUBERGE DE PROVENCE]

VALLETTA.

BY APPOINTMENT TO H. R. H. THE PRINCE OF WALES.

FURNITURE & DECORATIONS.

John Segond and Brother,

28, STRADA SAN GIOVANNI,

[OPPOSITE ST. JOHN'S CHURCH.]

Pianos from Erard's Manufactory.
Furniture on hire at moderate prices.

WHEELER & WILSON'S
SEWING MACHINES.

WILLIAM ROTHERHAM.
ENGLISH TAILOR.
NAVAL AND MILITARY UNIFORMS.
252, STRADA REALE,
Malta.

GODFREY CRITIEN,
34, STRADA REALE,
VALLETTA,
(Opposite the Union Club).

ENGRAVER, BOOKSELLER, & STATIONER.

A Large Variety of Fancy Paper and Envelopes. Card Plates, Monograms, Crests, and Inscriptions neatly cut. Paper and Envelopes stamped from Cypher and Crest in various colors.

XXXII.

EMIDIO CRITIEN,

JEWELLER,

GOLD AND SILVER SMITH.

58, *Strada Reale*,

[OPPOSITE DUNSFORD'S HOTEL]

VALLETTA - MALTA.

LAWRENCE VASSALLO

GENERAL GROCERY

AND

PROVISION WAREHOUSE

WINES, SPIRITS, ALE, AND PORTER,

289, Strada Reale,

[NEAR THE UNION CLUB.]

XXXIII.

THE
EASTERN · TELEGRAPH COY··
LIMITED.

TARIFF per SINGLE WORD from MALTA
on and after APRIL 1st, 1880.
EUROPEAN TARIFF PER WORD WITH GRUNDTAX.

	£	s.	d.
Algeria and Tunis—Direct Cable	0	0	3
Austria	0	0	5½
Belgium	0	0	4½
Denmark...	0	0	6
France and Corsica	0	0	4
Germany...	0	0	5
Gibraltar...	0	0	6½
Great Britain	0	0	6
Heligoland	0	0	6½
Holland	0	0	5
Hungary...	0	0	6
Italy and Sardinia	0	0	5½
Luxemburg	0	0	4½
Norway	0	0	6½
Portugal	0	0	5½
Russia—in Europe	0	0	8
in Caucasus	0	0	10
Spain...vià Vigo or Carcavellos	0	0	6½
,, Marseilles and Land-lines ...	0	0	5½
,, ,, and Barcelona Cable...	0	0	7½
Sweden...	0	0	6½
Switzerland	0	0	4½

In addition to the above rates per single word, an initial charge, equal to the charge for five words, will be levied on Telegrams for all places in Europe, for example:—a Telegram of Eleven words to Great Britain will cost 5/6, plus the initial or grundtax 2/6, total 8/.

XXXIV.

EXTRA EUROPEAN TARIFF PER WORD WITHOUT GRUNDTAX.

	£	s.	d.		£	s.	d.
Russia in Asia, 1st Region ...	0	2	0	Australia ...	0	10	9
Do. 2nd	0	3	0	New Sth Wales & Queensland	0	11	0
Cyprus	0	1	1	New Zealand	0	11	11
Egypt, Alexandria	0	1	1	Cochin China	0	7	4
1st region (Cairo, Suez, &Canal Stations	0	1	4	China...	0	8	4
				Manila	0	10	2
				Japan...	0	12	7
2nd Region (Upper Egypt)	0	1	6	Madeira	0	1	8
Aden	0	3	3	St. Vincent	0	4	1
Africa, Zanzibar :..	0	7	5	Brazil,—Pernambuco	0	9	1
Mozambique...	0	8	6	Bahia and Maranham	0	12	5
Delagoa Bay...	0	8	6	Rio de Janeiro, and Para ...	0	13	8
Natal—Durban	0	8	6				
Other places...	0	9	0	Santos, Sta Catarina, and Rio Grande do Sul.	0	15	9
Cape Colony, Transvaal, and Orange Free State	0	9	0	Other places...	0	16	2
				Uruguay, Montevideo	0	15	9
India, West of Chittagong	0	4	8	Other places...	0	16	2
East of Chittagong & Ceylon	0	4	11	Argentine Republic— Buenos Ayres ...	0	16	6
				Other places ..	0	16	11
Native Burmah ...	0	5	1	Chili	1	1	8
Penang	0	5	8	Peru,—Iquique ...	1	1	2
Malacca	0	6	3	Arica & Tacna.	1	2	9
Singapore	0	6	6	Islay, Mollendo Puno and Arequipa.	1	4	4
Java	0	6	11				
Australia, —Victoria, Tasmania, South and Western				Lima & Callao.	1	7	5
				Bolivia, Autofagasta...	1	4	10

COMPANY'S STATIONS:

CENTRAL OFFICE—7, Strada Marsamuscetto, VALLETTA.

BRANCH OFFICES—95A, Strada Santa Lucia, Do.

3, Strada Ghar Illembi, SLIEMA.

April 1st, 1880. By Order,

ROBERT PORTELLI,
Manager.

xxxv.

Peninsular & Oriental Steam Navigation Company.

INCORPORATED BY ROYAL CHARTER IN 1840.

The Company's Steamers leave Malta outward—viâ Suez Canal—for Port-Said, Suez, Aden and Bombay every *Thursday*.

For Galle, Madras, Calcutta, Penang, Singapore, China, Japan and Australia every alternate *Thursday*.

The homeward steamers are due at Malta from Bombay and Aden every *Tuesday*, * and from Australia, Japan, China, Singapore, Penang, Calcutta, Madras, and Galle every alternate *Tuesday*.

For particulars of Freight or Passage Money, apply at the Company's Office, 41, Str. Mercanti.

GEO. S. BROOKS,
Agent.

(*) During S. W. Monsoon from June till September, the arrivals will probably be on Thursday.

XXXVI.

LEYLAND LINE
FIRST CLASS SCREW STEAMERS
FROM LIVERPOOL
TO SYRA, SMYRNA, AND CONSTANTINOPLE,
AND
FROM LIVERPOOL, TO ALEXANDRIA,
CALLING AT GIBRALTAR AND MALTA.

LIVERPOOL AND THE EAST
PAPAYANNI & CO.'S LINE
OF BRITISH SCREW STEAMERS
SAILING BETWEEN
LIVERPOOL, SYRA, SMYRNA, & CONSTANTINOPLE,
LIVERPOOL AND ALEXANDRIA
CALLING AT MALTA.

These Steamers have good accommodation for passengers and carry a Stewardess.

ACHILLE CAMILLERI,
AGENT,

91, *Strada Levante*,

VALLETTA.

T. G. MICALLEF

COAL AND GENERAL MERCHANT
AND
STEAM SHIP AGENT, MALTA.

AGENT FOR

Messrs CORY BROS. & Co., Cardiff & London.
Messrs BAZIN & Co., Marseilles & Port Said.
Messrs FRAISSINET & Co., Marseilles.

LINE OF STEAMERS TO THE BLACK SEA, EGYPT, &c.

FRENCH PACKETS FOR NAPLES, GENOA, AND MARSEILLES,
AND
VICE VERSA.

XXXVIII,

MICHAEL & SONS,

BY SPECIAL APPOINTMENT PURVEYORS TO THEIR ROYAL HIGHNESSES THE DUKE OF EDINBURGH,

THE DUKE OF CONNAUGHT,

AND

THE DUKE OF CAMBRIDGE.

NAVY AGENTS AND WINE MERCHANTS,

GENERAL EXPORT PROVISION

WAREHOUSE.

(Established 1826)

7, Marina, Custom House Quay.

Agents and Purveyors to British and Foreign Yachts.
Agents for Messrs Pickford & Co., Shipping Agents all over the United Kingdom.
Agents and Purveyors to H. I. Japanese M's Navy.

The above Firm has recently removed to one of the largest houses in Malta, which will be found in every respect convenient for the Shipping Trade in general. A very large stock of stores on sale at wholesale prices.

MICHAEL & SONS are represented by Agents in almost every part of the Globe.

Registered Telegraphic address: "MICHAEL, MALTA."

XXXIX.

MESSRS.

HENRY S. KING AND CO.'S

MALTA
READING ROOMS,

20, STR. REALE,

Valletta.

Are open during the stay of the P. & O. Steamers in port for the convenience of passengers *free of charge.*

The "Kaisar-i-Hind" Cigarettes which in the opinion of Connoisseurs are second to none, may be obtained at this Establishment.

These cigarettes are made by hand from the choicest Turkish tobacco, and the paper used in their manufacture is specially prepared for the sole Manufacturers.

TURNBULL Junr. & SOMERVILLE,

20, Strada Reale.

XL.

MEDITERRANEAN EXTENSION TELEGRAPH COMPANY LIMITED

WORD RATE TARIFF
EUROPEAN SYSTEM

Composed of the rate applicable to the actual
number of words, plus an Additional Rate or
Grundtax of 5 words per telegram.

UNDER THE LONDON CONVENTION

From APRIL 1880.

		d.
Austria, ...		4
Belgium, ...		4½
Corfu, direct or Via Zante,...		4½
Denmark, ...		5
France, ...		4
Germany, ...		4½
Great Britain & Ireland, ...		6
Greece, (continental]...	Via Vallona	5
Sta Maura, Ithaca, Zante, Cephalonia, Hydra & Spezzia,	do.	5½
Andros, Tinos, & Kythnos, ...	do.	6
Corfu and Syra, ...	do.	6½
Continental Greece, Sta. Maura, Ithaca, Cephalonia, Zante,		
Hydra and Spezzia, ...	Via Corfu	6½
Andros, Tinos, Kythnos, ...	do.	7½
Syra, ...	do.	8
Continental Greece, ...	Via Zante	5
Sta. Maura, Ithaca, Cephalonia, Zante, Hydra & Spezzia	do.	5½
Andros, Tinos, & Kythnos, ...	do.	6
Syra, ...	do.	6½
Heligoland, ...		6
Holland		5
Hungary, ...		4½
Luxemburg,...		4½
Montenegro, ...		4½

XLI.

							d.
Norway,	...	...	...	...	...	...	6
Italy,	...	...	...	...	...	...	3
Persia, Via Russia }		Extra European System and without					1/8
do ., Turkey }		Grundtax,	...	...	...		1/8½
Portugal	...	...	...	...	...	...	5½
Russia in Europe	...	...	...	...	...		7
do Caucasus	...	...	...	...	...		8½
Roumania	...	...	...	...	...	...	4½
Servia	...	...	...	...	...	...	4½
Spain	...	...	...	...	...	...	5½
Sweden	...	...	...	...	...	...	6
Switzerland	...	...	...	...	...	...	3½
Turkey in Europe	...	...	...	...	Via Vallona		5
Do Asia Seaports		...	...	...	do		7
Do do Inland		...	...	...	do		9
Mytilene, Chios, Samos, Rhodes			...	...	do		8
Cyprus,	...	...	...	...	do		8½
Candia	...	...	...	...	do		9
Seaports of Turkey in Europe and Asia Via Otranto Zante							7
Turkey in Europe and Asia inland			Via Zante		...		9
Mytilene, Samos, Rhodes		...	...	do		...	8
Chios	...	...	...	...	do	...	5½
Candia Cable direct	...	...	...	...	...		9

EDWARD ROSENBUSCH C. E.

General Superintendent.

COMPANY'S OFFICES

CENTRAL OFFICE, 27 *Strada Mercanti,* VALLETTA,
(behind St. John's Church).
BRANCH OFFICE at the " BORSA " Str. Federico, VALLETTA.

XLII.

W. KINGSTON
CHEMIST & DRUGGIST.
BY APPOINTMENT TO H. R. H. THE PRINCE OF WALES.

AND THEIR R. & I. H. THE DUKE & DUCHESS
OF EDINBURGH.

ENGLISH DISPENSARY
243, *Strada Reale, &* 43, *Strada Teatro,*
(Corner of the Palace Square).

Physicians' Prescriptions and family recipes
carefully prepared.

ENGLISH & FRENCH PATENT MEDICINES.

Atkinson & Whittaker & Grossmith's
Select Perfumery.

JOHAN MARIA FARINA EAU DE COLOGNE
(*Opposite Julich's Platz*)
Agent for Vichy Mineral Water and
for Clarke's Blood Mixture.

BEST TOILET REQUISITES.

Hours of Business during the week
From 7. a. m. to 9. p. m.
On Sunday from 7. to 11 a. m. and from 5 to 9. p. m.

During the night at his private house 76, Str. Forni,
Opposite Morrell's Hotel.

XLIII.

SIG. S. MITROVICH
PROFESSOR OF FRENCH AND ITALIAN,
69, *Strada Teatro.*

References To Former Pupils.

G. BRIFFA
ARMY AND NAVY TAILOR & OUTFITTER
HABIT MAKER &c. &c.
28 & 236 *Strada · Reale*
Under the Union Club.

VALLETTA=MALTA.
Bills Cashed.
No connection with any other Firm.

ANTONIO ZARB
GENERAL GROCER
WINE AND SPIRIT MERCHANT
135, *Strada Teatro,*
VALLETTA-MALTA.

XLIV.

Naval and Military Industrial Exhibition.
Malta, 1880.
BOSSWARD'S
Orient Plate, and Tooth Powders
Honorable Mention.

BOSSWARD'S ORIENT PLATE POWDER.

For Cleansing and Polishing Gold and Silver, and Electro Silver Plated goods, Britannia Metal, and Block Tin Dish Covers, Mirrors, &c., &c.

Silver and Plated goods polished with this Powder will not tarnish, but will retain their pristine lustre.

The Proprietor feels great confidence in recommending his Orient Plate Powder as an article well worthy the attention of every House-keeper, Mess Caterers, &c., &c. It contains no mercury, or other injurious ingredient, and is quite harmless should it by accident be taken internally. Its daily increasing sale speaks most satisfactorily of its merits, and its cheapness recommends it above all others. It has only once to be tried to ensure its general adoption. To be had of all respectable Grocers and Italian Warehouses. In boxes 4d., 8d., 1s. 4d , & 2s. 8d.

BOSSWARD'S ORIENT TOOTH POWDER.

The most valuable discovery ever made. It thoroughly cleanses the Teeth, leaving them Pearly White, greatly improves the Enamel, and strengthens the Gums. It is not only perfectly harmless, but is beneficial to health. Agents Wholesale and Retail, W. KINGSTON, Chemist and Druggist, 243 Strada Reale, Palace Square, and J. E. MORTIMER, 18, Molo Marina, near the Custom House.

XLV.

M. A. ARRIGO,
37, STRADA TESORERIA,
VALLETTA-MALTA.

Importer of and Dealer in all sorts of Optical, Nautical, Mathematical, Physical, Geometral, and Land Surveying Instruments etc. Navigation Charts, Hardware, & Cutlery, also an extensive stock of Photographs-Views, copies of artistical works, Costumes, Stereoscopic slides Albums, for same elegantly and richly bound always on hand, Stereoscopes of all sorts etc. A most extensive stock of spectacles, eye glasses, pincenez, eye preservers, etc. and all articles connected with the optical line promptly served.

At the most reasonable prices, imported from the most credited London and Paris houses.

VINCENZO DI ANGELO BUGEJA
Metal, Timber, Paint, & Hardware
MERCHANT.
SOLE AGENT
FOR 'MUNTZ'S METAL COMPANY'
OF BIRMINGHAM.
•STRADA MERCANTI, Nos. 77, 168, & 169.
STR. CRISTOFORO, Nos. 147, 148D., & 177.
Valletta=Malta.

XLVI.

ENGLISH UNDERTAKER

Mr. MARTIN conducts Funerals
in the Best Style; Hearse with Plumes, Coffins,
Hat-Bands, Scarves, Gloves, Carriages, &c.
Apply in Valletta, at No. 126 Strada Stretta,
[BACK OF MAIN GUARD.]

☞*Monuments, Tomb-Stones, and Tablets of*
every description
at very moderate prices.

J. A. MOORE & CO.
BAZAAR,
103 & 50, STRADA SAN GIOVANNI
VALLETTA - MALTA.

Drapers, Silk Mercers and Hosiers. Table Linens, Sheeting, Calicos, Huckabacks, an Assortment of Excellent English Cutlery, and the best Electro Plated Goods.

WINE & SPIRIT MERCHANTS.

Price Lists gratis on application. Agents for the Orient Plate and Tooth Powders.

XLVII.

RISING SUN HOTEL, FLORIANA:

BY

W. REID.

PHOTOGRAPHY IN ALL ITS BRANCHES.

Studio Open from 8. a. m.

A Fine Collection of Views of Malta,
H. M. Ships &c. on View.

S. SCHEMBRI,

PICTURE FRAME MANUFACTURER

AND

DEALER IN PICTURES.

38, *Strada Tesoreria,*

(Under the Arcades),

Valletta=Malta.

Prints and Drawings Mounted, Glazed, and
Framed. Photographs of Every description.
Materials for Oil and Water Color Painting.

PIANOS FOR SALE AND HIRE.

XLVIII.

BY APPOINTMENT TO H. R. H. THE PRINCE OF WALES.

MICHAEL BORG

LACE MERCHANT & JEWELLER

Choice and extensive assortments of *Modern*
and *Antique* Lace, Coral, Lava, Roman Cameos,
Mosaic, Gold & Silver Filiagree Articles.
269, STRADA REALE,
Valletta - Malta.

MICHAEL BORG

DIRECT IMPORTER

OF

HAVANA AND MANILLA CIGARS:

AMERICAN, ENGLISH, & TURKISH TOBACCOS:
MANUFACTURER OF CIGARETTES

EXPORTER TO THE EAST

OFFICERS' MESS SUPPLIER

(Wholesale and Export only)

263, 206, STRADA REALE, & 16, STRADA ZACCARIA,
VALLETTA-MALTA.

N. B. Attention is respectfully solicited to the
Christian Name, there being other Firms bearing the
same Surname with which I have no connection.
MICHAEL BORG.

LaVergne, TN USA
03 June 2010
184811LV00003B/48/P